# Voice-Haunted Journey

** bp**

# Bilingual Press/Editorial Bilingüe

General Editor
    Gary D. Keller

Managing Editor
    Karen S. Van Hooft

Senior Editor
    Mary M. Keller

Assistant Editor
    Linda St. George Thurston

Editorial Board
    Juan Goytisolo
    Francisco Jiménez
    Eduardo Rivera
    Severo Sarduy
    Mario Vargas Llosa

Address:
Bilingual Review/Press
Hispanic Research Center
Arizona State University
Tempe, Arizona  85287

(602) 965-3867

# Voice-Haunted Journey

Eliud Martínez

Bilingual Press/Editorial Bilingüe
TEMPE, ARIZONA

ISBN: 0-927534-03-7
Printed simultaneously in a softcover edition. ISBN: 0-927534-04-5

Library of Congress Catalog Card Number: 89-81825


PRINTED IN THE UNITED STATES OF AMERICA

*Cover and text illustrations by Eliud Martínez*
*Cover design by Peter J. Hanegraaf*
*Back cover photo by Laura Stephanie Martínez*

**Acknowledgments**

This volume is supported by a grant from the National Endowment for
the Arts in Washington, D.C., a Federal agency.

*For Elisse, my wife*
*with love*

# Part One

Every novelist knows that at one time or another he will be confronted with the incarnation of one of his characters. Whether that character is based on a living person or not, it will draw into its circle those who resemble it.

Anaïs Nin, *Collages*

Put a novelist into the novel. He justifies aesthetic generalizations.... He also justifies experiment. Specimens of his work may illustrate other possible or impossible ways of telling a story. And if you have him telling parts of the same story as you are, you can make a variation on the theme. But why draw the line at one novelist? Why not a second inside his? And a third inside the novel of the second? And so on to infinity....

Aldous Huxley, *Point Counterpoint*

The writing of a self-portrait is not merely a very embarrassing, but even an impossible task. I should be a conceited braggart if I brazenly obtruded the good I might be able to say of myself; and I should be a fool if I exposed to the gaze of the whole world the defects of which I might also be aware. Furthermore ... no one can tell the whole truth about oneself. No one has as yet succeeded in doing it, neither Saint Augustine ... nor Jean Jacques Rousseau ... least of all the latter, who ... was at bottom really much more untruthful ... than any of his contemporaries.

Heinrich Heine, *Self Portrait*

Note: All the characters in this novel, the first of a series with the title "The Notebooks of Miguel Velásquez," are invented and fictional. Like countless characters in many novels they will inevitably resemble persons living and dead. Characters, as Robbe-Grillet has said, are pure fictional creations; they are true in proportion to their falseness. The reader should keep in mind, moreover, that ever since the knight errant of the woeful countenance imitated the characters of novels of chivalry, characters in fiction have been imitating fictional characters. Even writers of fiction and other people have been known to imitate fictional characters. There are those, in addition, who believe that a true autobiography is an impossibility. Consequently, even the real persons who make appearances in this novel have been dramatized for fictional effects, except when the quality of their real lives surpasses any possible fiction in the wildest imagination of the author.

# I

SUDDENLY ALEJANDRO VELASQUEZ SAT UP IN HIS COF-
FIN. Years later Alejandro's older brother would not remember
how many people were there, sitting in the funeral chapel in
Austin, Texas, perhaps twelve to fifteen people, he among
them, sitting next to his elderly mother facing the coffin. But
Miguel Velásquez would remember his mother vividly, sadly
heaving great sighs from time to time, sitting next to him, sob-
bing softly, holding a crumpled handkerchief to her eyes,
breaking out occasionally into mournful fits of uncontrollable
crying when someone came to shake her hand, to express con-
dolences and to embrace her; he would remember his mother
lamenting to God that He had taken her son Alejandro at such
a young age, reproaching Him for letting the elders live in-
stead; and years later he would remember above all his brother
Alejandro in the coffin, sitting up, looking all around, at the
front of the funeral chapel, seeing him, it seemed, for the first
time as a man, thinking that less than two months later he
would have been thirty-five years old. Miguel would always re-
member that journey home to his brother's funeral which
brought back a flood of memories of their childhood and of
adolescence and youth; he would remember the wake, and the
funeral afterward, at the Mexican cemetery in Pflugerville,
Texas where he, his sister and brothers were born, except for
his youngest brother, Eduardo; clumps of dirt slamming and
sliding upon the coffin lid.

Miguel Velásquez was a passenger, already at his assigned
seat on a PSA 737, watching other passengers coming aboard
and placing their carry-on baggage in the overhead compart-

3

ments or underneath the seats in front of the ones to which they had been assigned. Though he could not quite put his finger on it he felt that his brother's funeral had been typically Mexican. His thoughts transported him back to the funeral chapel, and he became oblivious of the other passengers on the plane.

Friends and family were mourning, but the death of Alejandro had brought the living together, and they were celebrating, in a sense, memories of the departed which they shared among themselves in conversation or silently, and these were memories of the kind, strangely enough, which one takes for granted when a person is alive, and which evoke so much of the life and many dimensions of personality of the person after he dies. Many years would pass before Alejandro's older brother would begin to make sense of thoughts and feelings which puzzled and bewildered Miguel at the time of his brother's death. At his brother's funeral he saw other relatives, those whom one sees mainly when some important occasion brings them together—a death in the family or a wedding, a fiftieth wedding anniversary or some other special event—and he saw childhood friends, too, whom he had not seen for fifteen and others for close to twenty years. How strange to see them carrying their childhoods about with them, and strange to find in those transformed faces of friends in their thirties, traces of the former faces they had worn as children. One could not help but glimpse in the faces of the elders, too, something of their younger selves, though of course they had changed much less.

Alejandro was sitting up in his coffin, smiling. He was looking all around the funeral chapel at the people who were mourning his death, as if he had just awakened not knowing where he was, wondering what everyone was doing there, and he seemed perplexed by the mournful expressions on people's faces. What a beautiful smile. What perfect teeth. He was smiling mischievously as he used to in life, sitting up and holding on to the sides of the upper half of the coffin, as if he were in a canoe.

Suddenly, Alejandro tossed his head back and laughed. He laughed joyfully, in that customary playful spirit for which he was well known as a child and adolescent. God! Alejandro always had the gift of laughter! And he would laugh, sometimes, even after the terrible swimming accident, when he was only twenty years old, that broke his neck and left him paralyzed

4

from the neck down for almost two years, when he dove into shallow water during a summer evening picnic.

From his coffin, Alejandro looked at his mother, doña Dolores. Next to her he saw and smiled at his older brother, who, not being astonished at all to see Alejandro sitting up in his coffin, returned his brother's smile. It was just like Alejandro, Miguel was thinking, to be playful and mischievous at his own funeral. He always hid his own great sorrows from everyone he loved, with laughter.

Only Miguel heard his brother's laughter. Only he saw Alejandro sitting up in the coffin, expecting him to jump out of his coffin at any moment. How warm was his brother's laughter. When they were children it was impossible to stay angry with him. Alejandro had been born with the gift of laughter.

In a few minutes the PSA 737 would take off to Oakland Airport. There Miguel would take a van to the Coliseum station, where he would board the BART train to Berkeley. A university professor, he was going to use the UC Berkeley Library to work on some scholarly articles long ago begun and abandoned, about Poe and Fellini, Buñuel and Bergman. In the eyes of his colleagues Miguel was a failed scholar. He had his own self-doubts which led him to identify with characters from some of his favorite novels. He likened his own temperament to those of strange anti-heroes and outsiders who failed at one thing or another. He felt a close kinship with eccentric beings. Whenever he travelled his thoughts turned to a novel on which he had been working unsuccessfully for years. I have been writing away my life, not living my life at all, he thought. He was like a character in a novel or film for which the novelist or the filmmaker had not found the right direction.

When he travelled he remembered his brother's funeral. Alejandro's death had imparted valuable lessons about the transitoriness of life, about love of family blood, about the passage of time and death itself, which made him ponder what Alejandro's life had been. Like Miguel, Alejandro would be in his late forties. Before long Miguel would be fifty. In recent years the question he had raised long ago had returned to haunt him. In one of his New York notebooks he had written ". . . I am twenty-nine years old. What have I done with my life? What does the writing have to do with what my life will have been when I die?"

5

Alejandro's death had sharpened his already keen sense of the passing of time. Eleven years later another death would further instruct him about living, dying, aging and grieving, would deepen his veneration for childhood and for his family in Texas. The two brothers were very close when they were children and adolescents. Miguel never ceased to mourn. When he travelled, he remembered and felt saddened about his brother's tragic life, his immense sorrows; and when he thought of their childhood, his thoughts were associated by contrast, strangely enough, as if inspired by his brother's gift of laughter, with childhood memories of the peals of laughter and the cheerful voices of children running and playing among great oak trees on the playground of the elementary school that was located on top of a hill near their house. Years later those memories would come back vividly when he became an inhabitant of wretched rooms in transient hotels and rooming houses, like some of the characters in O. Henry and Tennessee Williams short stories. In those rooms he remembered the immense Texas sky which first filled his child's mind with inexpressible longings to know the world, which very early developed in him, inexplicably, a sense of immensity and a fascination with the unknown. When he was a child his future was immense and foreseeable, immense like the blue Texas sky of childhood. In transient hotel rooms he was often comforted by the memories of being five years old. Watching the elementary school children playing every morning and afternoon, at recess and lunch times, from the porch of the dilapidated wooden house which his father and mother had rented, listening to the laughter and the voices—all of it made him yearn feverishly to attend school. The dreamy child wondered if that dreamlike year would ever pass, if he would ever be six years old. Years later, far from family and his place of birth, the grown man would remember that dreamlike year of his life as if it had been a single day. He would remember his mother's voice, speaking to him in the language of childhood, the year before he started school. How unbearable was his longing that year.

—When can I go to school, Mamá? What are those things, Mamá? The child was referring to the rectangular objects which the school children carried under their arms, to and from school.

—Next year, she answered, el año que viene. They are books . . . libros . . . You will go to school next year. You will learn to read and write, as I never have. I will never let your father take you or your brothers out of school, like other poor Mexican families, to follow the crops. When you are six, you can go to school. It will not be long, just a few months. Time passes quickly. . . . Ya verás, hijo. You will see, his mother said, how fast the time will fly.

Despite never having gone to school, despite never having learned English, his mother was an intelligent woman. Although she dwelled in a world of illiteracy, she had played a major role in Miguel's education. Doña Dolores instilled in her son a love of books and learning, and during those years when their family was poor and passing through hardships, she insisted that Miguel's father not take the children out of school to follow the crops. We can do without the little extra money they would bring, she used to say.

Miguel's father also transmitted to his son a love of books and learning. He went only to the third grade, at a Mexican village school, because the Mexican Revolution ended his education. Antonio Velásquez began to teach his son how to read and write Spanish when Miguel was eight years old, very shortly after he had begun to learn English at school. His father was Miguel's first important teacher, and because of him Miguel was able to learn to read and write two languages simultaneously, and to learn years later something of two others. Because of their mother and father, Miguel, his brothers and his sister, managed to move out of that world of illiteracy in which many American people of Mexican ancestry found themselves until not long ago. ¡Ay, Mamá! What if you and Papá had gone to school?

Doña Dolores was right. The time did pass quickly. Over the years Miguel travelled to many parts of the world. In New York, when he was thirty years old, he met and married Natalie Rosenthal. She was twenty-three.

Now he was vaguely conscious of the even droning of the airplane engine, warming up for departure. A man accustomed to travel, he knew the whole routine by heart. In a few minutes stewardesses and stewards would go through the safety instructions, point to the safety exit doors, point to the little compartment doors from which oxygen masks would drop in case of emergency, and show the passengers how to use the masks. Later they would begin to serve refreshments and spirits.

7

When he travelled alone the memories of his married life usually crowded in upon his thoughts. Almost three years after their marriage and after a year in Europe, he and Natalie became parents for the first time. Their first daughter, Sara, was born in New York City. Two years after that, Rebecca was born in Claremont, Illinois, where he was a graduate student at Claremont University. Had it not been for Natalie he would never have returned to graduate work. Yes, his mother was right. Time passes quickly. His daughters were teenagers. Their growing up drove home to him the passing of time.

Unforgettable image, little Sara three years old, on her tricycle, waving good-bye, her child's legs pedalling round and round. Waiting for the PSA 737 to depart, in order to bring that image back in all its vividness, he closed his eyes as he had done many times, and the scene came back before his mind's eye, like a film sequence. He imagined a long shot of the Midwestern neighborhood, evoking Middle America, with its beautiful turn-of-the-century, two-story wooden houses with large front porches and smiling people sitting there after dinner, greeting neighbors out for a stroll with once-cherished American neighborliness; friendly houses which contrasted dramatically with present-day homes in suburban America, with great, keep-away backyards enclosed by high walls to ensure privacy; yes, he could see the sidewalks, the street, the neighbors' cars parked on the street; and at the bottom of the picture frame, sweet little Sara, small in the picture frame; then in a long shot, in slow motion, the hauntingly lovely image of the child, hunched over a little, holding on to the handlebars, her little feet on the pedals going round and round, her long, beautiful dark brown hair tossing from side to side, in the opposite direction of her body swaying from side to side . . . in overvoice, *Hijita, mi corazón, such a perfect image of your childhood. There you go, moving away from me, hijita.* It was a prophetic image. That day her father knew. He had foreseen in that image of his three-year-old the passing of time. Memories of his children troubled him whenever he travelled, memories of missed opportunities to bring himself and his daughters closer, when he was a graduate student, an untenured professor, and later, when writing became an obsession.

—Daddy! Daddy, will you play a game with me, please, Daddy?

—Not now, m'hijita, Daddy is writing.

Becky, m'hijita. You were five years old. Your childhood, too, already slipping away then.

Like many professors Miguel woke up from time to time and discovered that books, scholarship and writing eat up the years. Between these awakenings the years had passed. His daughters had grown up. What had he done with his life?

I think of you too, Natalie, whenever I travel. You came into my life when I was burning it up, when I was disappointed with myself, because I had let people down. . . . I too have glanced out of windows, from rooms in wretched transient hotels, invoking from time to time those whom I have loved. I too have hurled prayers into the silence and solitude of the night, like one of my favorite French poets. *Ames de ceux que j'ai aimé, âmes de ceux que j'ai chantés, fortifiez-moi, soutenez-moi, éloignez de moi le mensonge et les vapeurs corruptrices du monde, et vous, Seigneur mon Dieu! accordez-moi la grâce de produire quelques beaux vers qui me prouvent a moi-même que je ne suis pas . . . inférieur à ceux que je méprise!* When you came into my life I had come close to wasting it irrevocably. You brought hope, which over the years I repaid with sorrows. Even then, before we married, I knew. Marriage was not for a man of my temperament and nature, because inevitably I would bring grief to someone.

—I must warn you, I must tell you that I can never be a good husband or a good father. I am going to burn up my life, I must. . . . I will always want to love many women, to travel and see other lands and skies. I know my terrible nature. You worry about my drinking. I am sorry. Oh, Natalie! Why did you not let me spare you a life with me? Why did you not leave me to burn up my life?

But Natalie would not leave him. She believed that eventually he would recognize the importance of family and a good professional career. Miguel was aware of the suffering that he brought to his wife and children. He wondered if Natalie and the children could possibly know the extent of his remorse, which made him lament, sometimes, his stubborn insistence on being true to his nature, his too-intense desire to live life fully.

When he pondered his remorse, he would think about a letter of farewell which he had planned to write in Paris to end their marriage. He never wrote it, but the letter was composing itself in his mind when they were travelling through Europe. It was in their second year of marriage. That year the miniskirt came out in the spring. They had flown from New York to Paris in the preceding fall, where they had picked up a new Volkswagen. They drove south to Madrid, where they spent six months. From Madrid they drove to Barcelona, around the Mediterranean, through southern France, on into Italy; across Italy to Brindisi and from there to Greece, on a ferry to Patras, on towards Athens, back to Aeghion, and from Aeghion to Delphi on a ferry across the Corinthian Gulf. Proceeding northward through Yugoslavia, beyond Trieste into Venice, and contining north through Switzerland and Germany, they went back to Paris, France, where they had started their European journey, where Miguel was planning to remain, at the end, because he wanted to spare Natalie the grief of a life with him, which she was already experiencing.

She lied in the letters that she wrote to her family back home, in upstate New York, saying that they were having a marvelous trip, that Miguel was such a wonderful person to travel with because he spoke four languages and he knew all the great art museums, the cultural history, the literature and the geography of the European countries through which they were travelling. She wrote glowingly about the vineyards, about Mediterranean beaches and picnics, about the cities they visited, the places they saw, all with strange-sounding names—the great museums, the Prado, Uffizi, Vatican, Sistine Chapel, Louvre; the great gardens of Europe, Tivoli, Parque del Retiro, the Tuileries; the great Cathedrals of Chartres, Rheims, Amiens; and buildings and plazas, and so much more—while in truth Miguel was being utterly miserable, wanting to be free, hoping to spare his lovely young wife from a life of misery, searching in his mind for the right words of farewell which would not leave Natalie thinking that there was something wrong with her, because he knew that in fact no man could ask for more in a wife because Natalie was thoughtful and tender and loving, because he knew that it was his wild and impulsive nature that made him unsuitable for such a warm and loving person. Miguel remembered how she cried, beyond Paris, when they were driving north through Holland, Belgium, another part of Germany, and on to Copenhagen, in Denmark. She had begun to sense that Miguel was going to leave her . . . *My darling*, the unwritten letter was to begin, *so that I will not*

*bring you grief . . . I must leave you . . . I will stay in Paris . . . I can-*
*not bear to see you crying, my darling . . . I will not be good for*
*you . . . I must always be free . . . I must . . . there is no other way. . . .*
But he was not going to be strong enough, or mean enough
perhaps, to stay in Paris, to say good-bye. Many years later,
leaving her was no longer possible.

Six or seven years ago he had thought of leaving her again.
But by then he knew that he never would, that he could not.
He owed his life to her. He thought of writing her a letter, as
he once planned to write the letter of farewell when they trav-
elled in Europe, but a different kind of letter this time, to ex-
press his feelings, to let her know that he knew how miserable
he had made her life with him. *Dearest . . . I know now that I will*
*never leave you . . . never. . . . I know. You have arranged our family*
*life around my solitary, unlovable nature, around my work, my art . . .*
*which may never come to anything. . . . No matter what I do, you be-*
*lieve in me. . . . I understand why the children became the center of*
*your world . . . because I did not wish to be . . . to occupy such a place*
*. . . as you wanted in the beginning, as you would have wanted. . . .*
*Oh! How you wanted to smother me with your love, of which I was so,*
*am even still, so unworthy. . . .* Not long ago he had begun to
wonder if perhaps in the long run he might not disappoint
her. . . . Would it be possible ever to make it up to her?

From Copenhagen they drove south to Paris, to the beginning
once again, and finally, they boarded an Italian liner at Le
Havre. Their European journey had come to an end. Despite
his streak of madness, they were together still, heading back to
New York, sailing across the Atlantic in July on a ship with a
huge swimming pool around which countless young, bikini-
clad European and American girls gathered, taking in the sun.
Young women of dazzling beauty, and Miguel could hardly
bear the sight of so much forbidden loveliness. He shuddered
with unbearable exquisite agony. He felt the flames of desire
leaping in his loins, suffered his body's trembling with an en-
ergy soaked in from the hot July sun, and he was anguished by
wild and voluptuous visions provoked in his delirious mind by
the suggestive rhythms of the great Atlantic Ocean, and by the
rocking of the ship. The wine, which he consumed in huge
quantities every evening with dinner, and the booze at the bar
every evening, made him even more miserable to be with, and

Natalie was beside heself, helpless, and she did not know what to do ... *Please, Miguel ... don't drink so much ... please, honey.* ... Great tigers of lust stirred, rose and crouched towards predatory readiness in his loins. ... He thought of Odysseus, bound to a mast of his ship, listening to the fatal songs of the Sirens.

From across the centuries came the warning voice of Lady Circe. *To the Sirens first shalt thou come, who bewitch all men, whosoever shall come to them. Whoso ... hears the sound of the Sirens' voices, never doth he see wife or babes stand by him on his return, nor have the joy of his coming; but the Sirens enchant him with their clear song, sitting in the meadow, and all about there is a great heap of bones of men, corrupt in death, and round the bones the skin is wasting.* The wanderer's curiosity was immense, however, and he chose not to fill his ears with wax, but he instructed his men, according to the lady Circe's instructions, to bind him in the swift ship hand and foot, and to bind him even more securely should he plead and beg them to loosen his bonds. *So bind ye me in a hard bond, that I may abide unmoved in my place, upright in the mast-stead, and from the mast let rope-ends be tied, and if I beseech and bid you to set me free, then do ye straiten me with yet more bonds.* ... And plead he did, and oh! how he must have suffered the sweet voices of the Sirens. ...

Great ocean waves crashed angrily against the Italian ship, splashing upward at him as Miguel stood by the railing, gazing into the ocean. He licked the salt water that splashed on his lips. He turned up his forlorn, delirious eyes to contemplate the immensity of the majestic sky. He could hardly bear the intensity of being alive. Young women in bikinis. He stood listening to the fatal Sirens' songs. All around him, while his drunken mind deliriously pondered the leap into the ocean, all around him was immensity of life, of nature, of an uncertain future. Immensity of insatiable desire.

Merciful drunkenness! Envelop me gently in your sweet diaphanous black shroud, bring tranquility to my insatiable soul, spread serenity through my spirit, let gentle oblivion flow through my feverish brain, bring me forgetfulness; above all, drive away lust, incorrigible and implacable lust, which has made its abode in my body. Drain me of this unbearable, passionate desire! No! No! Do not make me dance with you! Stop painting with your brush in my mind the most exquisitely voluptuous copulations! What memories of the flesh and the senses you conjure up to assault and torment me in my most inconsolate moments. Sweep over me, envelop me gently, bring me sleep and oblivion, sweet, merciful drunkenness. . . .

Even then, barely into their second year of marriage, when they travelled in Europe, Miguel had known his nature. He knew that he was one of those men like his grandfather, after whom he was named, whose destiny is to bring grief to others. His daughter Sara made him realize it.

—Oh, Mommy! little Sara asked a few years ago, why did you marry a man like Daddy? Why, Mommie?

His daughter's question made Miguel think of his mother, doña Dolores. She told him once, in a moment of candor, that the old man had made her suffer . . . me hizo sufrir mucho, hijo, nunca se lo podré perdonar. . . . She said that she would never forget or forgive the old man for that suffering.

Little Sara's question made Miguel ponder the resemblance to his grandfather that troubled his mother. The resemblance was amazing, and it was not just a physical resemblance that made Miguel his grandfather's double. It was temperament, too. His voice, particularly when he spoke angrily, was identical to his grandfather's voice, frighteningly so, his mother had said many times. What must it have been like, Miguel wondered, for Mamá to see her own son, the eldest, turning year after year into the man whom she could never forgive for four years of suffering?

—Your tía Celia forgets how she used to ask her own mother why she had married my father-in-law. ¡Mamá! ¿Por qué te casastes, con un hombre como mi papá? Her old age has made her forget the kind of man her father was.

His mother's experiences must have been painful indeed, because a few years ago when Miguel began to think about writing a family history, he could hardly get his mother to speak of the grandfather. No, hijo, no tengo nada que decir.

# II

SITTING IN AN AISLE SEAT toward the rear of the PSA 737, listening to the even droning of the airplane's engine warming up for departure, still waiting for passengers to come aboard, Miguel pondered his extraordinary resemblance to his grandfather. His tía Celia had taken care of her father, along with her mother, in their old age. It was strange when Miguel was a teenager to see the severity of his aunt's discipline toward her aged father, a former Mexican revolutionary soldier, known in young manhood for his courage, for deeds of daring in the field of battle, for his expert marksmanship and for his superb knowledge of horses. Was she getting even, unconsciously, for what happened in the past? Was tía Celia protecting the old man? Perhaps unconsciously, it was a little of both.

During the last years of her father's life, wanting to protect him from alcohol, tía Celia limited her father's drinking to one or two beers a day. How strange to see the old man in his late seventies, once powerful and domineering, so submissive to his daughter, who also resembled him in an amazing way. How far he had moved away from the man he used to be, the man whom the grandson discovered in the rumors of the family elders. Long ago in the fields, during the cotton seasons, abuelo Miguel used to pause from work and drink tequila when other people used to stop for a drink of water! *¡No, Papá! Una cervecita, y se acabó. No quiero que se me ponga borrachito.* The stories about his grandfather and about the Mexican Revolution were almost legendary. *He was a soldier in the army of Francisco Madero. Later, he went back during the time of Venustiano Carranza. Your grandfather was a maderista and later he was a carrancista. Are you writing down what I'm saying, hijo?*

The grandfather's manliness was truly admirable. He had been fearless and daring in battle, an excellent horseman, but beyond his manly attributes the grandfather was illiterate until the age of twenty-one, when he learned, with the help of his wife, to read and write. The former revolutionary soldier had wanted to honor Grandmother Estefanita by keeping a written record of his experiences during the Revolution. He hoped to publish these notebooks some day and to dedicate them to her. Miguel admired above all the love of books and learning that the grandfather transmitted to his son, Antonio, Miguel's father, and to his grandson. Miguel cherished his mother who never learned to read or write for never taking him, his brothers and his sister out of school to follow the crops, and he venerated his father for teaching him how to read and write Spanish. Despite the old man's terrible nature, Miguel loved his grandfather dearly because the man whose name he bore, whom he resembled remarkably, loved books and because he was a writer. There was also a gentle side to the old man, which his grandchildren saw. Usually in his cups, the old man often wept for love of his grandchildren. As he became older, Miguel loved this softness in his grandfather more and more.

Miguel first heard about his grandfather's notebooks when he was an adolescent. The elders used to speak from time to time of the notebooks of don Miguel Velásquez. At first, his grandfather's notebooks held out no interest for the young Miguel. They became important to the grandson only after he himself had kept notebooks for years. No one could clearly remember how many notebooks there had been, or what they contained. Over the years the stories in his grandfather's notebooks changed many times with the teller and retellings. The grandson would never know the contents of the notebooks, however, because they met with a horrible fate. One day a burro came into the farm house while everyone was away. *The door was open. The animal had stumbled on the notebooks, where Papá kept them, in an open barrel. When we came back to the farm we found the barrel on its side . . . and . . . and everywhere . . . the pages of the notebooks . . . in shreds . . . ¡puritos pedazos, hijo! . . . ¡Híjole!*

Many years later, lamenting this great loss, don Antonio Velásquez made clear to Miguel how much he had valued the notebooks.

—He wrote everything down, hijo, everything that was true, that was good . . . *and*, Miguel's father added, bad! Mamá was shocked by many of the things he wrote. Just think, Miguel, with your education, you could have translated them . . . and published them . . . in Spanish *and* English. Oh! What a great loss! If they could only have been made into a book! My father's notebooks, don Antonio exclaimed, why, they would have been as good as the Bernal Díaz book—you know it, ¿verdad, hijo?—the one about the Conquest. What is the title? Yes, that one, *La verdadera historia de la Conquista de la Nueva España.* I read it long, long ago.

Miguel marvelled that a man with a third-grade education had read *La verdadera historia.* Miguel also understood, only a few years after graduate school, what his father meant when he told Miguel not to read too much because he might become crazy! A few years later, his father would surprise him again, with his extraordinary memory, and by becoming a true narrador del pueblo. Don Antonio was an amazing storyteller. He remembered his own life vividly, and the stories that he told his son recreated at the same time the life of Mexican people in the United States. *You must write our people's story, Miguel. . . . Listen. . . . In the eighteen-nineties . . . a little before I was born, my father told me . . . write it down, hijo. . . . había un güero-güero . . .*

In recent years, don Antonio's sisters, Miguel's elderly aunts, Celia and Emily la güera, also remembered and told him stories about their father. Miguel was so struck by their accounts that he began to wonder if perhaps the family elders were motivated by some storytelling impulse, a more than common desire to preserve a people's history, by the telling of memories. They ended up convincing him that some people are born to remember and to tell, like the tlamatinime in ancient times. It was fascinating to hear his elderly aunts speak lovingly about their father, a terrible, strict and loud-voiced man who drank heavily and cursed. In her old age tía Celia referred to her father's heavy drinking and his cursing playfully. She understood, with the wisdom of the elderly, the stubborn old man who disowned his other daughter, Emilia la güera, because she eloped. Until his death, the old man insisted that her name never be mentioned in his presence, and he made threats about what he would do if ever tía Emily's children came into the house. His aunt Celia's devotion to her father led Miguel to think that perhaps it is possible to understand and to forgive fathers and mothers for grief they bring to their children.

Thinking of his grandfather Miguel, the grandson wondered how his daughters would remember him after his death.

My grandfather's voice is booming loudly shortly after my birth. He has been drinking. His laughter is loud and expresses great pride. After all, I am the first-born son of my grandfather's first-born son.

I am the first-born of my mother. A young woman, only twenty-seven years old, she has just suffered immensely in giving me birth because she was afraid, as she will be with each subsequent birth, that she will die in childbirth. She screamed when I was born. . . . *Yours was a very difficult birth, Miguel, my first, and you cried all the time . . . You were the first . . . I didn't know what to do . . . but your grandmother was there, gracias a Dios . . . She was so tender and kind, so different from your grandfather. . . . It was freezing and snowing on the day you were born. . . . And the other times . . . I cannot explain why, but each time just before one of you was born I began to fear for my life. I was so afraid of pregnancy, afraid I was going to die . . . die in childbirth. . . . I don't know why. . . .*

Was my mother's fear based on a very ancient genetic memory among our people, of the glorious destiny of women, who, according to legend, died in battle, who died as sacrificial victims, or who died in childbirth, like warriors with a prisoner in their wombs? Was she afraid when I was born that she would die and go to reside at the dwelling place of the sun, Tonatiuhilhuicac, in the western part of the sky?

Outside, on the day of my birth, the winter wind howls insanely. Our people call it el norte. My young mother is resting. Sitting next to her on the bed is my grandmother Estefanita, caressing my mother's forehead, gently pushing back her long black hair, comforting my mother. She is praising my mother because she has just given birth to a healthy boy. *Listen Dolores, just listen to that crying!* Oh, this one will have good lungs, my grandmother said when the doctor, a middle-aged man of German ancestry, spanked me and made me cry. Only a few minutes ago he cut my umbilical cord. Now I hear my grandfather's proud loud voice.

*¡Chingao! ¡Un macho! . . . ¡un macho! ¡Pero chingao! . . . Mira nomás . . . pobrecito . . . pobrecito prietito . . . Pero, ¿qué le vamos a hacer? ¡Que sea prieto este cabroncito . . . y que sienta orgullo! Pero yo sé que estos pinches hijos de la chingada me lo van a maltratar . . .*

*Bueno, ¿qué le vamos a hacer? ¡Mira nomás qué tanates! Este her-*
*moso cabroncito . . . ¡que sí los tiene! . . .*

I was there at my own birth! Was it a dream? With my
grandfather's eyes I saw myself, a newborn infant. In my
grandfather's face, with my newborn's eyes, I saw my future
face, as if I were looking in a mirror in which I saw and re-
membered the future. No wonder that my mother is troubled
by my resemblance to him. How disproportionately huge are
the skull and the genitals of the newborn infant, and how pro-
phetic of what destiny held ahead.

Miguel stroked his full, neatly trimmed beard with his left
hand. He looked about him at the other passengers who like
himself were waiting, some less patiently than others, for the
plane's departure. Did his remarkable resemblance to his
grandfather explain why he, the grandson, wanted to be a
writer? Was there something in the blood that compelled the
grandson to keep notebooks and to write? Some things could
not be explained. He accepted nevertheless the thought, a ro-
mantic notion indeed, that there existed a mystical blood bond
with his grandfather, and he surrendered willingly to a related
notion that this bond had shaped his life and destiny.

A few people were still coming aboard the PSA 737. The
thoughts and memories that were passing through his mind as
he sat there waiting for the plane to leap into the sky, espe-
cially his grandfather's words, spoken when he was born, made
him conscious of his appearance. Probably his mother or fa-
ther had once told Miguel what his grandfather had said.
Miguel's full beard, now almost completely white, and his
pepper-colored hair, once pitch-black, and his dark complex-
ion, plus his features all gave him the appearance of a for-
eigner, particularly in his own native country. He had travelled
in other countries, and his appearance had puzzled many peo-
ple, beginning in his own native state of Texas, and later in
other parts of the country. Over the years people had asked
about his ancestry. Are you Cuban, Puerto Rican, mulatto,
Greek, Japanese, Arab, Egyptian, Jewish?

Except for his full beard, Miguel was now his grandfather's
double. The resemblance to his grandfather gave birth to a
pleasant fantasy. If ever a film were made of his impossible
novel, the same actor could play the roles of grandfather and
grandson.

For the first time in many years, Miguel's skin was darker than it had ever been since his childhood years when, shirtless, he and other neighborhood children played in the sun. During the past spring he had started to take long walks during the late morning hours, wearing sneakers and swimming trunks. The hot sun caressed his naked chest, his arms and legs, his back. Childhood memories which the sun had engraved into his flesh returned. He was perspiring as he walked. The sweat, trickling down from under his arms, thrilled him voluptuously and renewed his energies. The blood and the juices of his body were flowing, oxygen was reaching parts of his body which he had hardly used for years because of working at a desk. Books and writing had made him forget how to live. The years had fled. It began to seem a long time ago that he would go to bed at night and feel when he awakened the next morning that months and years had passed during the night.

The sun had darkened his skin once again, and he felt healthier than he had felt in years. On his walks during the past spring and summer, gladly conscious of his darkening skin, he often thought how unfortunate were the words that he heard spoken by the parents of Mexican children when he was a child. *Stay in the shade, children. Don't walk in the sun . . . váyanse por la sombrita . . . porque se ponen negros . . . no anden en el sol. . . . Look at this child! So cute . . . if only he weren't so dark! He should stay out of the sun. ¡Pobrecito!*

Walking, thinking about his dark skin and about his renewed energies, he felt glad about the gradual transformations of the human spirit which the social movements in his country, during the fifties, sixties and seventies, had brought about. These were social and cultural transformations, in which one could take pride, brought about by young people. It is good, he thought, as he walked in the hot sun, that finally some Americans were able to say proudly that black is beautiful, that brown is beautiful, that yellow is beautiful. Sad though that too many Americans are still blind to the nation's historical past, and still insensitive toward people with dark skin. Even at the present time. To think that ten years ago, I myself could not understand what was happening in this country! Americans and historical amnesia. Must write an essay some day.

That spring and summer, walking in the hot sun, feeling the juices of his body flow, relishing the renewed connections of his body's rhythms with those of sea tides and waves, being joyfully conscious of the returning voluptuous palpitations of the strange blood power, he could not help but daydream. On his walks he fantasized.

When the surrealist artist Lorenzo Correa was in his early fifties he met an extraordinary young woman, less than half his age. He called her a child-girl-woman. She came briefly in and out of his life and transformed, he tells us, all the rest of his declining years. She was—and I quote from one of his notebooks—"the April sun of my September life." Lorenzo Correa, however, was writing autobiographical novels at the time, and he left several versions of a story describing a relationship between an older man and a young woman. It may never be possible to establish which of the many versions is the true one.

In one of the notebooks the young woman is said to have been a virgin. In two other notebooks, he describes the young woman as being experienced and unusually knowledgeable in the art of making love. She confesses to the older man, we are told, that she has had many amorous relationships. In one version of the love story, the young woman was born in New Mexico; in another, in a Mexican village in the state of Jalisco. Another version gives her birthplace as Tucson, Arizona.

Other unresolved problems need to be taken up later. As Lorenzo Correa's biographer, I feel tempted to conjecture, but this is a temptation I am obligated to resist. Perhaps one day the young woman will identify herself—she would be in her late forties now—or even write a book of her own and settle this question.

It is safe to conjecture, on the basis of Lorenzo Correa's notebooks, that during the short period of time during which the older man and the young woman were lovers he underwent a remarkable transformation. In addition to myself a team of scholars is working with a prestigious university press to establish his definitive biography. We are examining page by page, and some of us, word by word, the writings in which Correa seems to be everywhere present, as he describes this most revealing experience of his early fifties. The notebooks contain accounts of dramatic changes that were taking place in himself, slowly but perceptibly. He attributed these changes to autobiographical characters in novels that were never published. There are discrepancies, also, between what he wrote in the notebooks, on which he based the unpublished novels, and what he wrote in the novels themselves. Apparently Lorenzo Correa was a heavy drinker. Perhaps he was even an alcoholic. He wrote that he decreased his drinking gradually, and as he did so, he tells us, he began to enjoy feelings once more that he had not known in many years.

One day he woke up without a hangover, a notebook entry tells us, and eventually the hangovers ended. That he was able to reduce, perhaps even to quit his drinking, makes it impossible to say with certainty that he was an alcoholic. He tells us repeatedly that he, who had never been in love, is beginning to fall in love, that he finds it impossible to keep the young woman out of his thoughts. On a frequent basis, he tells us, he experienced a loss of appetite. He could not work, and he lost weight. In the notebooks which seem to be of that year, the artist omitted dates, very likely to protect the young woman's identity. It may be that he preferred for posterity not to identify the young woman to whom he referred as "the first and last love of my life."

His writing is flawed by long melodramatic passages and repetitiousness. Lorenzo Correa described in notebooks, for example, an "increasing, joyous awareness once again of the long bright and lovely days of April, of the afternoon sun lingering longer and higher in the sky, of the lengthening days that stretch into the early evening hours. "Oh!" he exclaims melodramatically, "Now the summer has arrived and reached its peak. How sweetly the daylight lingers on later and later into the evening, shortening the hours of sweet summer nights." Equally pathetic are other passages. He writes, for example, of his "awareness of lovely bright and sunny afternoons that invite lovemaking; awareness above all of the lyrics of popular songs and poems of love."

It is hard to believe that a short time earlier Lorenzo had written in a notebook that he felt a sense that life had lost its purpose, that life was absurd and not worth living, despite a certain measure of success as a scholar in Chicano studies. I quote:

"Perhaps the films and novels which I am using in my comparative arts classes have more to do with my feelings than I am willing to recognize. Undeniably, I must confess that in the present September season of my life my whole being longs, as flowers and plants long for the sun, to be free and to know love unlike I have ever known, new, deliriously passionate

21

love." And, "I know," Lorenzo Correa wrote elsewhere, "that this longing for something that I have never known, for something that I have missed in my life has always been there; I must be honest with myself once and for all. I have never been in love. I cannot fall in love. I will never know the fulfillment of this longing. Inside of me there is a boy who wants to know love such as he has never known. As a boy, as a young man, I loved older women. They were gentle teachers. They understood my nature, made me at ease when I was awkward and clumsy. I wended in and out of their lives; they understood. Am I destined perhaps never to know what it is to fall in love?"

Correa continues: "I cannot but compare myself to a writer of the last century who began to have moments of perplexity at about my age, who describes himself as if he no longer knew how to live or what to do. The questions 'why?' and 'what next?' trouble me as they troubled him increasingly. For me, as for him, things whose meaning had always been self-evident now seem meaningless. He felt that something had broken in him, something on which his whole life had rested, and now he had nothing to hold on to. I remember many times when drinking made life seem unreal. The nineteenth century writer became afraid of a force which was drawing him away from life, not that this force made him wish, exactly, to kill himself, he tells us. But he became afraid of going hunting, and of ropes hanging from rafters, of sleeping alone. That is the way I feel. And the writer, like myself, was perplexed, because he was in good health, perhaps in better health than I am. He, too, had a good wife, who loved him and whom he loved; good children and a good home. In his case, the writer was already famous; he was respected in many parts of the world. Look at me, I tell myself. I am a university professor, one who came from a world of illiteracy, one who knew hardships and poverty in childhood. I have travelled, know the world. Now, I am comfortable and middle-class. My wife and my children are wonderful. We have a good income. What more can I ask for? Why do I feel an intense rage from time to time, deep hatred, and helplessness? Can it be that the meaningless absurdity of life is the only incontestable knowledge accessible to man? What am I to do? There are times when reality seems to drop away from me, and I do not know where my life is going. Am I a failure?"

But, regarding the older man's love for the young woman who was half his age, there is considerable critical debate about whether such an affair actually occurred. For example, in a notebook from the year when he was twenty-nine, the older man wrote, "One day I will write a novel about an impossible love between an older man and a young woman half his age." Critics understandably seize on this statement, disregarding when it was written, to affirm that an extraordinary young woman did come into Lorenzo Correa's life. But what are critics to make of the formidable evidence in the later notebooks, that Lorenzo Correa may have abused his body with alcohol to such an extent that a full relationship with a woman could not have taken place? Above all, what are we to make of the notebook entry dated April 4, with the year omitted? It ends with this statement: "My fictional character, yes, he will live out my wildest fantasies, the most exquisite passions. I will have him fall deliriously, hopelessly in love, with a young woman half his age! He will suffer as he has made me suffer with his impossible demands as a character!"

# III

JUST A FEW MINUTES AGO, like the other passengers still coming aboard, he was moving toward the rear of the airplane, toward the smoking section, waiting for those ahead of him to check the row and seat number written with a green marker on their tickets against the information on the little tags above the aisle seats, waiting for other passengers to place carry-on baggage under the seats or in the small overhead compartments. He had found and taken his seat.

Soon the plane would depart. His mind was full of thoughts and fantasies, teeming with voices and images, with dreams and memories, alive with whole chapters and episodes and paragraphs for the novel he wanted to write. Many of them were already written, and although he had not really abandoned these countless fragments of his novel, he had set them aside with all good intentions of going back to them. But because he had gone on writing without going back to pages which he had left in vulnerable stages of development, these pages of the novel, the images, themes, memories and episodes had ended up obsessing him, like Pirandello's six characters rightly crying out for a life of their own, protesting against their creator who once having given them life had abandoned them.

Slowly, somewhat in the manner of a film dissolve which makes one scene fade out and slowly makes a new scene fade in, Miguel Velásquez began to change the focus of his mind's attention, slowly and consciously, away from the memories of his past and recent life, away from the thoughts and feelings which he wanted to turn into literature, away from the scenes and episodes of his own life, away from countless pages and chapters which he had already written for a novel that was becoming increasingly ponderous and unmanageable; deliberately, he changed the focus of his attention away from all that had been passing through his mind and memory. Now, as a respite from the wanderings of his mind into the future and the past, he consciously permitted himself to become aware of where he was, a passenger inside the PSA 737 whose destination was Oakland Airport. He allowed the murmur of fellow passengers' conversation, the even droning of the airplane engine, and a few isolated voices within the airplane compartment to wend in and out of his consciousness. He glanced out of one of the porthole windows, at the luggage vehicles, now empty, moving down below on the ground, away from the plane after loading the suitcases. Then he began to refocus the attention of his mind upon itself, as one adjusts one's ray of vision from looking at a lovely garden through a windowpane to the windowpane itself. He became keenly introspective, acutely aware of himself thinking, watching his mind watching itself thinking. As the garden will blur when one focuses one's ray of vision upon the windowpane, so too his sense of present time and place began to blur and his mind began to shut out the airplane sounds and the voices of his fellow passengers, until it closed off its consciousness of where he was.

Even though long ago it had become a fascinating method and an occupation, that of observing himself thinking; he never ceased to feel astonishment about the way the mind and memory work. Watching his mind, seeing it turn like a kaleidoscope, rearranging configurations of experience, clusters of images, groups of associated ideas; watching the proliferating memories which come involuntarily and which one can follow thereafter, consciously and voluntarily, seeing his mind and memory at work in this way made him cherish the magic of thinking and remembering.

Long ago he had learned to trust his mind, because over the years his introspective self-observation had taught him that left to itself the mind arranges, classifies, organizes and digests large amounts of knowledge, information and experience, in predictably natural and amazing ways. Over the years he had ended up being strongly and irresistibly fascinated with observations about how his mind and memory worked to an extent that these observations had begun to compete more and more with the memories and experiences themselves. In the same way the thoughts and ideas for his creative work had begun in

some cases to displace the subject of his writing. It was an unfortunate hazard that he attributed to scholarly training.
Now for example, he had succeeded in changing the focus of his mind's attention to itself. His mind relaxed, he slowly became oblivious of his fellow passengers, of being a passenger aboard an airplane that would soon take off. To set his mind completely free, he sat back comfortably in the upright seat, consciously turned the palms of his hands upward and he let the completely relaxed weight of his arms fall limply on the arm rests of his seat.

Mind and body became simultaneously relaxed. Consciously introspective, he willed no thoughts or memories, dictated no messages to his mind or memory. He began to watch his liberated mind thinking. *I am relaxed, alone . . . I was born to be solitary . . . it is my destiny to be restless . . . anonymous, as I am now, aboard this airplane . . . it is my fate to travel, in my imagination, to be everywhere at once . . . amazing powers . . . able, like the personae of Whitman's or Neruda's poems, to travel in a brief second of time . . . from the streets of Les Halles in Paris, France, to the streets of New York, Chicago or Mexico City, or from New England to Chichén Itzá and Machu Picchu; able in seconds to make love with several women from different foreign countries. . . . I am watching myself thinking . . . remembering, daydreaming. . . . I am a stranger with a foreign-looking appearance that would make me invisible in many parts of the world. I love the sense of freedom whenever I travel . . . I love the anonymity. I am liberated from the hostages of fortune . . . she said if you have an affair, Lorenzo, please at least be discreet. Again, like many years ago, intense longing for an exquisite adventure . . . for the rediscovery of passion . . . for forbidden pleasures. . . . Who would have known? At my age! Yes, I said, I will be discreet. . . .*

Attentively, one part of his mind was watching itself thinking. The foreign-looking passenger would be able to attribute his own introspective discoveries to his fictional character. And that was precisely one of his main problems, an obstacle to finishing anything. He wanted to turn every experience into literature.

Images and voices passed through his mind, entered his heart and spirit. They affected him strangely and magically as they became words and phrases, sentences and whole paragraphs, many of which he had written down in notebooks. Remembered conversations and long monologues, the whole tangle of memories, which he always connected with the traveller's sense of awe and wonder about new discoveries, about the sweet, magical quality of life. He had written down the words and phrases, the sentences and paragraphs, possible chapters for an impossible novel. Even in his dreams he was obsessed with the same irresistible impulse to write. Would it turn out to be a lifetime of wasted hours, years forever lost? Would art be able to recover the hours and years spent pondering the enigmas of human life, love, memory and regret, hatred and anguish, joy and sorrow, childhood and aging? Would his writing reveal the life experiences which long ago drove him to write in the first place, to give a meaning to a wasted life? No! I will not lament the experiences of my young manhood, not my rage, not my immense capacity to love, nor my immense capacity to hate.

Over the years, the writing had raised many questions in his mind. For example, he sometimes wondered why a novel should have to begin in any prescribed way. Why not have the novel begin with the problems of the novelist who does not know how to begin? Why not a novel whose first chapter is really the last? Is that what some novelists mean when they say they cannot begin? Are they suggesting that one cannot write the first chapter, which comes at the end, until after one has written the last chapter? Are they saying that only when a novel has found its own ending, its own form and configuration—that only then, at the end, can a novelist begin? Can Proust have written the "petite madeleine" overture at the end? Did Agustín Yáñez write his Overture to *Al filo del agua* after writing the last chapter? Can it be only at the end that a writer can write the first chapter? But is there not a danger that the first chapter of a novel might seek, inexplicably, to become a novel in itself? Might not the first chapter, written at the end, intimidate the writer, pressure him to let the writing itself follow its own logic? What was it one of Pirandello's characters said? Ah, yes! fictional characters are living beings more alive than those who breathe and wear clothes . . . beings less real perhaps, but truer! Yes . . . one may be born a character, and even if abandoned by an author, he can laugh at death. Once born, a character cannot die.

These were comforting words, because his own main character often rebelled against him, frequently made demands on Miguel about how his novel should begin. There was comfort, too, in knowing that Federico Fellini, his favorite filmmaker, once experienced much difficulty finding how to begin one of his great films. By association his thoughts began to stray, to a passage in one of Poe's essays, which Baudelaire "stole," as T. S. Eliot would say, to Cervantes, who is probably responsible for characters imitating characters.

At that moment his thoughts were interrupted by the voices of two men who were sitting behind him. On the bottom of the overhead compartments the No Smoking and the Fasten Seat Belt signs were on. At the front of the airplane the last three passengers had come aboard. Holding carry-on luggage in hand, they were coming down the aisle. At the front of the airplane, a stewardess was closing the door of the airplane. She turned a lever which locked the door tightly.

Behind the foreign-looking, white-bearded passenger two men were talking and laughing about an aging alcoholic who had not been able to board the airplane on his own. The dark, white-bearded passenger watched the last three people putting away their luggage and taking their seats. An attractive stewardess and a steward began to check that the passengers had their seat belts on. He could not help but overhear the conversation of the two men behind him. Their voices were boisterous, their laughter loud. The dark passenger, too, had seen the helpless aging alcoholic in the airport cocktail lounge. Without taking his eyes off the attractive stewardess he listened to the two men. At the cocktail lounge he had made an entry in his pocket notebook about the unfortunate aging alcoholic.

Sitting not too far away from me in this airport cocktail lounge is a man, poor fellow; he is rendered almost totally helpless by alcohol. Who knows how long he has been drinking. I have seen the glazed look in his eyes many times, in other men, in the mirror, too. I know it well. Perhaps he is asking himself, how did I get here?

An attractive young mother arrives at the bar with two children. The little boy is about four years old. His sister is perhaps a year or a year and a half older. There are several other people here, waiting for the announcement of their flights, waiting for the arrival or departure of loved ones. When the young mother moves away from the bar, a young dark-haired woman orders a "bloody Ivan." I read her lips. Then she turns and smiles in my direction. I wonder if she will sit next to me. I long for an amorous adventure; I think about ephemeral pleasures. She pays, leaves a tip in a glass, and holding what looks like a bloody Mary to me, she walks over and takes a seat at the little table on the other side of the helpless man. He is now between the young woman and me, facing her. He speaks to her. His voice is soft and weary, hardly audible. She smiles and they begin to talk. I cannot follow their conversation, but I can overhear some of it. The inquisitive children's playful voices interfere with my hearing. They are asking many questions.

"That's because you are a person," the woman says. "You have the power to fight back."

While they talk my mind begins to stray, to the little meaningless things that eat up our time at the university. Committee meetings, memos and junk mail that one has to read and answer in writing, things that interfere with teaching, research, helping students. Professors, always running . . . "vitality of life," the woman says. . . . especially during the past year, unable to catch my breath. The woman sounds like a psychologist or a counselor. Perhaps she is a Christian drinking tomato juice. Maybe a "bloody Ivan" is a non-alcoholic drink. I do not know. It is impossible to hear their conversation. I catch a word here and there. He tells her that he is a retired professor of American history. "Why do you drink?" she asks, and she talks about willpower and faith. Again the woman uses the words "vitality of life."

The unfortunate man is a fellow passenger. They are talking about him, the two men sitting behind Miguel Velásquez.

"Now I know how come people take 'n aisle seat. Git better service 'at way."

"Tha's why I allus take one. Case you needa go to the bathroom, too, or sumpin."

"Yeah. Sometimes you have a drink or two and you jes' gotta go. Matter a fact, I had three or four drinks 'fore comin' on. But you shoulda seen 'at fella, over 'bout aisle 'leven, in tha' no smokin' section. He's plain smackeroo. He maybe don't smoke, but he shore do drink. Ha! ha! ha! He don't know ifeez comin' or goin'. Ha! ha! Maybe he couldn't git no fu'ther back than the seat where he's at."

"Maybe he's afraida flying."

"Ha! ha! ha! He didunt know if he 'uz gonna make the plane'r not. He ast me to hep 'im git on. He shore is loaded."

Above the voices of the passengers the garbled voice of the pilot announces that the airplane has been cleared for takeoff. He asks the stewards and stewardesses to please take their seats. Now the engine races loudly. Two of the airplane personnel staff who have taken seats at the front are facing the rear of the airplane, sitting stiffly in their seats. One of them is the attractive mature stewardess. Slowly the plane starts forward, moves toward the runway. Gradually it picks up speed and leaps away from the ground, climbing upward through low clouds, flying south, circling over toward the east, toward the peaks of jagged mountains, circling slowly toward the north. The plane is climbing, cutting through clouds. The plane tilts one way, now another. A streak of sunlight comes in through the window, swiftly sweeps across the plane interior just for a moment. Then it is gone. The plane is climbing into thick grey clouds. Then the memories start to flow once more.

Scattered memories of other trips—to Chicago, New York, Mexico City, Austin, Los Angeles. To Berkeley also. Arrivals at Oakland Airport. Shuttle to the BART Coliseum station. BART train to Berkeley Station, then a bus to the Bayview Hotel. At the corner, on Shattuck, where I waited for the bus almost two years ago, in front of J. C. Penney, a tall man arrived. He too waited for the bus. He passed under a street lamp. Oh, God! His face! Out of politeness I avoided looking at him. His face! Poor man. Finally the bus arrived. On the plane, on the shuttle, on the train, and on the bus; every time, the voices and the memories, my whole life passing in review whenever I travel. Journeys forward into the past. Great chunks of life passing through memory in seconds. *One day a burro came into the house . . . destroyed your grandfather's notebooks. . . .* I understand now. The saying that people's whole lives pass in review at the moment of dying. . . . *Daddy, please don't drink . . . please don't smoke. . . .* It happens for the living too, for some of us, at least. *Yes, Dad . . . we don't want you to get cancer and die.* In seconds I am travelling all over the world . . . years of dead living . . . numbed living, except for the travelling, perhaps. All the airplanes in which I have travelled are arriving at all the airports. I am walking toward the airport terminals at Paris,

France. New York. Guadalajara, Mexico. Oakland. Mexico City. . . . I think of Pflugerville, Texas. I went home again. You can go home . . . *Hijo . . . You must write about our people, Miguel . . . . Hijo . . . no leas tanto . . .* his father laughed warmly . . . *porque te vuelves loco . . . sí, hijo. Seguro, m'hijo.*

It is a grey day. Here and there, in spots, as the plane climbs, bright, sun-filtered clouds. Amazing how the images come and go so fast. My life . . . a million fragments, sliced up into irregular pieces of an interminable puzzle, by this journey, like many others . . . and yet different. Why?

Not long ago he could hardly wait for the plane personnel to begin serving drinks. Now he waited patiently, and he thought about his friend, who had driven him to the airport. On the way Guillermo Carvajal talked about trying not to drink too much.

—Whenever you're about to drink beer or wine, or liquor, think first, my friend. It is thirst, ilustre amigo, that makes you want to drink. Fill up with a good big glass of ice water, or juice, and you won't need alcohol. It's healthier. Did you know that?

—Yes, Guillermo, I drink pineapple juice. Also if I take some pastry and drink milk I do not wish any alcohol.

—Really?

—Yes, milk, sweets and juices, and iced tea with plenty of lemon, I learned recently, lessen the desire for alcohol.

When they were near the airport, driving past the vineyards, Guillermo told Miguel that his ex-wife had telephoned the day before, at the office. She left a message to return her call. He thought that perhaps something serious had happened to one of the children. He was worried, he said, imagining the worst. When he telephoned, his eldest son answered.

—He wanted me, Guillermo said, to send him some money for school materials. I was relieved, Guillermo said. But I was also very annoyed with him because he had spent all his summer earnings foolishly on a stereo set. He didn't need a new stereo set. The one that I bought for him was just fine. He didn't have to buy another one. Sometimes I wonder if our children would be better off if we weren't able to give them the luxuries of life.

Miguel was half listening to Guillermo talking about the telephone conversation with his son. One part of his mind had drifted away to a telephone conversation that he remembered as Guillermo was driving past the vineyards on the way to the airport. The recollection of his own telephone conversation brought back other memories of that extraordinary spring when he met Sylvia. *Oh, Sylvia!* ¡*Cariño!* *What a foolish way for a man my age to behave. And how sad, that despite my age having made no difference to you . . . how could it have happened the way that it did?* And Denise, I wished afterward that I had lied.

There were pleasant memories too, connected with that spring. One day he had lunch with two friends, Frances and Mariana. After they finished their lunch, while they were sipping wine, the three of them collaborated playfully, with Frances taking the lead, in creating an imaginary story about a tempestuous, perfectly planned out, voluptuous love affair. Frances gave it a title, "The Perfect Scenario." She was imaginatively playful. Mariana and Miguel were amused.

—We must have an appropriately romantic setting, first of all, she said, and the man must be a Latino, right, Mariana?

Mariana agreed and so did Miguel.

Frances touched her finger to her cheek and looked up with pondering eyes. Without waiting for the other two to make a suggestion she mentioned several romantic settings.

—How about Carmel, by the sea? Paris, France? The Riviera on the Mediterranean? Then there's Acapulco, or Mérida, Yucatán. Hey! How's about Chichén Itzá? Oo-oo-ooh! Just think about that. Making love in the Yucatán jungle . . . en la selva . . . on top of an ancient pyramid, listening to the silent voices of our ancestors. Isn't that neat? But it would be better somewhere on a beach by the sea . . . ¡cueste lo que cueste! . . . The two lovers would have to find a place with a fabulous name, too . . . something like Motel Vista del Mar. Oo-ooh! I'm excited just thinking about it. . . .

Frances was so inspired that Mariana and Miguel let her continue. They waited for her, without speaking, when she took short pauses to add to "The Perfect Scenario."

—Yes, she continued, the setting's gotta be by the sea. It's so romantic, and you could have sea gulls that could . . . that could symbolize the freedom of the artist . . . and the script must have real intense, lusty scenes. That means we have to give the woman a really sexy dress that will drive the man insane. . . . a royal blue silk dress . . . and . . . and, yes, with buttons on one side all the way from the top to the bottom.

—For the man to unbutton, Miguel added.

Mariana did not say a word. She knew that Miguel wanted to enter into a playful dialogue with Frances.

—Yea-a-ah! Frances exclaimed. Now we gotta have some good music. Agustín Lara, singing "María bonita," "Noche de ronda," "Solamente una vez" . . . There's gotta be a little sadness, you know, 'cuz love doesn't last forever. Only the memory of love lasts forever. Only imaginary loves that we'd like to find last forever, cause if we find them they're gone.

She caught herself becoming too philosophical and she became playful again, laughing and fluttering her eyes.

—How about Liszt's "Hungarian Rhapsodies?" Miguel asked.

—Which ones?

—Numbers 6 and 11.

—Is there a 17?

—I think so, but I could be wrong. I know there are numbers 6 and 11. I used to play them when I lived in Mexico, after drinking half a bottle of Bacardi rum with coke and lime. I used to play them just before I went insane and began to smash ashtrays in a corner . . . so I could sweep them up easily the next day. . . . Ha! ha!

Mariana and Frances laughed.

—Oh, not you, Dr. Velásquez, said Frances. You're so gentle. I don't believe it. Do you, Mariana?

—Of course not!

—It is true, but let us get on with the scenario. What else, Frances? Mariana, you're awfully quiet. You must be having some mischievous thoughts.

—She's enjoying this, Miguel. I know her ver-r-ry well! She's gotta lotta fire, that small woman. Anyway, we gotta think about getting the man and the woman in bed.

Mariana smiled.

At this point Miguel took out his pocket notebook and his fountain pen, and he began to outline their conversation and the plot of the scenario.

—I don't want to forget having lunch with you two ladies. Maybe I can even write a novel about "The Perfect Scenario." I would have to give the two of you credit for inspiring me. Okay. Now, Frances, what else? Let's get them into bed. I want to write the rest of this story down. It's too good to lose.

The two women laughed to see him writing down in outline form the conversation that had just taken place and the story that Frances was telling.

—Well, what does this man look like? Mariana asked. What does he wear? Is he tall? Young?

Mariana and Miguel turned to look at Frances. She did not take long in answering.

—Wel-l-ll, Frances began. We already agreed he's gotta be Latino. Let's have him wear tight blue jeans . . . tight-fitting faded Levis, to emphasize curves. . . . Mm-m-m-m . . . and a burgundy shirt with fancy buttons and long sleeves, open low at the collar. . . . He's got a hairy chest, she said looking at Miguel, like Miguel's.

Frances giggled. Then she paused to take a sip of wine.

—Come on, Frances. You haven't told us how tall or how old he is.

—Wel-l-ll, Frances continued, he doesn't have to be too tall . . .

—About my height, perhaps, Miguel suggested.

—Yea-a-ah-h! Before I forget, he's gotta use Irish Spring soap so you can smell it on him . . . and age? . . . m-m-mm . . . a little grey. What the hell! He's over thirty and under sixty . . . and he's gotta bring along a book of poetry. He's gotta be very sensitive . . . romantic and intelligent, someone who knows how to fold a napkin . . . y vamos a comer primero . . . fresh oysters m-m-mm . . . y luego. . . .

—Yes-s-s! ¿y luego? Miguel inquired. What next?

The two women laughed as Miguel held his fountain pen ready to write down what Frances would say.

—Pos no pasa nada si comemos mucho . . .

—Come on, Frances, aren't you going to get the couple in bed?

Mariana laughed. She allowed parts of the dialogue to be strictly between Miguel and Frances. Miguel was writing down what Frances had just said. Mariana spoke and Miguel wrote that down also.

—¡Qué gasto de papel y talento! Mariana exclaimed, and they all laughed.


Wind turbulence now. The airplane is shaking and rocking, ascending still, cutting through the grey clouds; at the same time the journey is slicing up my life, fragments and pieces. Life, an interminable puzzle. The greyness brings back memories of other grey days, memories of a gloomy spring season not long ago, when I had already entered the September of my life.

Regrets. Burdensome as guilt. At the front of the PSA 737 I can see the attractive stewardess facing the rear of the airplane, sitting stiffly, chatting with her co-worker, whom I cannot see. It took a long time to stop feeling stupid about not lying to Denise.

Oh, Denise! I wish that I had lied to you that night when I met you. Then I might have written a few pages of happiness for my novel.

—What would you write about me, Larry, if you were to include me in your novel? I don't think anyone understands me.

—I would have to tell how we met . . .

—In front of the public library, at lunchtime . . .

—Yes. You had been reading a book during your lunch hour. You walked by my car and I asked about your book.

—What else?

—Well, I would have to write about my visit to your apartment that night, about how close we came to making love . . . on the sofa . . . after your child went to sleep. We had been drinking wine. . . .

—But . . .

—Wait, let me finish telling you what I would say about you. I would write how much I wanted you that night . . . and I still do, Denise. I would describe your beautiful, tousled, almost red hair . . . and your freckles, and your lovely Toulouse-Lautrec face. I told you that you remind me of Samantha Eggar. I fell in love with her in *The Collector*. I would describe what it felt like to run my hands over your bare arms and your bare belly, but you told me to stop, because you asked me if I was married and I did not lie. What I would write would express sorrow and regret that I did not lie, because I think we would have made love.

—But that isn't true. You did lie. You told me you weren't married. It was after we made love that you told me you were married. . . . Why don't you write the truth so people can know that you lie? You have no way of knowing how bad I felt for having been taken advantage of. . . . For a long time it was so hard to get over it; I couldn't help thinking about your hands . . . soft like a woman's hands. . . . You lied about your last name too, Larry . . . so I wouldn't be able to find you in the telephone book. There's no Lorenzo Correa in the phone book. You also gave me a number that rings every time I call, but there's never an answer. You lied, Larry, and we did make love. You lied, telling me you had a problem . . . that for a long time you couldn't. . . . You cried in my arms like a baby. Is that how you take advantage of women? By telling them what you told me? You made me feel sorry for you. . . . Then . . . then your soft woman's hands . . . they were all over my body . . . all over my bare belly . . . reaching up under my blouse . . . you were touching me . . . cupping my breasts with your woman's hand . . . first one and then the other. . . . I was not wearing a bra, because I was open . . . open to the possibility that we might make love . . . I took it off just before you came to the apartment. . . . told myself I would play it by ear . . . if it happens it happens, if it doesn't, I thought . . . and your mouth . . . and I kept wondering how is it possible that . . . that he can't . . . your mouth everywhere . . . your soft woman's hands . . . on my face . . . my neck . . . on the inside of my bare arms . . . on the inside of my legs . . . even through the jeans . . . before you undressed me . . . I could feel the hotness of your hands . . . then I closed my eyes . . . and you kept saying that even though you couldn't . . . you wanted to try anyway . . . my breast in your mouth, now one and then the other, and I placed my bare foot on your crotch . . . felt your hardness, and you shuddered . . . and you told me that maybe it was over, could be over . . . tonight, with my help, you said . . . then we undressed and you took advantage of me. . . . Damn you! You made me feel so sorry, so goddamn sorry for you. For months I could hear your animal cries. . . . They reminded me of cats in heat. . . . You lied! You lied about everything . . . and you took advantage of me . . . and only after . . . after we had made love . . . that's when you told me you were married. . . . That's why I told you I never wanted to see you again, even though I wanted to. . . . I felt like a complete fool. You made a fool of me. . . .

—But Denise, that is not the way it happened. . . .

—Come off that crap! Why'd you telephone me today? Anyway, write the truth, Larry. Is that your real name? Is it? Don't be a fucking asshole. Write the truth. It's the least you can do.

—The truth, Denise? I . . . I wanted . . . so much to make love with you that night . . . And that is the truth. . . . I wish that I had lied that night.


36

# IV

YOU WONDER if other men your age feel as you do. Aboard
the PSA 737 you experience anew the sensation of flying that
makes you introspective. The sorrowful grey clouds remind
you of your efforts to understand the meaning of your life.
Where have you been? Who are you? What have you become?
Where is your life going? Have you been deceiving yourself
about the writing? Do other men ask the same questions when
they think back and inquire into the meaning of their individ-
ual lives? Was there a choice, Lorenzo? Were you born to be
what you became? Were there choices along the way about the
man whom you were becoming and ended up being? Long ago
you became aware, you began to understand your nature and
you knew very well what consequences would attend your kind
of temperament. The script of your life was foreseeable and
predictable. You understood and decided to accept willingly
the consequences so that you could indulge yourself, obey the
impulses which would carry you through life. You understood
when you began to disappoint people who loved you that you
would bring grief to loved ones if you stayed among them. You
told yourself there would be regrets, inevitably . . . consuming,
unassuageable remorse at times. . . . You wanted desperately,
knowing your nature, never to inflict yourself on other human
beings . . . never a wife . . . never, never children . . . not even
friends. You knew that those who fail, as you might, blame
those who are closest. That was your own prediction about
yourself, that you might fail. You wrote the script. To protect
people who came into your life, who might begin to love you,
you took to running. You romanticized and glamorized your

failures. I am like a gypsy, you told yourself, like a homeless clown who comes with the circus or the carnival and then is gone after a few days. *Why didn't you leave me, Larry?*

You were always a thief of love, Lorenzo. You still delight in forbidden love. Women can tell. Perhaps desire flares your nostrils. It may be that the lust in your blood or something in your spirit, perhaps even from another life, is visible to women in your delirious eyes, something that also made you restless and homeless, that made you a dreamer and a wanderer. Something in the blood kept you always in awe about what you did not know, filling your mind and heart with terrible longings and indescribable dreams.

Is it enough, you wonder, the one thing that may possibly redeem you? The blood. Yes, the blood never let you get away. Always it drew you back from wanderings, back to your people, the people of your blood. And yet. . . . One day a few years ago you realized that you had become a stranger to your family in Texas, even to your wife and daughters. You lived with Valerie, Stephanie and Suzie, but could you say a few years ago that you knew them? Did you not once write in one of your stupid pocket notebooks that you could live without them? That you could forget them? Are they not now the creation of your miserable failures?

Wretched, abominable man. You knew that you did not deserve friends. Even a few close friends, and people with whom you work, were less in your life than people whom you meet when you travel out of town, and whom you will never see again. Strangers on planes, buses, trains, elevators, to whom you speak cheerfully, anonymously, breaking through their suspicions with cheerful laughter. They fascinate you because they cannot hold you. Everywhere, Lorenzo, wherever you travel, every place that you visit, you are the stranger, like the wandering apparitions in the songs of Leonard Cohen. *Yes, Daddy, we don't have many friends because of you. . . . Yes, Papa. . . . Guy Dad! You never wanna do anything with us. . . . They will be gone, soon, Larry . . . before you know it the children will be gone. . . . Better think about it. . . . How will they remember you? How do you want them to remember you?* You want them to know about the demons and obsessions, and that you suffer.

Like the gigantic boulder in a Magritte painting, a colossal metal file box, huge as a house, is suspended in the air, very high above the ocean. If a person were looking up from a ship or a boat in the water, he would see from that perspective the tiny figure of a man holding onto an edge of the opening to the grey-colored file box, his feet dangling in the air, holding on for his life. From the suspended man's point of observation, beyond his dangling feet, he commands a complete view of the ocean and the entire circular horizon. There, far below him, in every direction, is the ocean, nothing but water, no land anywhere in sight.

The man holding on for his life is Lorenzo Correa. The colossal grey file box reminds him of his research file cards, which he keeps in five-by-eight gray metal file boxes, just like the one from which he is dangling. He can feel the grip of his hands loosening, the weakness slowly coming into his arms. He wonders how long he can hold on. Not long thereafter he can hold on no longer, and he begins to fall, like Icarus, into the water below. He is thinking, rationally and methodically, as his body plunges downward. I am not afraid. I will never swim to safety, because there is no land anywhere to which I could swim. After I hit the water there will be no purpose to prolonging my life by coming up to the water's surface, swimming about until I am too exhausted to swim anymore, and then drowning. Would it not be simpler just to exhale all the air in my lungs as I plunge, so that when I hit the water I will simply sink? Far below the surface of the water, when I must involuntarily and inevitably inhale, the water will rush into my lungs, fill them up, and I will continue to sink and never come back to the surface.

He feels the weight of his body falling, dreading only the thought of being conscious of drowning and of his last moments of life. The thought of dying does not trouble him. He is horrified only by the knowledge that before the darkness and silence efface his consciousness, there will those last unpleasant moments of disturbing awareness when he will know that he is drowning.

These thoughts are passing through Lorenzo's mind as he plunges headlong, down toward the endless depths of water below. Soon his body will hit the water, he will be sinking, ever downward. Soon his brain will be on fire below the water, his chest will expand and with a supreme, terrible, frightening agony his lungs will swallow up great gulps of water, and he will open his eyes wide with terror and helplessness.

He was still high above the water, falling sheer downward when he began to gasp. Oh! if only this were a dream. If only I could wake up. . . .

I woke up with a terrible hangover. I looked around and I thought that I was dreaming, because my bed was in the large departmental conference room, where a meeting was being held. The faculty members of the Department were all there, about twenty-five of them. At the far end of the conference room Giuseppe, the chairman, was passing around a list for signatures, with course assignments for the spring quarter, even though it was only November. The list was strange, printed by a computer, unlike any I have ever seen. At first I could not find my name. There it is. But instead of my course on Renaissance art from Giotto and Niccolo Pisano to Michelangelo and Donatello, another course was listed by my name. Then I had trouble finding my name again. I had lost it. Now I had to search for it again.

—What is this course alongside my name? I asked, holding my finger to it so as not to lose it again.

—That's a 260, Giuseppe responded, the graduate seminar on the Baroque. You know that material well, Lorenzo. You know, Rubens, Vermeer, Rembrandt, Velásquez, and so on.

—Why did you change my course from the way it was to be scheduled? I already have the syllabus and the slides picked out for the Renaissance course. All my lectures are planned. It took me a long time to get everything together. The Renaissance course is important because of my present research. I have almost completed an article on landscape painting from Giotto to Masaccio! Now I will never be able to finish it.

I was worried about the amount of time I would need to prepare a course that I had not taught before. Why did he say I know the Baroque? While I waited for Giuseppe to explain why he changed my teaching assignment I was thinking that I should ask for release time to prepare for this new course. My request would certainly be in accordance with university policy. While I was debating this in my mind Giuseppe spoke, but he did not answer my question.

—Some students in your class this quarter have already come to me and complained about your teaching, Lorenzo.

What kind of an answer is that? Giuseppe's comment made me very angry. The anger turned to rage. I pushed away the covers and sat up in my bed. Everyone turned in my direction. The rage turned to fury and overcame my customary desire to avoid quarrels with Giuseppe in front of colleagues. Many times in the past I had been tempted to hold him accountable for conducting meetings improperly. He takes advantage of people's courtesy. He knows that they are afraid he will influence colleagues to vote against one another on merit evaluations. Even though my tenure evaluation was coming up shortly I was determined to speak up. I was extremely nervous. After all, keeping one's mouth shut for ten years does make one lose a little self-confidence. Damn him! Damn him! I must tell my colleagues how he fucked up my seminar class.

—Wel-l-l . . . d-do  t-t-tell-l . . . us . . . then-n . . . Yes, I was enraged. But horrors! When I spoke my angry voice was raspy and barely audible, as it is when I have an extremely bad sore throat or when I am about to develop laryngitis. On top of that the terrible hangover made me more nervous. It was frustrating to hear my barely audible, raspy voice. I was grieved that my voice seemed about to abandon me, conscious of not wanting to lose my voice or to become more nervous. I spoke angrily, determined not to be silent and passive, as one who is coming up for tenure is supposed to be. To hell with things now! Fuck getting tenure!

—Well, d-do . . . t-tel-l-l us then, Giuseppe, I repeated nervously, exactly how ma-n-ny s-stu-d-dents came to you . . . to . . . to complain? And would-d-d you be-be-kind enough to t-t-tell . . . tell us . . . how you . . . in your ca-p-pacity as chairman . . . received the . . . the complaints . . . an-n-nd how you handled the mat-t-ter-r . . . s-s-so as to mediate . . . be- . . . between a professor and students. Please d-d-do say it for . . . the . . . the . . . benefit of us . . . all. I am n-n-not concerned about your keep-ping com-m-plaints about m-m-me confidential. There is n-n-n-nothing . . . that I w-w-ish to conceal from . . . our colleagues.

There! I finally got it all out, but I hated my goddamn raspy voice. Meanwhile I felt a chill in my body so I reached over for the covers and wrapped them around myself for warmth. Suddenly, before Giuseppe could reply, I became even more enraged and could no longer disregard what he had done to me recently, just when I was coming up for tenure. I wanted at that moment for all the department to know it. Despite my barely audible, raspy voice I decided to blurt it all out.

Angrily I pushed away the covers of my bed. Everyone was looking at me, making me feel that I was on trial. Looking at the faces of colleagues in the conference room, I felt that I had to speak out.

—Do you know what our chairman did to me?

I paused to let the question sink in. Damn this raspy voice! My rage became more intense, and then my voice became clear and firm.

—When one student—a single student, mind you!—came into his office to complain about my editorial comments on a written class essay that I assigned, he summoned all the students in the class and told them I was teaching the class wrongly. He told them! And he called them into his office, without informing me! Without hearing my side of the story! He asked them to put complaints against me in writing! After that the seminar went from bad to worse. The letters of four students are now permanently in my file. They are vindictive, mean letters. What, I ask, do you think of our chairman now?

As I looked from my bed at all my colleagues' faces, I could see their embarrassment. It was that same I'm-sorry-that's-the-way-things-go kind of look that one sees on their faces when they talk of losing FTE instead of a thinking, feeling colleague, a human being! Unable to endure my appealing eyes, they lowered their eyes when I looked them in the face. Then something . . . I cannot explain it . . . something led me to anticipate what the chairman, who did not interrupt me at all, would say at the end of my outburst.

—I'm afraid Professor Correa is emotionally upset, as everyone can well see. Let's move on to something else. . . .

I felt totally helpless. Suddenly I got out of bed and began to run. I looked back just before slamming the door of the conference room. My colleagues still had their heads lowered, as if they were praying, perhaps for me. Dressed only in underwear shorts, I went to look for my blue bathrobe, which was in the closet of my home. I ran through many halls and corridors. At the end of a small hall, I could see a group of other colleagues holding a meeting. They were in one of the dining rooms of the University Faculty Club. Conscious of being in my underwear shorts, I told myself that there was no reason to be embarrassed. After all, it was not my fault that they chose to hold a meeting where someone might be walking by in shorts on the way to the gym shower.

Among the people at the meeting were several women, but I did not know either the men or the women. Just as I decided that I must walk past their room in order to get my blue bathrobe, one of the women, and after her several of the others, began to turn, one after another, to stare at me.

I am on trial again, I thought. The doorway provided a frame for a remarkably strange group portrait of people sitting at a table with a white tablecloth. I was reminded of the Rembrandt painting on Dutch Masters cigar boxes, of films by Bergman and Buñuel. The way they were staring made me lose courage about going for my blue bathrobe. I was greatly disturbed and embarrassed about how to cover up my body. I turned away from the judgmental faces of the bizarre group. With a terrible self-consciousness of being in undershorts, morbidly aware of the nakedness of my hairy chest and legs, I broke into a run, painfully conscious of my genitals bouncing from side to side, up and down, inside my shorts. Suddenly, I was running, like the frightened child in a de Chirico painting who is running across an empty, melancholy and mysterious street, on the way to some fatal destination. Ahead of me was the shadow of some menacing creature, an executioner perhaps.

A voice reached faintly into the chambers of the frightened man's consciousness. Several times the voice called out his name, as if from far away. Slowly the threatening scene began to dissolve. Half asleep and half awake, tired from all the running, he began to open his eyes. The taste of fear was still in his mouth. Again the voice called his name. *Miguel, you're trembling and perspiring. What is it, honey? Wake up! Oh! You must have a fever. Wake up, Miguel! Wake up! Are you having another bad dream?* Natalie was shaking him by the shoulders.

When he was going through his tenure evaluation he had many terrible dreams. Sometimes the dreams would be interrupted mercifully when he would wake up, two or three times during the night. These awakenings gave him only temporary relief, because the bad dreams would continue as soon as he went back to sleep.

Last night I arrived at a military-type barracks. Double bunk beds were all neatly lined up along the whole length of the interior. Judging from what I could see, men and women shared living and sleeping arrangements. I cannot explain why, but I thought that perhaps the housing facilities were provided without charge. Judging from what I observed, several lovely young girls, if they wished, could make love to any of the young men there. I say this hesitantly, basing my statement on what I observed when I arrived. I remember vaguely, I do not know why vaguely, that late last night girls were climbing into young men's beds. I saw them get into bed and under the covers. I watched the bed covers rising and falling over their bodies.

This morning a young, thin girl who was wearing a black transparent negligée came into my bed and woke me up. I was in the upper bed, on my back. She sat on my genitals. She leaned forward and brought her mouth towards mine. She dropped some saliva in my mouth, and then she stuck her wet tongue inside one of my ears, and then in the other. She seemed disappointed when I exhibited no sexual interest in her. Out of curiosity perhaps, or because I simply love to touch, I did reach over and around her legs, and I ran my hands over her buttocks, under the garter belt that held up her black stockings and under her panties. Nevertheless I felt no desire. When I caressed her buttocks she hugged me approvingly. It was daylight, so even if I had felt desire I would have been inhibited from making love. I confess that I imagined our making love under the covers, but I knew that everyone would know from the revealing movements, just as I knew last night. Furthermore, I would never want anyone other than the woman with me to hear my cries of love or to see my tears when I reach orgasm. To me sex is sacred. It must be a private matter.

—You're very different, she said, still sitting on my genitals. You show no fear, no desperate need to make love. What's the matter, honey? Can't you get it up?

No, that is not what she said, but it was something like that. I have no idea what she meant about being different. Then she was gone. She must have left. I cannot remember.

Later, when I was walking around, I saw several young women in another part of the barracks. The whole scene, the atmosphere, the lighting, the manner in which the women sat, wearing sexy negligees and underclothes, with their legs invitingly and seductively open—everything reminded me of a brothel painting by Toulouse-Lautrec.

Among the women was the girl who had come into my bed earlier. She was small and thin. Her black underclothes emphasized the pale white skin of her legs between the black hose and panties. She had black hair and looked Italian or Mexican or Jewish. Then for the first time I noticed that she had pimples. A few minutes later a man came in. He seemed to be in charge. He asked whether my evening had gone well. He said that the girls were there to please.

—I hope, he said, arching his eyebrows and smiling lasciviously, that one of the women has given you pleasure.

The scene changed. Later I found myself outdoors, inexplicably frightened, walking far from the barracks building, toward a pier, similar to and yet unlike the Santa Monica pier. Here the buildings are on the right side of the pier as one walks toward the Pacific Ocean. Suddenly I caught a glimpse of my own frightened image, reflected in a large picture window. My feet became heavy, as they used to in a recurrent childhood dream. Then in the glass window I saw reflections of two men pursuing me. I wanted to run, but I could not.

I almost woke up. Trembling with fear in my bed, unable to make myself wake up, I fell asleep again. Once more I was walking on the same pier. The two men were still pursuing me. They were within my peripheral vision. I saw them out of the corner of my eye, as I used to see a menacing figure in a recurring childhood nightmare. In my nightmare I was always afraid, running sluggishly around a track, barely able to run, because of fear and because my legs were heavy. I was always trying to get to a safe place at the end of the track before the unknown figure who always terrorized me.

In the glass window I saw that the two men were getting off a ship. One, a tall man, was wearing a dark suit. The other man, shorter, somewhat emaciated, had that appearance which develops in such an obvious way when one crosses the line into severe alcoholism in a short period of time.

—Miguel! Miguel Velásquez! Wait! Wait for us!

In the large store window their reflections were pursuing mine. I quickened my pace to get away and rushed into a bar. Hoping that I had lost them, I ordered a beer. A short while later, thinking that finally I had lost them, I saw one of them in the mirror over the rows of liquor bottles behind the bar. It was the tall man in the dark suit. He seemed the more vicious of the two men. The features of the other man were blurred. Finally, the two men began to walk over to where I was sitting. The smaller man was meekly following the taller man.

I do not remember everything they said, nor does it really matter. The taller man spoke to me.

—You have been selected, he said.

Selected for what? The man did not say. The other man had a nervous habit. He kept pinching his lips and thrusting his prominent chin out, like men do when they adjust the knot on a necktie. Again the tall man spoke to me.

—We have been instructed to act in our capacity as full professors and to grant you a few last wishes. After that our orders are to execute you. Or, he said, amiably, with a polite dissimulating smile on his face, you may choose to commit suicide, to die quietly and peaceably by swallowing a pill.

Probably arsenic, I thought. He said something about "deadwood" which I did not understand.

Now the man from the barracks appeared. When I asked him why I was to be executed, he refused to tell me. Then he disappeared. The two men who had been instructed to execute me were carrying pistols and rifles. They placed them right outside, on the wall of a small one-room building that had a bathroom.

Terror swept over me. Fear for my life quickened my desire to live, and I began to plot. Somehow having managed to escape, I was hiding from still another man with a pistol, in a junk-car lot. When he looked away I ran to a nearby building. I locked the door from the inside and went to the back where the bathroom was. A man was urinating in the bathroom, and one of my two pursuers came around the building and looked at me through the bathroom window, just as I was contemplating escape. He laughed.

—It's no use, he said, looking at his watch.

He told me the time of my execution. Why me? Why me? I was wondering how in the world I might get my hands on one of those rifles. Were they planning to make me run and then shoot me with a rifle rather than with a handgun? Is that what they want, for me to run so that they can shoot me with the rifle? In the back? To use me as a moving target, for practice?

The scene changed as if we were characters in a film. Close-up, interior of an automobile. The driver is not visible. But this is real. I do not want to die. In this scene I am in the back seat of a moving automobile, sitting between the two men charged with my execution. The emaciated man, who in this scene seems more healthy, keeps playing with the weapon, arranging and rearranging the handgun on his lap in an almost ritual manner, over and over, meticulously. From this point on my mind became set on seizing one of the weapons. Terrified, I wanted to wake up. I did, momentarily, but I fell asleep again.

When I looked around me, I was facing the sea, sitting at a table with the two men. The view of the sea was magnificent. One of them spoke.

—We are happy to grant your request for a last meal, he said. The setting reminded me of a Dalí painting, and of sea images in Fellini films.

On the center of the table was a pistol. I estimated it to be just within my reach, and I began to study the possibility of seizing it quickly and shooting them. What have I to lose, if they are going to execute me anyway?

Food was brought and placed next to the pistol. Directly in front of me were the two men. For certain as soon as I finished with the meal I would be shot. I would never take arsenic. Animal instincts of survival obsessed me with the desire to live. No, I do not want to die! How was I chosen and why? They refused to tell me.

No matter what, I must grab the pistol and shoot them. Now there are five men, but only two are armed. The others, something tells me, are passive. They mean me no harm, but neither will they offer help. They will not go against the two men who plan to execute me. I wonder . . . must I kill them also? Will the two armed men kill them if they do not try to stop me? What if I fail to escape? I must get one of my captor-executioners behind me. I must render him helpless . . . with a powerful blow to the groin, with my elbow . . . or my knee. Before or after I grab the weapon? Carefully, slowly so they will not become suspicious, I reach for a piece of meat. It is only an inch away from the pistol. Is the pistol cocked and ready to fire? The timing will be very important. If I am going to die, I must try anything. *No! No-oo-o-o! I don't want to die! I don't want to die!* Either way I will die, so why not die fighting?

At the very moment when I was prepared to kill I heard a voice. Whose voice is it? No, yes, it is Natalie's voice. Where are you? Natalie! *Wake up, Miguel! You're having a bad dream!*

I was not completely awake . . . terribly frightened . . . awful fear in my guts. Half asleep and half awake . . . still trying to decide which action to take first . . . what to do? Shall I drive my elbow into the man's groin first, and at the same time seize the weapon, then shoot the other man? Or should I grab the weapon and shoot first? Shoot them both? Even before I do anything I have already enacted the whole scene in my mind. I had struck.

One man is clutching his groin, bending over in pain. What about the others? One of them might have to kill me. I must reach for the pistol, seize it. I don't want to die. I want to live. But if I escape after killing them I must run for the rest of my life.

Gradually I realized that I was awake, in my own bed, and the choices were unnecessary.

—Miguel. You're trembling. See, honey, you shouldn't drink so much before going to bed. You were crying in your sleep, calling my name. Oh! just look at you! You've been crying in your sleep. Your eyes are all red and you're trembling. . . .

For several minutes the fear of death and the obsession to kill in order to live, the terror of being compelled to kill human beings, left him physically and emotionally weary and troubled.

Who was the tall man? Giovanni? The others? Was the emaciated one the Austrian, Bauer? They say he has a drinking problem, headed towards his third divorce. What does this dream mean? What did the girl mean? What does this dream have to do with tenure? Having no sexual desire? Why? So many months, just writing letters to the Dean, to the Chairman of Privilege and Tenure, because they have denied me tenure. Cannot even tell Natalie. Mustn't worry her.

—It's all right, Natalie. Turn out the light. Go back to sleep. It was just a bad dream.

I am a passenger aboard a crowded electric train car. The train is moving quietly on tracks that will intersect ahead with other tracks. A few yards before the tracks intersect, a red light is flashing. The train begins to slow down. It does not resume its normal speed. Night has fallen and the train is practically stopped.

The operator tried without success to get it back to normal speed. Behind our train the two wavering lights of another approaching train were visible, yet no one was alarmed. Everyone remained calm despite the train's coming closer and closer. It was approaching slowly. There seemed to be no danger of a collision. Inside our train, among the passengers was a lovely girl whom I wanted to meet. She reminded me of a young girl from the South whom I met recently at a department store, who in turn reminded me of another southern girl who was abused by her father when she was fourteen.

Finally, apparently convinced that our train was not functioning properly, the operator tried to open the doors to let us out. But the switch that opens the doors did not work. He decided, consequently, to break open a small overhead window, perhaps to get at an emergency device that will open the doors. Perhaps breaking the glass will open the doors.

When the glass broke the doors opened and the people began to spill out to safety. Everyone walked out calmly onto the crowded street. People were relieved and smiling, and they began to walk away, safely in both directions, to left and right.

I was walking between two people, in the opposite direction from that taken by the beautiful girl whose friendly eyes glanced back towards me and met my own. She was wearing a light-colored, grey-beige skirt that fitted tightly around her strong, well-defined young buttocks. She smiled in a way that acknowledged my attraction. I believed the attraction to be mutual, but despite her friendliness I hesitated to go and introduce myself. She paused, smiled, began to walk away, stopped, and turned to see if I was going to follow her. Lack of self-confidence froze me to the spot. Then she continued on.

Then I became aware of walking slightly behind two different people. They continued walking ahead until they were not visible anymore. Being with other people inhibits me from pursuing beautiful women. That is why I travel alone, in case the possibility of an amorous adventure presents itself. These people will wait, or come back for me; it does not matter. Giving it more thought after a few moments of indecision, I turned around and started to catch up with the lovely girl.

There, a few yards ahead, was the beautiful girl. She smiled encouragingly again. I returned her smile awkwardly, with uncertainty and indecision. She was smiling and slowed down so that I could catch up with her. What more can she do to encourage me? Damn my nervous reluctance! Why am I so damn shy at times? Then she began to walk away, stopped momentarily once more, and looked over her shoulder to see if I was following her.

When I did not move she continued on. Then I began to follow her. She is so lovely and encouragingly friendly. What is the matter with me?

The sidewalk was crowded with people. It was difficult to catch up with the girl. I could see her wending in and out of the crowd. Ah! there she is. I can see her grey-beige skirt. Then she was lost from sight again.

Suddenly, among a large crowd of people, women with horror-stricken eyes began to run wildly and to scatter. There was no screaming but there was great fear on the running women's faces. Several frightened men also began to scatter, to run away. There was panic everywhere. I could not see clearly what was going on until several people cleared the area. Then it became clear.

It was a horrible, a violent scene. Several men were seizing women left and right, and men as well, to assault them sexually. Some of the victims were being assaulted right there on the street. The sidewalk, the closed steel doors of the sidewalk elevator on a raised concrete platform, the downstairs buildings, the iron grill fire escapes, and the whole scene reminded me of the Lower Eastside streets of New York. On top of the closed steel doors of a large sidewalk elevator several men were preparing to rape female and male victims. I wanted to help. I imagined myself going heroically from one of the attackers to the others, striking them, pulling them away from the victims. What could I do against so many? Helpless, I was helpless. Like a coward, all I could think of was to run away, immediately, before I too became a victim. The mere thought was repulsive.

Everywhere, before the terrified eyes of scattering people, several men with wild leering faces were removing women's clothing, preparing to rape them. Over there one man was rubbing a woman's private part with a lubricant. To the right, among twelve to fifteen victims being simultaneously violated was the beautiful girl. A wild-eyed man had just pulled down her skirt from behind. She was terror-stricken and helpless. All the victims were helpless; some were being violently raped from behind. I too was helpless. How can men do such violence to human beings? What can I do, alone, against so many of them? Then, seeing among the victims, men too, the most abominable thought struck my mind like a thunderbolt. If I tried to help, the attackers would turn their violence against me.

50

The strategy of the rapists was clear. They probably agreed beforehand to attack simultaneously, to lend support to one another, to eliminate with tumult and mass hysteria any possibility of help for the victims. They had succeeded.

Just as I was sneaking away to avoid attention, making my cowardly dash for safety, I woke up with the grotesque scene vividly before my mind's eye, full of the terrible details, the attackers' grotesque, leering faces, their busy, malignant hands forcing women's naked bodies into vulnerable positions, men fully dressed ripping away the clothing of more and more women, the horrified and helpless look on the victims' faces. Some of the attacking men have already lowered their trousers or unzipped the front. They were ready to violate.

Oh, God! This is the most abominable of crimes! How can men do such violence to one another and to women? And I was totally helpless.

# V

ONE MORNING, a little after five o'clock, he woke up and for a long time he could not go back to sleep. Bureaucratic responsibilities at the university had turned him into a restless sleeper. Very often in his dreams he composed memoranda, letters of recommendation for students, the minutes of committee meetings, angry letters to merchants and businessmen. He also dreamed of strange beasts devouring each other, of angry lionesses stalking him on the streets of his childhood neighborhood in Texas or coming into his bed, like one lioness which took his erect penis into its mouth; he saw millions of strange tiny creatures squirming with eerie life in his own suburban backyard; he experienced terror because of unknown men peering into the bedroom window while his naked wife was dressing; he saw his daughters being threatened by huge snakes or getting away from him in runaway automobiles they did not know how to drive, or falling from the roofs of houses, or being kidnapped or attacked by evil-looking men. Often he found himself in bed with women, and being excessively aware of others watching, unable to make love; frequently he passed through landscapes that combined scenes of places that he once knew; he travelled roads that seemed untravelled, that passed strange, uninhabited areas, leading him to who knows where; he dreamed of attempts on his life, of experiencing great, immense rage, and of killing for survival. In his dreams he is late for appointments, he loses his way rushing, trying to get to airports; elevators, with him among others inside, break down or go berserk; trains are derailed; crowds of people are violently assaulted; he tries to run away, he stumbles, he is dying or about to die, he wakes up shrieking during the night, and more. . . . He does not know where he is going or what life holds ahead for him.

That morning he could not take his mind off the work that had to be done that day. He could not forget the unpleasant meeting of the day before, or the action he had felt forced to take. He wondered if he had done the right thing . . . *there are disturbing similarities in your proposal and mine* . . . afterwards . . . lunch with Pete Alvarado . . . *you did the right thing, Larry* . . . *and bringing it out like you did . . . in front of witnesses so that everyone could judge for himself . . . yeah, I gotta hand it to you, Larry . . . that was the professional thing to do* . . . Pete was lying, of course, being devious as usual, pretending not to take sides . . . *no one'll be able to say you're talking behind his back.* . . . but what if I am wrong? And yet, that I would have done such a thing, he reasoned, indicates that Almafuerte's conduct in the past gives credence to my suspicions . . . *I did not name the charge against him . . . I do not want to nail him* . . . he told Pete . . . *but he has gone too far-.* . . . *I wanted the rest of you to know how far . . . and because of our silence . . . well . . . he was getting bolder and . . . more blatantly quarrelsome and unreasonable* . . . and unable to get back to sleep, he began to think that perhaps he should get up; after all, he had gone to bed early and he felt rested. He would be able to get a little work done before the children and Natalie were up. It had begun to get chilly at night, so he brought the blanket up high against his neck for warmth, and he wondered where Pete really stood in this matter; after all it was quite serious, but he and everyone knew Pete. Pete was one of the cleverest people at the university, and even when someone asked him a question point-blank, he always managed to squirm out of giving a clear answer. . . . Oh, well.

Then he snuggled under the covers and did not get up, and he went back to sleep and began to dream.

He was with another person. It was not clear if the other person was male or female. He felt only a presence. They were standing in a setting that suggested the craggy rocks and wilderness so beloved of the romantic poets, atop a great boulder that permitted a spectacular panoramic view about them. It was a splendid view of wooded areas everywhere that reminded him of the painter Thomas Cole and the American Native and Hudson River schools of nineteenth-century American landscape painting. Down below was a river that cut through the wooded country. In the river, far away, two people were swimming.

A man in a sweat suit arrived on the scene, and as he was jogging by he made strange grunting sounds that brought to mind the sounds made by participants in kung fu martial arts. The jogger was muscular and because of his resemblance to Burt Lancaster, the jogger could have been the same man who appeared in the film which Lorenzo had dreamed earlier that same night. While he was watching the film, Lorenzo had searched intently for Jewish features in the face of the movie star whom he thought did not look very Jewish.

From down below a voice cried out. The swimmer who was farthest away in the river below was warning him to leave. He was waving his arm and saying in Spanish, Go away! Go away! But he was using the singular *¡Vete! ¡Vete!* Why doesn't he use the plural *¡Váyanse! ¡Váyanse!* Why? Several times he heard the warning, just the one warning word in its singular form. The other person who was standing next to him must have vanished. Lorenzo was alone. The alarming word frightened him, to run, to escape. Down in the river below, he could almost see in close-up, the menacing face of the other swimmer who posed some unknown danger for Lorenzo. Indeed the face had the determined look of one who is intent on revenge.

Lorenzo's fear brought a weakness into his legs. Once more, the weakness in his legs made him think about his recurrent childhood dream . . . always having to run around a track that circles an open field . . . endlessly having to run for safety, forever having to reach the end of the track, before the threatening person, who was always running against him in the opposite direction. As in the childhood dream which always attended an illness and fever, so now Lorenzo knew that he would not be able to depend on his legs.

He wanted desperately to get away. He wanted to run while a great distance and precious time still separated him from the dangerous man who was swimming rapidly in his direction. Down below, the man's arms were rising and plunging alternately, into the water, quickly, up in the air, quickly into the water. Soon the man would reach the craggy rocks and boulders down below and begin to climb up to where Lorenzo stood, riveted helplessly to the spot. The weakness in his legs prevented him from running away. He was afraid that if he began to run his legs would collapse. He just stood there, helplessly, wanting and thinking about running away, but unable to do so.

At that point he awoke once more, still trembling with fear. Two hours had passed. It was a little after seven o'clock when he rose and went into the bathroom. After brushing his teeth, he turned on the shower. In the shower his mind turned to the two meetings scheduled for that day, the Chicano Studies Advisory meeting at noon, which would bring him into contact with Almafuerte again, and the Faculty Senate Affirmative Action Committee meeting, of which he was the chairman. Soaping himself vigorously, building up a rich lather, Lorenzo thought sadly of the pained, anguished look of disbelief on Dan Almafuerte's face, when he confronted Dan, and later, when Lorenzo saw him, rotating his small left hand at the end of his arm, held slightly away from his body, as he was walking slowly across the campus, his wife alongside of him, listening carefully to her husband's account of the unfortunate meeting earlier in the day. She was gazing intently in front of her feet while Almafuerte, like a blind man, was looking upwards, unseeingly. How sad that it had come to a confrontation.

Lorenzo rinsed the soap from his hair. Almafuerte would never forgive him for the irrevocable insinuation that the others preferred not to pursue. It was done. Lorenzo would always be incompetent in the politics of academia. Being naive about campus politics, often to the point of stupidity, he could not even see that the menacing swimmer of his bad dream was Dan Almafuerte, who would spend the next three years making life miserable, turning Chicano staff, students and people from the barrio communities against Lorenzo. One simply does not surprise and embarrass colleagues publicly. It is customary to work quietly, "speaking confidentially, of course." To rally support against an enemy colleague, one must learn the art of dissimulation.

In these matters, Lorenzo was downright stupid. He surrendered to his rage too often. He expressed contempt for colleagues with silence and glaring looks. To avoid shaking hands with people he did not respect, he would deliberately shift an object from his left to his right hand, or stick his hand in his pocket. He had left men standing with hands extended. ¡No seas pendejo! one of his Chicano colleagues told him. But how long did Dan think he could go on being arrogant and quarrelsome, being disrespectful towards students and staff who did not share his views, and expecting Chicano Studies faculty members to remain politely quiet while he went about placing them all in a bad light because of his conduct? How long?

How sad, Lorenzo thought, as he took water into his mouth and gurgled. At his age he wanted to be gentle. He had learned to avoid people who brought out in him his great capacity for hatred. No, there had been enough hatred in the past. He was older now. He had mellowed. He wanted to put his life's work together, aiming for his fiftieth birthday, only a few years away, as a time to begin that task. After that let the years and the work come and go as they will. After that, whatever might be possible—what the hell—the rest will be a gift of Providence. Why the fiftieth birthday? A symbolic year in a person's life? Perhaps. The thought could not be explained. It was simply there.

Above all, the novel that had taken possession of his life mattered, the novel in which he had been writing away his present life rather than living it. He wanted to find his writer's voice, the right tone for the writing, to work at the writer's craft.

He turned off the water, pressed his hands against his body and rubbed them downwards like squeegees to remove some of the water. Then he stepped out of the shower, took his heavy bath towel from the rack and began to dry himself.

At times he was troubled about his academic career, about his relationships with colleagues, some of them kind and thoughtful people. While he was writing his novel his colleagues and scholars in the same field had gone on to write countless articles and books, leaving him farther and farther behind with each passing year. Life, and the days and weeks and months and years, had passed him by, like a rushing train.

He glanced in the mirror and thought of the meetings scheduled for the morning and afternoon. If only he could be just a scholar, or just a teacher! Perhaps then he might have had some success. Perhaps that would have made him a good husband and a good father. He thought of the midterm examination which he had to type, scheduled for the following week.

The reflection of his blurred face turned one way and then another in the mirror. Also, he had taught two two-hour sessions of creative writing at his daughter's elementary school.

The gifted children's Halloween stories were waiting for comments in a manila folder on his desk. There was a six-hundred-page novel to be reviewed, written by a colleague who was being evaluated for a merit increase; and there was still another meeting concerning personnel evaluations in his other department; and everything required time to read; he still had to prepare for his classes. In one of them he was using a book he had never read, because that was the only way he could force himself to read it! Force himself! The thought made him cringe. Time! Time! In the same class he was using three other large novels which he wanted to reread but had never used in classes before. Soon, he would have to take some of his scholarly material and reshape it in order to present it at a conference only two weeks away; then there was the graduate student coming up for his doctoral comprehensives; and today there were many little errands that he had to run—going to the bank, the post office, the campus parking office, then the meetings. So many things.

After drying off his body he put away the large towel and he took a smaller towel to dry his hair. He also had to call the principal of Suzie's school to see what kind of program she had organized for the gifted and talented children.

He was still staring at his reflection in the bathroom cabinet mirror. The shower made him feel good and clean. His face came closer to the mirror. He squinted. Yes, they were coming along, the furrows of time around his squinting eyes, around his nostrils. He was one of them, a member of an aging department. His tousled, uncombed hair was pepper-colored, his beard was almost white. The hair on his chest was almost all white too. On his naked belly he saw, as he backed away from the sink, a few scattered grey hairs, and white hairs on his scrotum also. He glanced up again into the mirror. His blurred reflection reminded him of figures in Zurbarán paintings.

Suddenly he understood the meaning of the Rip Van Winkle story. One goes to sleep at night, and when one wakes up the next morning days, weeks, months, and years have fled! Oh! . . . I grow old! . . . I grow old! . . . I will wear the bottoms of my trousers rolled!

The pilot's garbled voice came over the speaker system. Miguel Velásquez glanced up and saw that the No Smoking and the Fasten Seat Belt signs had been turned off.

"This is the pilot, Captain Richards. Thank you for flying PSA. Our plane has reached its assigned flying altitude of 31,000 feet. You're aboard a PSA 737, Flight 509, destination Oakland Airport, and then on to Reno, Nevada. It's a very pleasant day for flying . . . weather's just perfect . . . visibility is clear. We should be arriving at Oakland in approximately forty-two minutes from now. It's sunny there, and the temperature's seventy-seven degrees. We hope you have a pleasant flight. We'll be serving refreshments now, and spirits for those of you who care to make your trip a little more relaxing. You'll notice that the 'no smoking' and the 'fasten seat belt' signs have been turned off, but we recommend . . . "

The plane had found a steady course and all the clouds were gone. It was truly a beautiful, sunny day. Miguel loosened his seat belt. Sometimes the chapters of the novel seemed to fall together in his mind. Not long ago, on another trip to Berkeley, he thought of a title, "Voices," to convey the sense of his own experience. Other times it seemed foolish to conceive of a novel of voices. Was it a worthwhile enterprise to make a written record of voices that came to his mind whenever he travelled, or when he walked the streets? And what would one call a novel that obsessed him even in his dreams, that continued to write itself even when he slept? A lucid novel? A dream novel?

After many years, he finally realized that the writing of a novel was an awesome, solitary enterprise. His main character gave him difficulties, because the character felt that the novel must include everything. Initially, before his tenure evaluation, Miguel had conceived of a simple, straightforward narrative. But now! Was his a hopeless task, to write a novel which he could not begin? A beginning must be good, to seize the reader immediately. He wondered if most writers have trouble beginning, or knowing how to tell the story. What narrative voice should I use? The first person or the third. Perhaps the second person. Was it to be an autobiographical novel? Where could he begin? In the present? The past? He knew that his most difficult problem would be to find a way to tell the story. What if he wrote it in the form of a filmscript, from the point of view of a camera?

The passenger in the aisle seat across from Miguel saw him take out his pocket notebook and his Parker fountain pen. He took the top of the pen off and began to write.

NOTES. Why, when dreams have always been important to writers and painters of fantasy, and in this century to film-makers also, why has no one thought of the most appropriate term to describe a work of art about a work of art, which incorporates the consciousness of the creator (or of his spokesman, the narrator or a character or characters), in the process of consciously creating a work of fictional art. The most appropriate word to describe such a work, a novel or a film or a play, seems to be *lucid*. As in a *lucid dream*, in which the dreamer is conscious that he is dreaming, and in some cases dreaming a dream over which he exercises some control, like a writer creating fiction. A work of art, then, in which the creator appears like the lucid dreamer, watching himself consciously creating, with conscious control over the images—even though he is sleeping and dreaming—over the scenes, the action, the characters, and over what develops in his fiction, watching his mind weighing which of many alternative possibilities the work of art itself wishes to take, letting it lead the creator forward towards choices, selections, directions —is this not a *lucid* work of art? A *lucid novel*. A *lucid film*. A *lucid painting*. A *lucid poem*. A *lucid play*. Are not the lucid dreamer and the lucid artist alike then? Do they not share an imaginative, creative mind that works independently of attention, that works best when it is idle in the best possible sense, because when it is unburdened, it is then that the mind does on its own the work which one cannot force it to do?

Miguel Velásquez stopped writing. He glanced towards the front of the airplane, at the tops of his fellow passengers' heads. Across the aisle from him, a fellow passenger was still watching him, wondering what Miguel was writing in the little pocket notebook.

I must ponder this a little more, Miguel thought, give my mind an opportunity to digest these reflections. I am not sure that I have expressed my thoughts well.

He put away his fountain pen but he kept the pocket notebook in his hand. He flipped through the pages until he came to an entry dated Thursday, June 9. The curious fellow passenger wondered what Miguel was reading.

Thursday, June 9. Today I confirmed the rumor which I heard about the middle of May that Roberto Roquefort has been looking for a woman to charge me with sexual harassment. It is no longer a rumor. Today, I had breakfast with Mariana. When I told her about the rumor, she said to me, "Please, Miguel, this must be a private conversation." A man called her on the telephone, she said, asking if she would bring charges against me. She said that she was deeply offended and that she passed a very restless night. She would not tell me who telephoned her.

Monday, June 13. Today I learned the name of the person who first overheard three women discussing this distasteful matter.

"She's a quiet person who hardly talks," Richard said. "The three women saw her. They must've known she could overhear them, but they probably didn't think she'd say anything. She came and told me."

Richard told me her name and the names of two of the three women. The person who told him did not know the name of the third woman. According to Richard's friend, the exact words spoken by one of the women were: "Miguel would be easy to hang a sexual harassment charge on."

Later in the afternoon. I covered myself on that possible charge by calling the staff personnel office. The director of that office will discuss the matter with the affirmative action officer on campus.

On Thursday, June 9, the young woman who was recently offered a teaching assistantship telephoned me. Richard, she and I had lunch the next day, on Friday. She agreed to accept the assistantship, and because of certain improprieties when it was awarded to her, she also agreed to decline the position later. There is talk on campus that Roberto has gone to an academic senate committee to bring charges of some kind.

"It's confidential," Richard said. "I can't talk about it. But Roberto's gonna get a warning that if he persists, counter-charges will be brought against him."

Wednesday, June 29. I have been covering myself by telling many people that an invented charge of sexual harassment might be brought against me. Two days ago I spoke with Eleanor Alvarado about it. Today, I had lunch with Mariana and Frances. After a wonderful, playful conversation about a perfect scenario for two Latino lovers, I mentioned recent developments in the continuing scandal surrounding Chicano

Studies. Mariana told me the name of the man who telephoned asking her to bring the sexual harassment charge against me. His name is Henry, Roquefort's right-hand man. But she hedged and changed the story she told me in private conversation on June 9. At least I know the names of the main persons involved. Tomorrow I will call the director of the personnel office.

Perhaps some day, he thought, raising his eyes away from the notebook, all this will go into the novel. Perhaps not. The one abominable Chicano character of my novel, should it ever get published, will set our literature back enough as it is.

He flipped through the pages of his pocket notebook. He paused and read a few sketchy notes in which he had outlined events of another year.

What strange seasons the spring and summer were of that unforgettable year. Borges at Domínguez Hills. Memories and regrets that still trouble me when I remember. The eruption of Mexico's El Chichón volcano. Denise. Sylvia and the García Lorca play at the Inland University Theatre . . . cariño, cariño. . . . The visit with the doctor to discuss my physical examination. Have I done irreparable physical harm to myself? Sylvia and I at José Durán's home. Who would have known? At my age! Summer visitors, Kathy and Doug, Lew Pierce and his daughters. Outdoor barbecues and conversations, good friends. Always, thoughts about the novel.

# VI

At the front of the plane a steward was starting out with the liquor cart. He was moving it from side to side in order to center it in the aisle. Soon the attractive stewardess joined him.

Miguel Velásquez flipped the pages of his pocket notebook rapidly. He caught glimpses of other notes which evoked experiences that he wanted to develop fictionally. Glancing up toward the liquor cart, he thrust the little notebook into the pocket of his coat. *Hijo, no se te olvide traerme una botellita de whiscle . . .*

The sight of the liquor cart carrying small bottles of whiskey evoked his grandfather's voice from long ago. The memories began to stir in him. The sensation was inexpressibly strong and pleasurable, connected with travel. He closed his eyes and savored the nostalgic moment, letting the mounting sensation sweep through his spirit. In his mind's eye he saw a long, narrow dirt road in the middle of great fields of fertile land. The road led the eye towards the two-story house where he was born, and because of the distance the house looked like a toy house on the horizon. The house was surrounded and shaded by chinaberry trees, and the whole scene was dominated by the immense blue Texas sky. The remembered scene thrilled him with the sweet sadness of nostalgic memories, a bittersweet sense of loss, and his childhood longings for faraway and unknown places. How strangely had the little whiskey bottles evoked his grandfather's voice and the house where he was born.

The liquor cart was making its way down the aisle, with the little liquor bottles all neatly lined up behind cans of soft drinks, whiskey and vodka and gin and brandy and more. He glanced from one side of the airplane interior to the other.

The scene through the porthole windows, of bright sunshine and great distances, made him joyful. The warmth of the sun, too, which from the inside of the PSA 737 he could only imagine, added to the sensation, very much like that which one experiences when, after a long absence, one returns to a childhood place, or when, far from home and one's place of birth, one thinks of his father's face; or of the one small room where a family of six children slept in the same bed and of the mother bending over to cover them up.... He heard his grandfather's voice clearly. *A-a-cuérdate hi-i-i-jo ... acuérdate, hijo, de traerme una botellita ... de whiscle....*

His grandfather's voice took him back to childhood days when every Sunday the whole family used to visit the two sets of grandparents in the country. Sunday visits, unbearably long to the children who could find only mischief to get into while the grownups talked, sitting around the table in the kitchen forever, it seemed to the children, until at last, just before dark, when they were all inside the old Model A, his grandfather would take Miguel's father aside and whisper, as if the grandmother did not know what he wanted, the same unforgettable words each time, reminding him to bring a little pint of whiskey the next Sunday ... *que no se te vaya a olvidar ... hijo....* And of course Miguel's father never disappointed the once hard-drinking old revolutionary cavalry soldier.

Vividly, like scenes from a movie, the memories of childhood returned. Among them, this farewell scene always stood out in Miguel's mind. He could easily imagine the scene filmed with a zoom lens. Countless times over the years, in many parts of the country, the memory of this scene had come to comfort him. This memory made him a child again, standing alongside his brother Alejandro and his sister Isabel, the three eternally waving good-bye to their grandparents from the back seat of the old Model A which his father owned long ago. Their grandmother and grandfather and the two-story farmhouse kept getting smaller and smaller as the car lurched along on the long narrow dirt road, until he could barely see them when the car arrived at the intersection of the dirt road with the old Hutto highway.

Mexican people called it "el jaro jaiwei"; it was a two-lane hardtop road that always smelled of asphalt. At the intersection his father always looked both ways after stopping the car, after shifting into first gear, then he would slowly let out the clutch, press lightly on the accelerator pedal, bring the car out into the highway and turn south towards Austin and home. The smell of asphalt and engine oil engraved the whole scene indelibly in the child's memory. He would always remember the slow lurching movements of the old Model A, which settled down when his father shifted into third gear and found the right pace for it. The string of farewells became one scene ultimately, a single memory that he would discover many years afterward and treasure for the rest of his life. Mingling and unmingling smells of gasoline and engine oil and asphalt. It was enough in later years for any one of the smells alone to enter his nostrils to evoke the Sunday trips to and from his grandparents' homes in the country, the sweet murmuring sound of the tires on fresh asphalt, the unforgettable sweet-sad Sunday visits in the country, and the journeys back home through wooded and unpopulated areas long ago, before the construction of the great Interstate 35 made the old Dallas Highway a thing of the past and transformed Pflugerville into a suburb of Austin.

At the front of the PSA 737 the steward pushed the liquor cart a few rows ahead. On the other side of the cart the attractive stewardess was serving drinks to two of the passengers.

A different farewell scene stood out in his mother's memory, but it too was conjured up by the same string of farewells repeating the same scene at the end of each Sunday visit. One day a few years ago, when he was sitting in the kitchen with his mother Miguel asked her what it was like to live with the grandfather. A faraway look came into his mother's face, and Miguel could read on her face that there were painful things connected with those first four years of marriage with his father, when they were poor and had to live with the grandfather. Miguel wished that he could read his mother's thoughts. He wished that she would share them with him. He wanted to know his grandfather, everything, whether it be good or bad. For a long time not even Miguel's father would talk about the old man. Miguel had to listen carefully for spontaneous comments about the grandfather. Slowly, over the years, a portrait of the grandfather began to emerge, like a portrait on canvas, a few brushstrokes at a time, from little bits of information buried in conversations about other things.

That day he was sitting at the kitchen table with his mother, like the grownups used to when he was a child. Miguel wanted very much to know his mother also. On a previous visit, Natalie, who had just finished reading *The Thorn Birds*, had made him curious about her private life. *Mamá, when you were a girl and a young woman, what were you like?* Miguel probed thereafter, but his mother was reticent. A little bit at a time, during each of his recent visits to Austin, he began to break through her reticence and shyness. That particular day, after a very long silence during which Miguel waited patiently, she told him how she felt on the day when they finally moved out of the grandfather's home and away from Pflugerville.

*At the end of every Sunday visit I used to remember the day we moved out . . . When we were leaving, to come home, it reminded me. . . . The moment I got into the car I would remember how finally, after four years, we moved away . . . I will never forget, I thought to myself . . . as we were driving away . . . they are over! Over at last! . . . four terrible years under the same roof with a madman . . . a foulmouthed, hateful . . . mean drunkard . . . ya no lo podía aguantar . . . Thank God, thank God! They are over . . . those four unbearable years. . . . I thought they would never end. That's what I was thinking when we finally moved away. I told myself I would never forget or forgive him . . . me hizo sufrir mucho. . . . And do you know what he said to your father, his last words? Right in front of me! He said, you must always wear the pants, Antonio . . . you must make your wife . . . do as you say . . . be the man in your family . . . let her know from the very beginning who wears the pants! Do you understand, Antonio? he asked. Can you imagine! ¡Ay, hijo! you look just like him. . . . forgive me . . . forgive me for my thoughts.*

His mother's voice echoed in his mind as he contemplated through one of the windows the beauty of the day and the immensity of the lands down below, thirty-one thousand feet below, is that what the pilot said? He could not remember. How remarkable that his mother, who never went to school, who could not read or write, should have pushed her son so irrevocably in the direction of his own destiny, towards a world of books from which she herself was forever excluded. With growing pride, the son began to understand the world of doña Dolores Velásquez. His mother, he discovered, connected him with his whole family and his people. She taught him to see with her eyes, to understand with fresh insights the country of his birth and the country of his ancestors, and himself above all. Many things which he might otherwise have taken for granted or forgotten because of his education and travels, because of books, acquired a fresh, memorable and enduring value because of his mother. At that moment, sitting towards the back of the airplane, he found his thoughts linking his mother and his family with that amazing discovery, one day, in the university parking lot on the way to his car, when he realized that the joint appointment in Chicano Studies had changed the whole direction of his life. That discovery took place unexpectedly, not long after the tenure evaluation which truly opened his eyes to American education and universities and professors.

The tenure evaluation shook his sense of what really mattered in life. It brought back long-buried memories which had comforted him during the years when he was disappointed in himself. These memories were connected with the love and wisdom of his family and his people. His appointment in Chicano Studies made him aware that his American success story, as some people could reasonably view the path of his life, the attainment of a professional position, a middle-class life, a home and family, travel and a knowledge of the world, among other things; these, he realized, would never have been possible without the great sacrifices of his mother and father. Indeed, his university appointment ensured his never taking for granted the world of his mother and father, his grandparents and his ancestors; ensured his never becoming blind to his people, their struggles and hardships in the country of his birth and in the country of his ancestry. Looking back on it, he remembered that his joint appointment had begun—after Chicago, Mexico City, New York, Europe—with the culture shock of coming to Ríoseco, California. Paradoxically, as he drove about the city during the first weeks and months, becoming slowly acquainted with the city's neighborhoods—the streets, freeway exits and landmarks; its happy-hour places and restaurants, and the city's inhabitants—he always found his thoughts turning back to other countries and cities, to places where he had lived, to people whom he had known and to the things he had done, and following an impulse which had taken hold of him long before coming to Ríoseco, he continued to fill notebooks which he hoped one day to turn into a novel.

Miguel looked to the front of the plane, then he brought his head and rested it against the back of his seat. How the years had flown by. Soon the liquor cart would be at his side.

Voices. What's your novel about, Miguel? . . . Is there any sex in your novel? . . . Is the novel about people you know? Are we in it? Yeah? You're gonna call me Irwin how come you don't use my real name? Sure it's all right Preston's my name I don't mind. The tape? You wanna borrow it you mean Shawna's Bat Mizvah tape oh I keep forgettin' it yeah sure you can borrow it I'll get it to you on Tuesday, okay? . . . How did you and Miguel meet, Natalie? In New York? He was dating a friend of yours and she wanted to know if it was okay to bring a Mexican to your party yes she brought him and after that? . . . No fair telling she said smiling it's a little too personal and she laughed ha! ha! . . . What's it like, Natalie . . . being married to a Chicano? Is your husband's novel about the university? . . . Am I in your novel? Damn! when are you gonna finish it so's I can read the parts about me? . . . No he didn't get recommended for tenure . . . too many things going against him I tried though but. . . . Were you spanked when you were a little boy Daddy? Please tell us and then we'll go to sleep ple-e-ease Daddy! . . . You can't do it, Miguel it's madness too much for one man just get a few articles out so you can get a merit increase two articles a year one day you must make general full professor at the university like a general in the military . . . Get away from me, Lorenzo, don't touch me! Why don't you paint anymore, or write your novel at night? You're drunk again get away from me find yourself a mistress all you do is talk about writing and about the masterpieces of painting you're gonna do all you do is drink every night I'm tired of waking up every morning to your alcoholic breath cleaning up the half-full whiskey glasses in the morning watching you pass out every night . . . oh, Lorenzo! . . . One part of your mind is trying to tell you something . . . if you interpret the dreams, what your dreaming mind is trying to tell you is that you are slowly killing yourself. . . . You remember your dear friend, Alfredo. In the year before he died he told you, I've begun to read the obituary columns he said I'm curious about how old people are when they die and about the causes of their deaths, and you had a dream about him Lorenzo that he was dying but you didn't really know until it was too late and when you spoke on the telephone he said he just wanted to hear your voice, no, no special reason for calling he said, you did not know at that time you would never see him alive or hear his voice ever again, he was like your own brother. . . . Hey! Did you read Giovanni's zoo article about the department? Which animal is you?

Like the city from which it took its name, Ríoseco University turned out to be a fascinating place, too. The world of the university and the life and foibles of professors were favorite topics of conversation among the secretaries who addressed as "professor" the men and women of culture and learning who called the secretaries by their first names.

A few years ago he began to ask some of the secretaries what it was like to work at the university. He soon learned that they are marvelous storytellers.

—What's it like? Well, what do you mean, Professor Velásquez? What is it you wanna know?

—Just personal impressions. A little bit of gossip, he teased and winked. You know, some juicy stories.

—Well-l, at first I didn't know what to expect, coming from business to the university, but when I first came to work here, Edith Steinmann said, the other girls who'd been here a long time told me not to be shocked by anything. Nothing! Edith, they told me, we've got the scoop on 'em all, and we're gonna give it to you. You're gonna see what professors are really like, they told me, and boy! I'll tell you, did I ever learn what they're like! If any secretary wrote a book about the university and about the goings-on, they told me, you can be sure it'd be a best-seller. Name anything that sells books and you've got it, right there, they told me, in the department where you're gonna work, and all over campus. . . .

It was true, and he himself had given them plenty to talk about. Miguel Velásquez often wondered what the secretaries and his colleagues said about him.

One day at a cocktail party the subject of Miguel Velásquez's novel came up.

—I'm beginning to wonder if there is such a novel. Not that he couldn't bring it off, Gregory Scott conceded, but he's been talking about it for years; it's gotta be just talk.

—Oh, but there is a novel, declared Martha Goldstein. He's just slow, says he's in no hurry. He's got a very good idea about what he wants to do. He told me it's about a Chicano from Texas who goes to Chicago and New York where he leads a dissipated life. A "magnificently degenerate life," he told me. In New York his character meets and marries a Jewish girl. His wife is Jewish, you know. Then they go to Europe for a year. After that she talks him into going back to graduate school, and they end up at a university in California. Sound familiar?

—He told me, said Lennie Shapiro, it was a "going home again" novel. The return of the prodigal son. He says it's based on his experience of going back to his childhood barry-o neighborhood in San Antonio, Texas. It's mostly about his father who's eighty years old and his mother who never went to school, and it's about the hardships of Mexican immigrants. The story begins with the Mexican Revolution and comes right up to the present. It starts in Texas and ends in California.

—That's not what he told me. He said the whole novel takes place aboard an airplane, in the mind of a character who's going back to New York. He's got a joint appointment in Chicano Studies and Art History at some university. He told me it's about his tenure evaluation. He thinks about it on the plane to New York. The airplane journey, he says, reminds him of another time in his life when he took a Greyhound bus from New York to Chicago. Lots of memories come back.

—He told me it takes place in Berkeley, where the character remembers his experiences from when he led a dissipated life in Chicago and New York. As he walks around the streets of Berkeley and on the UC Berkeley campus, the city and the campus bring back memories. He says everything reminds his character of something else.

—I wonder if it's got any sex, Edith Steinmann said.

—Yeah! I wonder, too. After all, you know Miguel. . . . Several of them smiled.

—Well, if there's such a novel, Guillermo Carvajal says it's got quite a bit. According to him, it's gonna be the most pornographic novel of the century. Guillermo also says it's been influenced by morbid writers such as Baudelaire, Rimbaud, Kafka, and by Robbe-Grillet and company, as Guillermo puts it. He's told Miguel he should make a life-affirming literary work, not another piece of morbid garbage.

—Yes, yes. I heard it had sex. But . . . it's about an older man who's impotent because of alcoholism. One April the older man meets a young girl, and when he gets into bed with her he discovers he can't . . . well, that . . . do you get the picture? So if his character ... you know ... how can the novel have any sex? Sexual frustration, maybe. And what about Miguel? Is he, I mean, writing about this from firsthand experience? Is that how come Miguel is always joking that even if the opportunity presented itself, well, that he's too old?

Even though the thought was not pleasant, the question was taken humorously. They laughed.

—Miguel once said, a long time ago I might add, that it was based on a trip that he made to Mexico some years ago. A journey by airplane, forward into the past, he called it. It has sections on pre-Columbian Mexican history and on the conquest of Mexico. A lot of the novel is set in Mexico City, where he was a student many years ago. The streets of the city remind his character of his student days when he was studying Latin American art history and culture. He says he's done a lotta research on Mexican pre-Columbian and colonial history, and on the travel literature and chronicles of exploration, discovery and conquest. He knows a little bit about contemporary writers of Latin America, who, judging by what I hear, are quite good.

—I heard that the protagonist of the novel is a writer who discovers after many years of trying to write a novel that he'll never be able to write it. It's about the writing of an impossible novel. At the end he just gives up. He realizes finally that he's a failure.

—Miguel told me that it's about a man in his early fifties, or about to reach the age of fifty. After seven or eight years of having no interest in women he experiences a sexual reawakening when he has a summer romance with a twenty-two-year-old girl. Imagine that! Miguel laughed when I asked him, are you sure he's not in his middle forties?

—Guillermo's the only one who's read any of it. Or listened to Miguel read some of the pages. But you know how he tends to exaggerate everything. In typically Latin American fashion, he's always using superlatives and flowery language. But Guillermo says it contains some good parts. Maybe he'll be here later and we can ask him.

—Someone said Miguel's writing it in English and Spanish. Who's gonna read a novel in two languages?

—He told me it's got a few passages in Italian and French too.

—Who's gonna know those languages? God! I have trouble just with one language. Won't it be hard to publish a book like that?

—It's hard placing a novel, period!

—Miguel says that his father has only a third-grade education, but he started to teach him to read and write Spanish when Miguel was eight years old. You oughta hear the way he goes on about his father and mother. He worships the ground they walk on. And he talks a lot about his grandfather, too. Says he was a cavalry soldier during the Mexican Revolution. He says the novel's gonna set down the hardships of Mexicans in Texas, tell their side of the story.

—One day Miguel told me the hardest thing about writing a novel is finding names for the characters, and finding a way to begin. He doesn't even have a name for the protagonist yet. I told him to try the telephone directory.

—I wonder if the novel's autobiographical.

—From what he's been telling us, I think it's gotta be. It's his own story, at least part of it. He's said that the task of writing a novel is torture sometimes, but he says dreams help him. He told me he's been writing down his dreams for the past four or five years. He's gonna put a lotta dreams in the novel, but readers aren't supposed to know they're dreams.

—Guillermo also says it's about the Mexican Revolution.

—I wonder if it's gonna be about what it's like to be a Chicano. I still can't figure out why they wanna be different.

—I tease him about being Chicano, said Gerome Stone. His office is right across from mine, so I keep asking him when he comes to the office if he's been working on the great Chicano novel. Oh, look! There's our distinguished visiting French novelist. He's become very good friends with Miguel. I doubt that Giovanni has invited Miguel. Or Dimitri Radke. Look, there goes Giovanni to greet him. Our distinguished French novelist is looking all around. He's probably looking for Miguel and Radke.

—Oh! and here comes Guillermo, said Edith Steinmann. Speak of the devil; maybe he can shed some light on our questions about Miguel's novel.

Many years after his graduation from Ríoseco University, Dannie Rodríguez told Miguel Velásquez that he was not really a

Chicano when he became a professor of Chicano Studies. They were visiting with José Colín Velásquez at his apartment.

—Hey, tío! José called Miguel "uncle" even though they were not related, because of having the same last name. You guys want some good José Cuervo Especial? I've got some limes too, José added.

Dannie said beer was all he wanted, but Miguel accepted the tequila invitation.

—Look, you guys, I'm gonna put some carnitas on the grill. Help yourselves to beer and tequila. Hey, Miguel, the limes and the salt are over there, next to the stove. Beer's in the fridge. Okay, guys? Están en su casa.

Miguel found a knife and cut a lime. The salt was next to a little bowl of cilantro and onions that José had chopped up for the delicious salsa picante that was still in the molcajete. Miguel took the lime and salt to the table and sat down with Dannie, who continued with what he had begun to say.

—As I was saying, you weren't a Chicano when you came here, Miguel. I watched you becoming a Chicano. You've always been a loner, so you didn't care about the community. Even now, you don't know about the community, cause you never went on protest marches or demonstrations . . . never made no political speeches. Even in Chicano studies classes . . . and I think I took almost every one you taught, you were always off in your own world. Sure you came to some student parties, and we had fun, but you'd go off and tell us about what you used to do in Chicago or New York . . . and when you talked about lo mexicano it was always a little too intellectual for a Chicano, man, cause you also talked about France or Spain or about some other European country and the United States and you'd bring in their cultures, their history or their art. The vatos used to talk after class and say, Hey, man, what's that gotta do with Chicano studies? I used to look at you teachin' and ask myself, is this is a Chicano? Man! You were the strangest, and my compadre, you remember my compa, Juan, he thought so too. I remember once when you were talking about Mexican mural painting and you mentioned something about . . . hell, I don't remember, something like surrealism, and things I cain't remember no more. . . . I still got my notes, and all the textbooks. . . . I like to read 'em over now and then, to remember the old MEChA days when we used to march and protest and we were active, cause that's when I was taking your classes . . . I'll never forget how you nearly blew my mind when you said that Spaniards were mestizos. . . . Hell-ll-l man-n! That wadn't tha way I learned about mestizos! As far as I knew they wuz jes Spaniards . . . gachupines, ese, and then you come along talkin' 'bout the ancestry of the Spaniards and my red hair and freckles, and my uncles' bushy eyebrows and thick black beards, all the hair on their chest and their balding heads! Man! You nearly blew me away! . . . I hadn't ever heard 'bout the backgrounds of the gachupines . . . Arabic, you said in class, Roman, Greek, Jewish, Germanic . . . 'n hell, I don't know what else. . . . I think you said something about the güeros and misigoths or gossips or . . . what? Yeah, somethin' like that. Huh? Ostrogoths and visigoths, yeah. Anyway, you came into Chicano Studies when the programs were just gettin' set up in California, and you talked about Chicanos being American citizens of Mexican ancestry, ese! . . . At that time we wuz just startin' to stop being hyphenated Mexican-Americans, 'n you come along tellin' us some bad stuff, ese, 'n that we are a very diverse people . . . hey, man! . . . at a time when we were trying to create unity of all Chicanos you wuz telling us we're all different. At the very time when the Plan espiritual de Aztlán meant a lot to students, ese, you criticized it . . . 'n you used to criticize the language of "El Louie," before you learned to like Montoya's poem!

The door opened and José came in with the sizzling carnitas on a plate.

—I'll just cut this meat up, won't take long, then we'll have some frijolitos right from the pot, some hot tortillas; we'll put some carnitas and cilantro and cebolla and some hot chile, and . . . Hey! you guys been having a heavy talk, huh?

—No, it's not really heavy, Dannie said. We're just remembering when Miguel came to Ríoseco University. I used to ask myself if Miguel could possibly be from Tejas, where I'd heard Chicanos are so traditional. I thought maybe he was some kind of South American who got on the Chicano bandwagon, 'cause of his last name. There was a lotta opportunists in them days. Lotta people all of a sudden were changin' their names, like from Peter to Pedro and Chuck to Carlos, and from Mary to María and from Jee-meenez to Jiménez, and Purr-r-rez to Pérez. Anyway, you've changed a lot since I first knew you, he said, turning to Miguel. A lotta years've gone by since I took your classes. All I can say, as a friend . . . is you were not a Chicano when you came to California. Mexican, ma-ay-be-e, maybe. . . . Chicano! No way! Sorry. Sorry for being so blunt. I've been meaning to tell you.

—Too-o-oo heavy! José said, as he placed a plate in front of each man, with a flour tortilla bulging with carnitas, cilantro, cebollas and salsa picante.

The PSA 737 was moving smoothly towards its destination. His mind was relaxed, and his thoughts drifted from his former student to the plane and then back to the university, to the unpleasant time of his tenure evaluation. Others had told him stories about the physical and psychological symptoms that attended the process. He discovered it for himself. At that time the meaning of Kafka's *The Trial* began to become clear to him, and at the same time, he went back to one of his favorite plays by Ibsen for comfort. How strange, he thought, that just about every absurdity through which one's life must pass has been written about. He too became an enemy of the people, an enemy of the pillars of society and his colleagues, and in later years he could look back with fascination at what happens to some professors when they bare their teeth to judge a colleague who is up for a merit evaluation or for tenure.

Edith Steinmann was right. Certainly one could write a novel about the world of the university. Miguel had yet to find a fictional name for Edith. She would make a great character in a novel, he thought. He admired her wonderful sense of humor, and because she was, in the case of graduate students, like a favorite aunt. She was always ready to listen to their troubles, ready to cut through bureaucratic red tape to push through some official document, able to bend the regulations and to laugh. She always found time to type letters for Miguel, which he appreciated. It was even rumored that if one got a letter to her for typing when it was two or three days past the deadline, she could set back the clock, type and get it there before the deadline! And what a storyteller! Edith knew about all the bizarre goings-on and the personal animosities among professors, but she was always in good spirits. If only I could stand back and watch, like her. What a fascinating place, this university! He liked to tease her when she answered the office telephone.

74

—Hello. Department of Modern Languages and Literatures. Edith speaking. May I help you?

—Hello, department. He always called her "department," and she would recognize the familiar greeting and respond cheerfully.

—Hi there!

She once told him that when she was a child the muscles of her right eye were weak. The weak muscles used to cause the eye to rotate and wiggle a little. Her family doctor, she said, had recommended exercises to strengthen the eye muscles.

—Eventually the eye problem went away, she told Miguel. Now it only goes around and around whenever I have more than three martinis. Then it goes like this.

Edith looked up at him to demonstrate. She squinted the left eye playfully, arched her right eyebrow, grinned and wiggled her right eye. They both laughed.

Eventually Miguel developed the habit of playfully asking Edith, after lunch, to let him see her eyes.

—Okay, Edith. Let's have a look. How many martinis did you have with your lunch?

It amused him to imagine her as a character in a film, gazing up from a huge movie screen, sitting behind a desk, playfully making her right eye dance round and round, and the two of them laughing and laughing. Close-up of Edith Steinmann's eyes. They fill the whole screen. One eye is going round and round. Now her eyes stare directly at the camera. Fade out. Fade in, close-up of the person who plays the role of Miguel Velásquez's character aboard a simulated airplane interior. There is a faraway, dreamy look in his eyes. The camera brings his face into a close-up. He smiles. In voice-over: *She is a great person! She really is!* Cut. The camera assumes his view. Subjective shot of other passengers on the plane, then of the lovely day through a porthole window. Ahead, the liquor cart was coming closer.

It would be easy in a film to suggest what is taking place in the mind of a character. He had once seen how movies are made with simulated airplane interiors. The camera would rest on a dark, foreign-looking passenger in close-up. His smile of amusement would confirm the screen images of a woman playing the role of Edith. The viewer will be installed inside the mind of the character, as critics say, and understand that the character is thinking of her. In a novel the writer uses interior monologues to let his characters speak for themselves, or to suggest a character remembering what another character, or other characters, have said. In a film, the effects of an interior monologue would be achieved by using voice-over. Meanwhile, the camera would remain focused on the remembering passenger's face, and alternately on the imagined speaker's face, in close-up. The passenger's face would register his responses to the voice. Voice-over would give the film an incantantory quality.

Yes, a film could easily suggest the mind of a character who is haunted by thoughts, memories, voices, longings, dreams. Face of the passenger in close-up. Lorenzo Correa is remembering a dream that he had in the spring two years ago, shortly before he met the young woman half his age, after the García Lorca play.

# VII

LIKE SOMEONE who gradually regains consciousness after an indefinable period of time, not knowing where I came from or what my immediate responsibilities were, I arrived at the set where a film was being made. Many people were preparing for a scene to be acted out on stage and videotaped for television. On a monitoring screen I recognized the effects produced by a special lens that make the actors' faces appear fishlike in close-up. The distorted faces, with their wide-open eyes and parted lips loomed strangely forward on the screen, which to my mind suggested imminent danger, psychological stress and anguish. Then, in a half shot, the camera brings into a close-up one of the actors who then looms high and forward on the picture screen. In an extreme close-up his strangely grotesque, fishlike face, with its huge bulging eyes, fills the screen.

Gradually, the man's grotesque face turned into the head of a horse. Dissolve. There, filling the screen was the head of a horse, in extreme close-up. Its nostrils were flared.

The camera tracks back and the scene changes. One understands why the horse's nostrils are flared. The powerful and spirited horse is being conducted to a mare that quietly awaits him. When he is behind the mare she turns her tail aside to receive him. The viewer observes on the screen the flashing of the horse's eyes, the leaps, the bows, the ears erect, the mouth opening with convulsive gaspings, the flared nostrils; and when the final consummation of nature's work is about to take place, when the male horse rears up, the camera cuts on the horse's convulsive gaspings and takes the viewer to a bedroom where the clothing of a man and a woman are scattered on the floor, on chairs. One does not see the man and the woman, only their clothing. Heavy breathing is heard, the murmur of a woman's voice. The groans of love, made by a man and a woman.

Inexplicably, I lost consciousness again, perhaps for a long time. I did not know how much time had passed. When I regained consciousness I was watching a film. Far away, scaled almost to insignificance in a vast desert where there is nothing in sight for miles, the figure of a man on a horse is moving slowly from the right to the left side of the screen.

I was riding the horse, apparently without concern for its health. I could not explain what made me feel that way, or what I was doing. Where was I going?

The sudden awareness of being on a horse startled and frightened me because I had been afraid of horses since childhood. I rode a horse without a saddle and I was afraid of falling off. Then it scared me because it neighed. That was a long time ago. In the present case, however, I soon became comfortable with the horse and felt good about my horsemanship. My grandfather would be proud. He would never forgive me for my childhood cowardice if he knew.

I had the distinct impression that we had come a very long distance, and that we had a long way to go still. I wondered where we were going.

My hands were stroking the sides of the horse's great neck. I could feel the great power of the horse between my legs. The great neck was pleasantly warm, almost hot. Without warning, the horse began to run backwards.

—How can you run backwards? I asked. There is no way for you to see where you are going if you run backwards.

—It's all right, said the horse nonchalantly. Don't worry. All I have to do is lift my head high, like this, and look over my shoulder.

When the horse raised its great, powerful neck to look over and around me I became terribly afraid of not being able to hold on. I wondered if something had frightened the horse. Were we running away from some danger? Wild dogs perhaps? I became more afraid because suddenly my face was to the horse's rump. I had nothing to hold on to. Or was I riding a headless horse?

Some time later the horse stopped, turned around and began to go, rump forward in the opposite direction. I became acutely conscious of thinking that I was thinking. I noticed that sometimes the horse was white. Other times it was of palomino color. Then the rump became the neck and the head again.

The great power of the horse between my legs, and the height, gave me a joyful sense of power. Everywhere, no matter where I turned, I saw barren and desolate land that stretched on for miles. After a long time I lost all sense of time again. I wondered how far the horse and I had travelled.

The scene changed. I was in the film, but I was also viewing the scene. In the film a man was walking. A tired horse was following him. Glancing over his right shoulder, the man saw that his horse was unwell. It looked tired. Then the horse began to shrivel, as if it were a great inflatable toy. In the distance the sadness in the animal's eyes was obvious. Its hind legs became limp and useless.

Poor animal, dragging its useless hind legs. Why did I neglect it? When did I last give the horse any water or food? My God! I cannot remember. How thoughtless can anyone be? How far can a horse go without food and water?

—Try and stay on your feet, I said, thinking that surely we would come to water soon. But there was nothing in sight.

Much later we arrived at a stone fountain with running water. It had a silver faucet. But then a strange girl came by and distracted me. I went off with the girl and left the horse by the stone fountain.

The girl and I spent a lovely, innocent afternoon outdoors. Afterwards my memories were not clear about what had occurred, but I vaguely remembered a long, friendly conversation. I could not remember anything that we talked about. Nor could I remember if I desired the young woman. We had a picnic, but I do not remember eating. After spending a few hours together, we walked along until we arrived at a huge iron gate. The gate was located near some boulders, and it was here that we said good-bye.

—It has been a delightful day, I said, with a polite handshake.

I complemented myself for being able to spend a few hours with a young woman without wanting desperately to make love. Not that I was not thinking about making love; of course I was. I remembered that I was thinking of wanting and not wanting to make love. Sexual desire was still important, I told myself, but it no longer has the unbearable urgency it used to have. Now I can enjoy a young woman's company without distress.

After the girl left I continued on, leading the horse toward a nearby railroad station. A short distance ahead another young woman distracted me and caused me to neglect the horse again. As she and I walked along I embraced her, felt desire, but I did not pursue it. Her body was delightfully warm against mine. Poor horse, I thought.

My memories of the two young women were not clear. The two seemed to come together in my mind. At times they resembled each other. I regretted my faulty memory, thinking that it was faulty like when I go to bed after having too much to drink. I wake up not being able to remember what happened even before I drank too much.

Where did I leave the horse? No sooner did the question cross my mind, wondering how far I left the horse from the railroad tracks, when the loud crashing sound of an approaching train made me look up and turn towards the noise.

Not far away the train was approaching at a great speed, fiercely snarling, exhaling great angry puffs of steam, shaking the ground, making windows clatter, and then it rushed by, getting smaller and smaller in the distance until it became lost from sight.

Inexplicably I sensed that something terrible had happened to the horse. I must go back and find it. I should have fed it. How long has it been?

While I was worrying about the horse a stranger came up to where I was standing.

—A horse's head was struck by the passing train, the man said. The train was going awfully fast.

Oh, my God! It is my fault. How could I have been so irresponsible? I mustn't mention the accident to anyone. I will pretend that I know nothing. No one will be able to blame me. Even so, who would want to blame me? It is probably guilt, I thought. I must find the horse. Where should I look for it first?

At that point I began to run. The horse was not at the water fountain where I had left it. I became confused and did not know where to look or what to do.

Another stranger came along. He told me that a man took away the horse that was struck by the passing train.

—Can you describe the man who took the horse? I asked.

—Yes, he said. He was a tall man, about six feet tall, dark hair, bushy eyebrows, and let's see, what else? Oh yeah, he had beautiful teeth, and he wore dark glasses so's you couldn't see his eyes. He seemed kinda sad though, even if I cain't rightly tell you how come he seemed that way. You kin jes tell 'bout some people. He's one of 'em.

From the stranger's description I knew that it was my brother Alejandro. Ever since he died he has come to visit me regularly. It will be good to see him again.

While I was looking for Alejandro I ran into two of my other brothers, Tony and Andrés. They were standing by a barn on a farm that was near the train station.

We greeted in the customary Mexican way, with an embrace. Then I asked them if they had seen Alejandro.

—Sure, said Tony. A real horrible thing happened. A train hit a horse's head and broke the whole nose. Alejandro took the horse to Dr. Howard.

—Oh, my God! I exclaimed. That was my horse!

Looking toward the front of the airplane he saw that the liquor cart was making slow progress. He remembered other dreams from about the same time, when he used to tire easily and seemed always exhausted. In one of the dreams he was in a bathtub with Denise. There was no water in the bathtub. He was naked. Denise was not.

—Let me undress you, he said.

—No, please don't. If only you would be patient. Why can't you wait until I can get to know you better? Please.

—You are lovely, Denise. I would love to touch your hands and feet, your belly, your thighs, your hips, your pubic hair. I would like to spread your legs, to touch the soft flesh there, gently with my hands, and here . . . let me touch you. . . . There, doesn't that feel good?

She closed her eyes and shuddered.

—No, please don't, Lorenzo.

But he continued to implore gently, until finally she consented. He helped her when she began to undress.

—I want you, Denise, so much. I want to include you in my novel. I want at least a few pages to express tenderness and affection.

When she was completely undressed his eyes travelled lovingly over her body. His hands moved tenderly across her lovely, naked flesh, caressing all the wonderfully soft parts of her arms and her legs, which now were open and inviting. Kissing him passionately, she had found a good position. He was about to enter her. He brought his body closer to her body. The warmth of her soft skin delighted him. She exerted a pleasurable pressure with her legs around his waist.

Unexpectedly he awakened with unfulfilled desire and he lamented that he had not lied to Denise. Sadly, he wondered why he repeatedly awakened from his erotic dreams just as he was about to make love.

He glanced admiringly at the attractive stewardess who was approaching down the aisle. Many things used to keep him in a state of exhaustion, especially that year when he met Sylvia and Denise. Perhaps his friend Guillermo and the others were right. Was he trying to do too many things? Was he placing a burden on his creative and physical energies? Were the dreams commenting on his diminished energies?

Many times during those years his self-confidence wavered, and he preferred being solitary. Did he really have a choice? He knew that his many projects were ambitious and impractical. Yet he persisted. How could he alone believe that one day he would carry them out? Why could he not be content with a well-ordered life, a good career?

The years were slipping away. Before long he would be fifty. What would he have accomplished? What in the world ever led him to tell people that he was writing a novel? In the beginning he had thought it would be easy. After all, there was so much to write about. He had lived intensely. He had suffered. He had travelled. He had known many nights of love. But was that enough?

His energies, he could see in retrospect, began to wane at about the time that he turned forty, when the writing became intense and obsessive. He went nowhere without notebook and pen. Every morning he would write for several hours until he was exhausted. Over the years the notebooks had proliferated. His waning energies coincided with a trip to Mexico. That year he had quit smoking. His drinking was moderate. But two years after that he began to drink heavily again when he came up for tenure. Again, as it had happened over the years, he wrote more and more, in response to a spiritual necessity.

In Mexico City he retraced his steps. The great capital of the country, from which he had been away for nearly fifteen years, had changed considerably. He saw the city with new eyes, and he discovered new things about Mexico City, about himself, and something about the passage of time. The anticipation of his trip to Mexico had brought back memories of his student days at the National University, UNAM. He was inspired to write, as he always was when he went back to places where he had once lived. Going back to places made him experience with extraordinary force the awe and wonder of the traveller and the explorer. Going back reminded him of arriving at a city for the first time. Arrivals and returns turned his memory into a kaleidoscope of recollections, images, voices.

The trip to Mexico turned out to be a journey forward into the past, and because much of the past always lives on into the present, the city came alive with memories. He retraced his steps from Colonia Polanco to the Zócalo. From the apartment building where he used to live, near the Bosque de Chapultepec, he walked to Mazaryk. He headed east and took Mariano Escobedo to Reforma, and at the glorieta he was overcome by a sense of loss. The statue of Diana was gone. He walked past the old palaces on Reforma, crossing familiar streets with the names of international rivers, until he came to Insurgentes. At the glorieta he walked around the monument to Cuauhtemoc and continued on.

At Bucareli he stopped for a long time before continuing on to Avenida Juárez. On Bucareli, fifteen years ago, he had seen two cars wending in and out of traffic. Each car was filled with lovely, laughing girls. From time to time the cars would stop, and the girls smiled and flirted with men. Two or three beautiful girls—they were all between the ages of eighteen and twenty-three—got out of the cars. Laughing, flirting, the cheerful girls went from car to car, stopping traffic, passing out little address cards, talking to men, spreading moments of joy among them, filling their heads with images of voluptuous pleasures. Ladies of the night in broad daylight. They were beautiful to watch. The scene had been deeply engraved in his memory, and it thrilled him to have it pass across his mind's eye, to hear the girls' laughter. Such are the joys of the traveller who goes back and finds again what once was there.

Ahead and to his left were the Alameda Central and the Palacio de Bellas Artes. Lost in recollection, he continued on. The streets were crowded with people. At San Juan de Letrán he stopped for the light. When it turned green he crossed. The tiled building on the corner, Sanborn's, brought back other memories. He was now on Avenida Madero, walking toward the great Zócalo. That night he would go to the Plaza de Garibaldi to see the mariachis, and the next day he would visit the Universidad Nacional Autónoma de México.

His walk was strangely marvelous and wonderful. Old memories came back and thrilled him. Long ago, his flesh, his body, his legs, his senses had recorded and stored up the memories. Strolling leisurely along on Avenida Madero, his whole being alert, he experienced a renewed deepening of his sense of history and the past. The streets of Mexico City, the sight of familiar buildings, the names of the streets, the smells of antojitos coming from small eating places, and the faces of the people, stirred and thrilled his spirit, produced a warm sensation of coming home to the nation of his people, his ancestry. Configuration after configuration of remembered days from his young manhood turned in the kaleidoscope of memory. He was warmed by his knowledge of the city, the streets, the buildings, the university, the people. The history of Mexico was everywhere, its Mediterranean and its pre-Columbian past, the Conquest, the colonial period, independence from Spain, the war with the United States, the reform period, and the Mexican Revolution. The storm and pageantry of Mexican history palpitated in him, had followed him about; it was in his blood, in body and mind, in his spirit. His student days in Mexico were memorable. A few years later, when he was pacing the streets of Chicago and New York City, the memories of his student days in Mexico often came back, and he had watched his knowledge and the configuration of that history and of his experience change when he and Natalie went across Europe. Fifteen years had added to his knowledge of Mexico. Travel and books had enlarged his understanding of Mexican history. It was more alive than ever. So powerful was the effect of his return to Mexico that he was compelled to fill still another notebook with all that he did and saw and felt. With the fresh experiences of his fortieth year he combined those of his twenty-fifth and twenty-sixth years and between the two points

"Would you care for a cocktail? Or refreshments?"

Miguel opened his eyes and brought his head slowly forward, away from the back of his seat. At the time that he met Sylvia, he was beginning to think of himself as being no longer young. She was much too young then, but two years after that his age had not mattered to Sylvia. Even so, the difference in their ages made him self-conscious. You came into my life at a strange period, Sylvia . . . I kept thinking, at my age . . . I mustn't make a fool of myself. But you were such a wonderfully wild niña-mujer-hembra. . . . You made me understand how we older men feel too, and remember how I told you that men make fun of women in their forties? But that is because they have no sense until they are men in their forties. Then they will know that men, too, make love in their forties as if each time will be the last. When it is their turn, will they laugh?

He turned towards the voice. The dark-haired stewardess was standing in the aisle, leaning slightly over a heavy woman in the seat on the other side of the aisle in the same row of seats as his own. Her back was toward him. He admired the body and legs of the attractive woman. The neat rows of small whiskey bottles on the liquor cart evoked other memories.

Sylvia Esquivel, born in a village near Guadalajara. Twenty-one years old, and he in his forties. They met at a dinner banquet and dance. They danced several times. She was cheerful and her eyes were seductive. Her body pressed against his, but she was too young, he kept telling himself. It was new at his age for a young woman to show an interest in him. After years without desire, what if? Two years later she was in his arms, oh! She was young and beautiful . . . and the doorbell kept ringing. Make love to me in French, she said. I am going to Paris this summer. . . . Edith Piaf was singing. *Non, rien de rien, non, je ne regrette rien, ni le bien qu'on m'a fait, ni le mal, tout ça me vien égal . . . non, rien de rien . . . avec mes souvenirs . . . car ma vie . . . aujourd'hui . . . ça commence avec toi . . .*

When you went to Paris to stay for six months, I imagined you, Sylvia, walking proudly on the Champs Elysées, being admired by men as you pause to look into a great department store window. And when you returned from Paris and went to Washington D.C. I remembered other young women like yourself, fascinating, hungry to know life, and . . . in your case, how sad . . . but I am glad that you came into my life, even briefly.

You helped me to understand some of my dreams and fears. I will always be grateful, cariño, for running into you after the García Lorca play at the Inland University Theatre, and for those ephemeral moments we shared. Will you remember too, how we met accidentally, at the Neighborhood Cantina? We made a date and I confess that with the foolishness of older men, I wrote to my friend, Claude Sorel, the French novelist. Ah, mon ami, I wrote, je crois que j'ai trouvé le grand amour fou dont rêve chaque quarantain. . . . Cariño, a few days before our date, I had a dream.

I was watching a football game on television. I was one of the players. Near our goal line a member of the opposite team threw the football. It spiralled through the air towards me. I see myself running, in slow motion, to intercept the spiralling ball. I caught it, but it was underinflated and shaped like a balloon. Close-up shot of feet running across ten-yard lines. On the screen in a long shot, I saw myself running with the ball, dodging players who were trying to tackle me. Out of the corner of my eye I could see players from the other team running to head me off. The ten-yard lines flashed brightly white in the lower part of my eyes. The flashing white lines passed slowly under my feet, as in slow motion, one after another.

I was running, dodging, off to one side, then to another, zigzagging. Several more bright white ten-yard stripes passed under my feet, and flashed whitely in the bottoms of my eyes. My legs became tired. I had been running with the uninflated ball for almost one hundred yards, wondering if my legs would hold out, wondering when my breath would begin to give out, worrying about getting physically hurt if someone tackled me.

Somewhere, the image of a girl? A school? A meeting? Who is she? Am I imagining things? Without my knowledge everyone disappeared while I ran the last few yards. My legs were tired, but my breathing was not labored. I kept on running, all the way across the goal line. I expected loud cheers at any moment for making a touchdown. Across the goal line I bent down with outstretched arms and touched the ground with the soft, penis-shaped, uninflated football. A touchdown! I did it!

No one cheered. The stadium and the field were empty. There was not a soul in sight. What happened to the players and the football crowd? Why is the stadium empty? Did I intercept the ball and run in the wrong direction? Did I make a touchdown for the other team? Let me see. I ran and caught the ball, turned around and . . . yes, I ran in the direction that the ball was thrown. Was I on the thrower's team? Or did I make a mistake and run in the direction of his team's goal? What happened to everybody? Why did no one cheer for me when I made the touchdown? Where is everyone?

On the television screen, a long shot of a huge empty stadium around an empty football field. In the distance, barely visible because he is so small, scaled down to insignificance by his surroundings, a man, who is standing just over the goal line, removes his helmet and scratches his head.

The young woman came in and out of his life, like a dream from which one is rudely awakened. He wrote in his notebook:

Sylvia, I will always remember, barely noticing you out of the corner of my eye. You were standing nearby, off a little to the side, after the García Lorca play, when I was greeting some friends. You looked familiar, like a marvelous character out of a novel, with full, black, long hair. Young and beautiful. Later that night, when we met accidentally at the Neighborhood Cantina, you told me that you remembered our first meeting, two years before. You were so lovely that night, two years earlier, when you were nineteen years old and you walked up to me and introduced yourself, telling me you knew of me from your brother who had been a graduate student in one of my classes. We danced and your full transparent dress swirled around. You brought your young body close to mine and your eyes were sleepy with drink, and with love dreams perhaps. Two years after that we saw each other again, and this time too, you were dreamy-eyed and ready for love. You even asked my age, compared it to yours, and said that it did not matter. We made a date.

I remember you, standing in front of me, in the bedroom of my friend's house, loosening your dress, letting it fall to the floor, standing there nakedly, a masterpiece of nature that my eyes were privileged to see, and I was thinking how young you are, cariño, child-woman, an unexpected treasure; niña-mujer, hembra, you took away my breath. And I tasted your mouth, your breasts, cariño. . . .

I remember everything, Sylvia. I wrote about that short-lived evening and about our conversation afterward, shamefully, with infinite regret, in the last pages of one of my notebooks. That notebook entry has preserved the grief itself in my mind like a terrible scene from a film or like a refrain that is repeated over and over, multiplied infinitely, until one is about to go mad. I will never forget you, so exquisitely young and naked. Oh, cariño!

He had to find out what was wrong. He went for a complete physical examination, and he explained his concerns to the doctor.

—So, the doctor said, you're concerned about . . .

—Yes, Doctor. It is not the first time; I think it started a few years ago when I came up for tenure at the university . . . I was having an affair then . . . no, my wife didn't know . . . well, perhaps she did. There were several times when . . .

—You couldn't . . . hmmmmm. I see.

—It happened just a few months ago. That's why I decided to have a complete physical. And even when I dream . . . I always wake up, before it happens. Even in the dreams, also, I feel inhibited. Someone is always watching me. . . .

—What about alcoholism, Professor?

—I am a hard drinker, I know that.

—That doesn't answer my question, Professor.

—My wife thinks that I am an alcoholic.

After serving soft drinks to the three people on the other side of the aisle the stewardess turned to Miguel and his fellow passengers. She was standing in the aisle, in front of the liquor cart, leaning over slightly towards his row of seats, an attractive woman, probably in her middle thirties. She resembled Christie, the attractive dental technician, whose voice he recalled, talking about herself as she was cleaning his teeth. I bet you look great in a bikini, Christie, he told her. Marvelous, healthy tan. A young California woman. Beautiful green eyes. He loved the feel of her arm on his chest. Christie could feel his heart pounding on her arm. See what you do to me, Christie? he told her.

"Would you folks care for a cocktail?"

The stewardess was smiling. She reminded him of older women in their thirties and forties whom he had known when he was in his late teens and early twenties. He was attracted to them as a young man, and now, as an older man he could no longer think of them as older women. He would always cherish the "older women" of his young manhood. They had taught him to be gentle and tender with women. And it was from women, in fact, that he had learned about life. Even recently, he had learned from a young woman what it is like for an older man to feel infinite tenderness and gratitude. He thought of Pirandello, who said somewhere that it must be sad for a young man to dwell in the body of an old man, to be driven by the desires of the flesh that lives on. Ah! what a wretched condition for a man—he had read it in one of the Sicilian's plays—to feel no longer young and yet to feel desire with shame. Phrases from the aging Yeats's poetry, that Miguel Velásquez had memorized when he was a young man, came to mind and moved him immensely. Since long ago, he had known that one day he too must pace the battlements of old age and lament that an aged man is but a paltry thing, a tattered coat upon a stick unless . . . yes . . . unless soul clap its hands and sing, sing, sing! . . . Who can know the year . . . when an old man's blood grows cold? . . . sick with desire and fastened to this dying animal . . . because I am mad about women . . . I am mad about the hills . . . a young man in the dark am I, but a wild man in the light . . . Oh, troubled heart!

The stewardess's hazel eyes were cheerful, and her warm womanliness made him conscious of his appearance, his year-round natural "tan," and the full white beard and the pepper-colored hair of an older man. He wondered if she was one of those wonderful American women who are attracted to foreign-looking, older men. Her friendly smile acknowledged graciously the compliment of his eyes. He wanted to express admiration with words. He resisted the temptation to tell her that she was attractive. But his eyes told her.

He waited while she served the two passengers to his right. Just at the moment when he was about to order a drink he heard a child's voice coming from the front of the airplane.

"Daddy!"

The magic word startled him. Even now that his daughters were teenagers, each time he heard it, away from home, it made him think of when they were little.

"Daddy," the child said. "Daddy, I gotta go."

He recalled how they used to worry about his smoking. *Daddy! Please don't smoke too much. You'll get cancer.* And the other would also say, *Yes, Daddy, when are you going to stop smoking, Dad? You said you would.* He loved to hear them sound their g's. They objected sometimes when he corrected their pronunciation, but most of the time they listened. Sara, Becky. Hijitas preciosas. Natalie, too. *Please, Miguel, don't drink too much while you're away at Berkeley. Please, honey.*

"Yes," he said, looking admiringly, boldly, into the stewardess's smiling eyes, leaning over slightly to the right to reach for his wallet in his left back pocket. "I would like a Canadian Club and water, with plenty of ice, please."

She unfastened the little plastic lock on the back of the seat in front of him and brought the plastic tray down gently.

Her hair was full and came slightly forward. The healthy complexion of her neck and face, sensually inviting, again reminded him of Christie. He felt her warm womanly closeness. She turned to the liquor cart, while he took out money from his wallet. She took from one of the neat rows of little liquor bottles a small Canadian Club. By association he recalled the small refrigerator in the hotel room at Guadalajara, full of similar little bottles of liquor, lined up in several neat rows. They had reminded him of one of his favorite writers. The stewardess turned, leaned over and placed the small bottle on his tray. Once more he felt the woman's warm closeness. At his request she filled a plastic glass generously with ice and poured water from a pitcher into it. When she leaned over to place the glass of water and a package of peanuts on his tray, she was close enough to kiss. She knew what he was thinking, because she too understood the special, unspoken language of eyes, glances and gestures with which a man expresses wordless admiration for a woman.

Their hands touched when Miguel paid for his drink. She looked into his eyes and thanked him. Then she moved the cart to the next row of seats behind Miguel. There was mutual gratitude, one might say, in that small, yet wonderful meeting of male and female spirits that brought to Miguel's mind a vignette from an Italian short story, published in a special 1960 edition of the *Texas Quarterly.* The setting was the market near the Piazza Monte d'Oro, he was almost certain. A beautiful girl is moved by the misfortune of a handsome young man. Because he is a cripple, the beautiful girl drops some coins in the beggar's hat, but because he is a handsome young man he looks at her with the adoring eyes of a man. Their eyes meet, his acknowledge the coins, and hers, the compliment of his eyes. The beautiful girl's gaze, in which there is no trace of pity, elevates the handsome young man's spirit. The poor giving alms to one another.

"And you, sir. Would you care for a cocktail?"

"Yeah, I think I'll have a bloody mary."

Miguel took the plastic glass and drank all the water, leaving only the ice so that he could enjoy the undiluted taste of whiskey on the rocks. He opened the little bottle and poured the whiskey over the ice. To chill it he tossed the whiskey around the ice with circular motions of his hand, and with the little plastic stirrer he moved the ice around in the glass.

Placing the drink on the tray he pushed the sleeves of his coat and his shirt away from his watch. Dolores, his sister-in-law, had given it to Miguel after his brother's funeral. In the little calendar window he read the date, September twenty-first. On this trip he was looking forward to the first day of fall quarter classes at the large UC Berkeley campus. On Alejandro's watch it was ten twenty-three in the morning.

# Part Two

Il a vécu tantôt gai comme un sansonnet,
Tour à tour amoureux insoucieux et tendre,
Tantôt sombre et rêveur comme un triste Clitandre,
Un jour il entendit qu'à sa porte on sonnait.

C'était la Mort! Alors il la pria d'attendre
. . . . . . . . . . . . . . . . . . . . . . . . . . . . .

Et quand vint le moment où, las de cette vie,
Un soir d'hiver, enfin l'âme lui fut ravi,
Il s'en alla disant: Pourquoi suis-je-venu?

Gérard de Nerval, *Epitaph*

# I

ALEJANDRO IN HIS COFFIN AT THE FUNERAL CHAPEL, not even thirty-five years old, and you, Miguel, were standing by his coffin, looking at his handsome face, pale from the make-up, at his thinning straight hair that once was full and curly, expecting him to open his eyes at any moment, to wink playfully at you, then to sit up, smile as he used to and laugh.

Later, by the gaping hole at the Pflugerville Mexican Cemetery, after taking your turn to throw a handful of dirt over the coffin lid, while others were taking their turns, your thoughts turned to what you were doing on the day that your brother died. Clumps of dirt slamming, sliding and slipping across the coffin lid, slam, slide, slip. You will never forget those pounding sounds, or your elderly mother's arm and fist raised up towards the Almighty, her fist clenched angrily at first but then the gnarled hand began to open up, opened beseechingly, palm upward. Nor will you forget the mother's anguished cry reminding you of an Edvard Munch painting, her cry floating through the dreary grey November air, and your mother asking questions for which there were no answers.

—Why, Diosito mío, did you take him? Why didn't you take me? I am old. I am old. His whole life was ahead of him.

You remember your father too, trying to hold back the tears, and not being able to hold them back; he dashed away in his customary way to weep where no one could see him. But everyone knew, Miguel. Your brothers were standing next to you, tears in their red eyes, too. Tony, Andrés, Eduardo, and your sister, Isabel, your brother-in-law, Vicente, and a few of the surviving elders of the family, and your contemporaries who were already beginning to look like their mothers and fathers; there were family friends too, and many of them were people, you could not help but remark again to yourself, whom one saw at funerals usually, and at wedding anniversaries sometimes.

As you look around the airplane now, other memories come back. About a month after the funeral you received a letter from your sister-in-law. Dolores enclosed a comic birthday card that your brother had picked out for you. *Alejandro found this card two months before he died*, she wrote. *He liked it right away, so he bought it even though your birthday was still four months away. He was planning to send it to you.*

When Dolores' letter and the comic card arrived in the mail Miguel was astonished to receive his brother's birthday greetings, in a sense, from the grave. Alejandro had postdated and signed the card. It was to be just one of many surprises to come from Alejandro, who took to visiting Miguel from time to time after his death.

The comical card was long, with an emerald-green, velvety felt surface and yellow borders on the outside. In the center, above the middle of the card, a cartoon character is standing on top of a bottle. His squinting eyes suggest that he is cheerfully inebriated. He is laughing. At the upper left corner, in boldface type, appear the words BIRTHDAY CHEERS, and in each of four small circles, cut out of the emerald green felt surface appear the words "doctors say" "we'd live longer" "without" "booze." He opened the card. Inside, on the right side, centered in boldface type also, in black letters, the card said BUT I'VE KNOWN MORE OLD DRUNKS THAN OLD DOCTORS. At the bottom of the card in Alejandro's own handwriting, were the words, "Happy Birthday, hermano," and his signature.

You close your eyes aboard the PSA 737 and your thoughts take you back to the Mexican cemetery, to the sounds of shovels scraping against the hard rocky ground, where you closed your eyes too, letting your thoughts drift back and forth from what you were doing on the day that Alejandro was dying, to the clumps of dirt pounding on the coffin lid, back to the pounding of your heart on the afternoon when you and Alejandro were hemispheres apart. While he was in the intensive care unit of Woodridge Hospital you were at a friend's apartment, with Gail Sanders, a neighbor's lovely twenty-three-year-old wife. Standing in front of the gaping hole, watching the dirt slowly cover up the coffin, you were remembering that

Alejandro had been in the hospital several times. Your mother and your brothers telephoned that Alejandro was dying. But his will power was keeping him alive, as it kept him alive on the night of his terrible accident. Each time he went into the hospital he recovered and you were relieved.

You stared down into that gaping hole and in your mind's eye you saw your neighbor's lovely wife arriving at your friend's apartment, smelling as usual of soap and cleanliness, because she always went home first after work to shower and change. Aboard the PSA 737 you think back on how intense was passion in those days. You could hardly bear the waiting. You fell into each other's arms, your hearts were pounding against each other; you were breathing heavily and loudly, you perhaps more so than she, and being eager, you kissed her hungrily on the neck, the face, the mouth; your hands were everywhere, exploring lovingly inside her clothing, your chests were heaving in and out, the two of you were ready, and you began to undress her, one garment at a time, beginning with her blouse, under which her breasts were free and strong and proud, until she was standing there wonderfully naked, and before she could finish unbuttoning your shirt or unzipping your pants, you were down on your knees, pressing your face against her firm and shallow belly, and her heart was pounding there

like the clumps of dirt crashing down upon your brother's coffin lid, which made you think how strangely life works, and because of guilt, you felt at first some responsibility for your brother's death, thinking that you were being punished for your exquisitely sweet adulterous afternoon. You had learned, long before, from an English writer, that none of us is properly to be judged for what happened in the past; you already knew that you would never disobey the vital impulses of your recalcitrant spirit, that in seeking the freedom to be the man you had to be, you were destined to violate others' codes of honor, the conventions of other people. Long ago you learned that no matter what, you had to obey and be true to your nature. From deep feelings connected with your brother's death and from your once insatiable longings, you learned and continue to learn some lessons about guilt, about the strange ways in which life works, and about death.

Not long after your brother died you read poems about death, and chapters in the biographies of artists and writers, the sections that dealt with how they died and their funerals.

You began to understand. The imagery, the words and phrases were familiar, unforgettable, purifying. Mysteriously, in the language of your childhood, words brought comfort that derives from the magical utterances of art

*golpes de terrones caían sobre la caja negra, terrones polvorientos golpeaban la superficie del ataúd, en el fondo de la fosa, fosa como boca gigantesca tragándose a mi hermano, golpeaban y se desbarataban, derramábanse los terrones polvorientos sobre la caja negra, tragándose a mi hermano que apenas había llegado a la flor melancólica de su madurez*

Standing before the gaping hole you were reflecting on the distance between your brother's hemisphere and yours. In Alejandro's hemisphere, somber, winged companions were hovering over him, strange white-robed figures were circling about him, and barely able to hear their strangely incomprehensible murmuring voices, he was watching the white-robed dreamlike shapes moving things around, medical paraphernalia with strange names he knew not, watching them pumping blood into his circulatory system while Death sat down upon his chest, driving liquid fingers into his feverish brain. He closed his eyes

he saw as in a dream the water all around on the day when he dove into shallow water and broke his neck. He could not move his arms or legs, his body was down at the bottom, he was holding his breath wondering why no one came, then legs came splashing around him and arms were reaching towards him down in the water, picking him up, pulling him out of the water, his friends were laughing at him and telling him to stop fooling around and to stand on his own two feet saying stop playing games with us come on Alex come on Alex stop your fooling around until he said Bessie I can't feel anything in my arms or my legs Bessie and Isabel screamed she was crying and

Alejandro shut his eyes tightly. The pain was excruciating. He heard the murmuring voices and the needle went into his arm and shortly thereafter a little numbness, a sense of well-being, a sense of what-the-hell began to envelop him mercifully. The narcotic began to work its magic, mercifully bringing insensibility to pain, to sorrow and regret, to the knowledge that his life had been lived too fast and that soon it would expire. It was too late to regret that one cannot start life over. He wondered why the terrible accident had happened to him. Why me? I was only twenty years old. It ain't fair. Suddenly Alejandro laughed and weakly he ordered the white-robed figure closest to him to bring a telephone.

—Gotta talk to my brother! Git me a telephone. I gotta tell 'im mahself, hear! Don't want nobody but me to tell 'im.

Death sits upon Alejandro's chest, driving liquid fingers into his vital organs, the liver, heart, lungs, intestines, poisoning his blood; delirious Alejandro is hallucinating, while far away in another hemisphere, his brother is dashing his body against her body, her legs are wrapped around him, he is moving his hard erect flesh in and out of warm-soft sea flesh, feeling the pleasure of her body against his own, the liquid fingers of her desire clutching his own, her body and his, obeying the eternal and timeless rhythms of the sea while

in another hemisphere Alejandro is dying. Opening his delirious eyes, he hears the fluttering wings of dark companions who hover unseen above the strange white-robed figures who circle Alejandro's hospital bed. He is coughing up blood between drug-induced smiles of relief, eliminating blood through other orifices, while Death sits upon his chest driving her liquid fingers into clefts and fissures and broken veins and capillaries, driving wild with her fingers the white blood corpuscles, squeezing away Alejandro's life, while

in another hemisphere, you and the young woman are locked in each other's arms performing the act that nature designed for the perpetuation of life; you remember by the graveside how your bodies were rocking in harmony, in that remarkably clumsy position, when suddenly, you burst alone, and after shattering into petals of flowers, into precious diamonds, jewels and pearls, you tell her apologetically that the first time was for you because you had been so impatient, so full of desire, but then you promise to fulfill her to her heart's content because you will be able to hold off for as long as she wants until she is happy, and that is what you did on that magnificently glorious adulterous afternoon, which reminds you by the graveside of another similar afternoon when after having been with Gail you returned home to be greeted by the telephone ringing like the cry of a vulture in a drunken man's hallucination. You picked up the telephone and heard your brother's voice *hey, I'm calling from the intensive care unit, Woodridge Hospital, hey, Brother, just wanna tell you somethin' funny, okay? Hiya doin' ese? Hey listen, this is funny, I'm surrounded by strange beings in white they're standin' all around my bed and maybe you can hear the wings too the way they's clamoring so loud I think they's comin' fo to carry me home ha! ha! remember that song from*

*when we were kids, huh, Mike? well they's here and I can still sing*
*real good, huh? and it'd be a pleasure to sing the whole song for you if*
*you like cuz I still remember it but what's that? I can barely hear you,*
*brother, w'az goin' on, sportee-o?*

and Alejandro described the winged apparitions so persua-
sively that you could almost hear the loud clamor of their beat-
ing wings and you could imagine the doctors and nurses in
white standing around your brother's bed looking rather omi-
nous to his delirious eyes, while

listening to your brother's voice and his feigned, drug-
induced laughter on the telephone that day, your mind was still
on the hours you had just spent with Gail, your body was con-
tent, and it was enough to close your eyes to see the young
woman arriving as she always did and to inhale in your imagi-
nation the smell of cleanliness and soap on her body which left
a wonderful aftertaste in your mouth. While your brother was
on the phone you could not turn your thoughts away from her,
remembering how you undressed her, how she unbuttoned your
shirt, caressed your chest and your ribs, and then unzipped
your pants, and by your brother's grave you remembered that
you wept uncontrollably after the doctor took the telephone
away from Alejandro because he was not able to talk anymore.

You did not know that would be the last time you would
ever speak with your brother, and you will never forget Alejan-
dro's last words as you overheard him telling the doctor who
was advising him not to talk anymore, because he was too
tired, Alejandro wanting to spare you an expense, saying that
he *just had one more thing to say, okay? Hey, man! This is my older*
*brother . . . the eldest in the family . . . I jes wanna tell him I don't*
*want him wasting his bread if I kick off he don't needa come to my*
*funeral hell he's gettin' old, ha! ha! but he's still a student . . . and he*
*ain't got no bread. . . .*

Miguel Velásquez brought the glass of whiskey to his
mouth. He took a big sip, held it in his mouth and savored it.
He swallowed and the coolness went down all the way to his
stomach. Unlike years ago, he could pass by a bar now without
stopping for a drink. To make sense of drinking he was com-
pelled to study the effects of booze on his mind, its effects on
his perceptions of reality, on his dreams, lovemaking, writing.
Drinking was a kind of wild dance, a dangerous one to be sure,
but one from which he learned many things about himself,
about life and memory, about women and love.

The taste of whiskey brought back recollections of places where he lived when he was younger, reminded him of passionate longings for exquisite agonies. He relished the reawakened stirrings of the great tigers of lust in his loins. An endless string of drinking places from many parts of the world passed in procession across his memory: cantinas, cocktail lounges, bars, taverns, neighborhood places, campus pubs from many years ago, followed by labyrinthine bureaucratic offices where he worked, festive bohemian parties from undergraduate days, spirited art gallery receptions during his wandering years and professional conferences more recently, then wretched rooms in dilapidated hotels and rooming houses for transients, from years ago, and more. How different the trip to Mexico had been when he was forty years old, when, after nearly fifteen years, he saw Aurelia and her sister Kika, both past their prime. His heart went out to the two women, because of their kindness towards him when he was such a forlorn young man, desperately in need of giving and receiving tenderness. They knew him the year when he began to write and drink. He was twenty-five.

The empty little whiskey bottles on the plastic trays again brought to mind the hotel in Guadalajara at the end of his trip to Mexico, the small refrigerator in his room, full of little whiskey bottles, all lined up in neat little rows, like the little bottles on the airplane whiskey cart which only a moment ago went by. *See these photographs, Mike, I was just twenty years old. That's when they ruined my whole life.*

Limping about with difficulty, holding a glass with vodka and orange juice in his hand, Alejandro led his older brother from one room to another, proudly showing him the house which he and Dolores had just purchased. By then, thirteen years after his terrible accident and two years before he died, Alejandro was almost completely paralyzed. A sad song was playing on the record player . . . *tengo una pena clavada en mi pensamiento . . . como carcajada que se hace lamento, como si llorando se rieran de mí . . . mi pecado y mi culpa serán conocer demasiado el dolor . . .* Playboy magazines were scattered in every room, belying the dark secret which years ago Alejandro finally blurted out in tears.

*Goddammit, Mike! How would you feel if you were twenty and couldn't make it? If you couldn't fuck! That's right. Dig, man? At first, after the accident, I thought it was just boozin' it up that did it. But it happened when I didn't. Dammit! I was just beginning to develop a little self-confidence . . . it was so beautiful. How's a guy supposed to*

*feel when he discovers what it's like and then he cain't do it no more.*
*Would you wanna live? Shit. What would you do if a woman grabbed*
*your whatchamacallit and nuthin' happened? Or if you were naked*
*with a really neat lady and you couldn't do nuthin'? She's ready and*
*you ain't. Shit! You look at her, you touch her all over, she's hot to trot*
*and you ain't worth a shit . . . and she's lookin' in your eyes . . . not*
*sayin' nothin' . . . just waitin' . . . and you cain't do nothin'. Just the*
*other day a woman came on strong to me and I didn't pay her no*
*mind . . . ¿qué pasa papacito? ¿ya no se te para? . . . Shit, man!*
*How'd she know? Whatcha gonna do, Mike? Me, I wanna blow my*
*brains out! Hear! Whatcha do, Mike, if you were in my place? Tell me,*
*man. Dammit! I just found out how beautiful it is . . . so beautiful . . .*
*and suddenly it's gone . . . and the goddamn doctors say it's all in my*
*head, that I oughta see a shrink. Imagine!*

They were back in the living room. Alejandro pointed to
the armchair in front of the television set.

—This here's where I relax, Alejandro said. I get to read
magazines and watch my favorite shows in that chair. I'm re-
tired, you know, ha! ha! Ah gotta lotta time on my hands, yep.
Come on and I'll show you the master bedroom.

Alejandro led his brother toward a narrow hallway which
took them to the bedroom. On top of the dresser was a photo-
graph of Alejandro at the age of twenty-one. It was a black and
white picture, eight by ten, in a gilded frame. It was the only
photograph of Alejandro taken without his glasses since his ac-
cident. He was handsome, smiling and his teeth were beautiful
and perfectly shaped and white. He was wearing a dark grey
pinstripe suit. Alejandro, however, had covered up his warmly
affectionate eyes. On the glass of the frame, with a black magic
marker, he had drawn a pair of sunglasses over the eyes. Dur-
ing the last few years of his life Alejandro could not bear for
anyone to look into his eyes, not even in this photograph.
Surely he knew how profound was the sadness in his eyes.

—Hey! I look pretty fine with them shades, huh? I'm a
pretty good artist even if I say so myself, huh, Mike? I drew
them shades on myself. With a magic marker, ha! ha!

After a few moments, perhaps because he noticed the way
that his brother was looking at the photograph, Alejandro
changed moods. In an attempt to hide his sorrow he had felt
compelled to make light of what the glasses on the picture
meant. He became serious again.

—I used to carry a pistol in the car, Mike, with two bullets
in it. Look! If you think I'm afraid of death . . .

Alejandro raised his hand and with his index finger he pointed to his temple, as if he were holding a pistol. Then he snapped his thumb as if it were the trigger of a pistol, and with his mouth he made a faint popping sound.

—I was gonna blow my brains out, Russian roulette style, he said, like in the movies, ha! ha! Tried it five or six times. Guess my time hadn't come. Eeeneewayze, brother, Daddy found it and he took it away from me, so's I decided might as well go on livin', ah done decided I'm onna live till I gits to fortee . . . couldn't kill myself . . . so-o-o, what kin ah do-o-o but git to forteee, eh, sportee-o? Done decided, yep!

Miguel was at a loss for words about his brother's feigned playfulness, but then Alejandro reached over and tousled Miguel's hair. It was a warmly fraternal gesture and Miguel turned his eyes away from the photograph on the dresser. When he looked at his brother he could barely see his eyes through the dark glasses. He smiled and his brother became playful again.

—Now come on, Mike, and let's get back to some serious drinking in the living room. Later on I gotta get my rest, ha! ha! Go on, you go first. Fix us another drink, willya? It's in the kitchen. A little vodka and orange juice. Gotta drink my orange juice, you know, for my health. Eeeneewayze, ah got a story I wanna tell you. Ain't never told you about it. Case you're interested.

The story that Alejandro was about to tell was one he had spared his brother too, carrying it around like a painful illness. Like that other secret which he finally blurted out one day, this one too helped Miguel to understand his brother's sorrowful life. *I coulda killed that damn woman, Mike, when she guessed, when she told me right to my face ¿qué te pasa papacito ya no se te para? and she laughed.*

Miguel went into the kitchen and fixed drinks for his brother and himself. He had no idea what his brother was going to tell him. Smiling, he handed his brother a drink. Alejandro had already taken his favorite armchair.

—Sit down, Mike. Have a seat. Make yourself at home, Brother.

He took a chair close to his brother. Around the living room *Playboy* magazines were scattered everywhere, and several ashtrays were filled with ashes and Viceroy cigarette stubs.

Alejandro took out a partly crumpled pack of Viceroys and offered one to his brother. Miguel took out some matches and lit his brother's cigarette first and then his own. Miguel's mind was still on the photograph of his brother in the living room. He understood now why his brother had taken to wearing very dark prescription lenses years ago, even at night.

Another record dropped onto the turntable. Alejandro took a large drink from his glass. Then he raised the cigarette to his lips and took a big drag. He inhaled deeply and held it for a while. He was obviously listening to the words of the Mexican song now playing... *Dios puso penas en nuestras vidas... para olvidarlas con el amor....* Then Alejandro raised his head and slowly he blew the smoke out through puckered lips.

—Remember, Mike, that time when you came to visit me, when I was stationed in San Francisco? Yeah, that's right. You hitchhiked. Uhuh! That's what you told me, that some fine lady had picked you up. Well, just a few days before you came to see me the base commanding officer had signed my promotional certificate. I was gonna get promoted to corporal the day after you showed up, but they wouldn't give me leave that night to go on the town with you. You had come a long way, Mike, to see me. I was gonna get out a corporal, it was only a few months before I got out. Well, shit, I told 'em to shove them corporal stripes. After that they started shoving me around and giving me shit details. That's when they ruined my whole life, Mike.

—You mean you didn't get promoted because we went out? You didn't have a pass?

—That's about it, Brother.

—But you should have told me that you couldn't go out.

—Hell, it don't matter no more. Hey! Don't cry, Mike. It wasn't your fault. Maybe I shoulda told you. Anyway, Brother, it's all in the past... Yep, promotion was all set... and the AWOL, the brig afterwards, they were part of it. I didn't give a shit after they didn't give me the promotion. Chicken shits. Hell, what's a shitty stripe? And later on they took the one I had, after the other Velásquez and me went AWOL. Remember him, the one from New Mexico, the one we useta call Velacue? Them girls from New Mexico, man, they called us both Vela-cuties. Man-n-n! New Mexico was full of girls. In Velacue's hometown they saw an unfamiliar face, one they hadn't ever seen in that town. Mine. A Texas boy. He's cute, they said.

And the girls chased me. Boy, they made me feel like some-
thing special! A different girl ever-r-ry night. New Mexico was
something! Hey! Come on, stop crying, big brother. Come on
now, or I ain't gonna finish my story. Come on, now, easy.
Wasn't your fault. Honest. There, that's better. Anyway, as I
was saying, beautiful girls, different one every night. So when
Vela-cue wanted to get back to the base, I didn't. Then, when I
wanted to, he didn't. Goddamn! I thought I was somebody for
the first fuckin' time in my life! We wuz always partyin', and
fuckin', man-n-n, like there ain't no tomorrow. And kick-ass,
too. Vela-cue and I were bad. We got into a few fights, kicked
ass. Four big guys tried to jump me one time. Come on, moth-
ers, I said, one at a time, but they wanted to kick my ass to-
gether. So I ran, brother. Four at once! I ain't stupid. When we
went back to the base, they put us in the brig till we got out.
Shit, Mike, to tell you the truth, I felt like I had finally gotten
out of your shadow. I used to think how maybe you shouldn't
of protected me so much when I was a kid. I used to wish that
you had let me fight my own battles. You were always kickin'
ass for me. But the Marines changed all that. And goddammit,
the way I shot up. I never would've known. Six feet of solid
muscle. Man-n-n! I could kick ass! I still can, Brother, and no-
body better ever fuck around with you. Ever! Hear me? You
just let me know if they do. Hear me? I'll protect you. God! I
thought I was really somethin'. Started livin' too fast. Too-oo
fast. I don't blame anyone, Mike, except myself. Honest. If I
could do it over again, I probably would do it all over, the same
way. Hell, I think I lived a whole lifetime in New Mexico! Is
that possible, huh, Mike? I brought back enough memories
from New Mexico to last me a lifetime. Hey! You ain't even
touched your drink! Afraid I'll drink you under the table? Ha!
ha!

Alejandro was always playful with his brother about being
able to drink him under the table.

—Yeah, Alejandro said. I guess that if you live just one day,
really live one day of your life, it'll give you enough memories
to last a lifetime. That's how I feel about New Mexico. I really
lived!

# II

HE REMEMBERED the telephone calls from Texas, before Alejandro's death, and after he died came the letter, photographs and memorabilia from Dolores, his sister-in-law, and a letter also from Isabel, his sister. Tossing the ice around in his drink, he recalled many conversations after Alejandro's death about him, with his brothers and their wives, with his nephews and nieces. After his brother died his visits to see his aging parents and his family in Austin, Texas became an annual pilgrimage, and each year he saw the city and the neighborhood of his childhood disappearing. Every time he went back he found the city changed, almost beyond recognition. Despite changes of the past twenty-five years and more, it was enough to visit the old neighborhood near Eleventh Street and Red River, now the site of a fashionable outdoor concert theatre and restaurant; enough to pace the same streets again, even though they were irrevocably transformed, for his limbs to remember and to bring long-buried memories to the surface again.

The smooth flight of the PSA 737 turned his thoughts to chapters that he had written for his projected novel in his proliferating notebooks. Alejandro occupied a special place in his writing. Like the memories of his brother, the chapters were jumbled up in his mind. He wanted to find the right tone to express the love for his brother, the right sequence for the memories. For the tone he went to certain favorite poets in whose works he found comfort and inspiration. He read certain passages over and over, from works by Rilke, Machado and Vallejo. A suitable narrative sequence for the episodes was difficult to find, because the writing followed a logic of the mind all its own. His mind composed whole chapters independently of his attention, usually in fragments that fell neatly together by inserting themselves into what was already written, somewhere! In some cases months or years would separate several episodes that belonged together. He wrote so much, and he could remember having written certain episodes, but he could not remember where. On the back of a napkin? In a small pocketbook or in a large notebook? Sometimes he sketched out outlines of episodes in the margins of books or bureaucratic memoranda, or incorporated his ideas into his class notes. Many times he would find things that he had written long before and be amazed, because he did not remember writing them.

The drink in his hand had barely touched his lips. Somewhere he had read that a writer should be able to write from memory, without notes. Thinking about his brother's widow, he wondered whether he lacked the talent for literature.

A month after Alejandro's death, Miguel received a letter from Dolores. Dear Miguel, the letter began. I'm sending you the picture that I had made for you, and a few of Alejandro's favorite Mexican records. He used to play them over and over. The picture is one of my favorites of him. Alejandro looked so good, so strong and healthy. I gave a copy to Isabel and the boys, and to Mama and Papa too.

Well, I have moved back to our house. After thinking it over I have made up my mind not to sell the house. It is full of memories. And Alejandro and I worried too much when the loan was going through. We were both happy in the house and I feel closer to him. Sometimes I can almost see his beautiful, smiling face trying to hide his pain from me, trying to show me that nothing was wrong, always telling me how happy we both were just the two of us forever. He used to say Honey, we don't need anyone else, just the two of us. He would always say that when he would go he would take me with him, because he knew that I would never be able to make it without him.

So now I wonder, was he right? Did he know what he was talking about? I'm trying very hard to go on without him. It's very hard for me to do this after fourteen years. We would always talk everything out, all our plans, and he was always there whenever I needed him. I worked for him, and if I had to do it all over again I would do the same thing—only I would try to help him stop his drinking. Miguel, I loved Alejandro, with everything I have, I feel empty without him, I feel like part of me died with him. I don't think that I will ever stop loving him. I still can't believe that I will never see him again. Way in the back of my mind I keep thinking he's all right, he'll come home soon, but it's just some silly dream, I should know that he has left, that he's resting now, no more pain, no more worries, no more anything.

Sometimes he used to say, Honey, I wonder if there really is a heaven, do you think that I will go to heaven? He would say that if he had to do it again, he would do everything different, only it was too late, and he knew it. So I pray that he is in heaven and that God will take care of him, and some day I will join him. I know Alejandro wouldn't want me to be afraid of death. I pray that he will forgive all our misunderstandings, and all our little fights. The only thing that bothers me is that I was always working and didn't spend enough time with him. How I wish that I could have taken care of him day and night, be with him always, but I guess that's the way life is—never perfect.

Well, Miguel, I have cried on your shoulder enough, it's been a very long time since I have written a letter, so forgive all my mistakes. I hope that you and Natalie and the girls are doing fine.

Papa and Mama have both been wonderful to Alejandro and me. Miguel, it did hurt me to leave them, but I've got to start my own life, I can't stay with them forever. I feel like an outsider when I see the boys, your brothers and their wives. Dolores, I say, what are you doing here? Where do you belong? Remember, I tell myself, Alejandro is no longer here. So I say to myself, be strong. Alejandro always wanted me to be strong, and no matter how everything looks, he used to say, always keep your worries and troubles to yourself, never let anyone see you cry.

Well have a nice holiday, and give my love to Natalie and Sara and Becky. Love, Dolores.

P.S. We are planning on going to Tony's for dinner. Mama doesn't want to go, but Alejandro would want her to be happy. Papa is working every day, so that helps him. I wish she would go, it would be good for her to get out of the house. Maybe she wouldn't think of Alejandro so much. She's like me, everything reminds her of Alejandro.

And sitting there, somewhat drowsily, in her favorite armchair, doña Dolores Velásquez often found her eyes roaming across the photographs of her sons, her daughter, her grandchildren, from one photograph to another. Every now and then when she thought of all the hardships of the old days she would heave a great sigh. Each November as her birthday was approaching, she would find herself looking away from the photographs of all her other sons and turning to look at the photographs of her dead son, Alejandro. How strange that he had died on her sixty-third birthday. After several years she could still not get used to the idea that she would never see him again. She still expected him to walk through the door any second now.

She looked at all the photographs of Alejandro. In the photograph over to the left, on the second shelf, he was seventeen. In the other one, on the top shelf, occupying a special place, Alejandro was twenty-one years old. Fixing her gaze on this photograph, in which he is wearing a dark gray pinstripe suit, a white shirt and tie, the photograph in which he will be smiling forever, so beautifully, doña Dolores could not keep from thinking of the countless times when the door to the living room would swing open suddenly and Alejandro would be standing there, unsteadily on his feet, over the threshold, so tall, so handsome, partially paralyzed by that horrible accident from which he was supposed to have died that very night, or surviving, after which he would be a quadraplegic forever. But he exerted his will, and he recovered miraculously, never completely, however, when he was not even twenty-one years old, after having been to Korea and back. For years he was a walking miracle, but he hated pity and he could not bear for anyone to look upon him as a limping cripple.

Doña Dolores turned her blurry eyes away from the photographs, turned her head towards the front door, and she imagined him standing there, so tall and handsome, framed by the doorway, his left hand with fingers spread out resting always on his stomach which became larger and larger over the years as muscle began to shrink away from his once powerful arms and shoulders, and from his chest and his legs, as he began to lose more and more weight over the years, dropping from nearly two hundred pounds to one hundred and twenty pounds when he died, and she remembered that special way of his, the way that he used to tilt his head slightly, and she could not forget the dark glasses that hid his beautiful, sad eyes, his full, curly black hair and his melancholy smile, which at times she did not suspect that he forced, to conceal his great distress from her, a big smile which revealed his perfect teeth, the smile with which over the years he finally could no longer conceal his great and unbearable sorrow; yes, she could never forget how the front door used to swing open suddenly and he would be standing there unsteadily on his feet, and she expected him to come in, walk over, put his arm around her and kiss her and greet her in English.

—Well, well. How's my momma today? . . .

Oh! how he used to joke and tease her playfully, to try and ease her sorrow caused by his own helplessness and poor health. He knew, and it added to his grief. Sometimes he would arrive before noon and already he would have had a drink or two to ease his own troubles and grief, and she would ask him gently, half-heartedly scolding him, if he had begun to drink so early in the day, to which he used to reply, in English.

—Of course not, Mama. Oh, how she wished when he was alive that he could be a baby again, so that she could hold him and comfort him. I ain't got no bread, Momma. How's a man gonna get a drink without bread? His smile was unforgettable. He used to feign laughter, and she would ask him, in Spanish, if he had eaten yet.

—¿Almorzaste, hijo? Would you like me to fix you something to eat, Alejandro? ¿Unos huevos con chorizo? ¿Con frijoles? El chile está muy picoso, como te gusta. . . .

The door, the living room, the kitchen, the breakfast that she cooked long after Antonio went to work, the Mexican novelas on television that his sudden entrances used to interrupt—everything reminded her of her dead son.

Exactly two months before Alejandro died, nine months after the birth of her youngest daughter, Isabel la güera wrote to Miguel. Miguel read his sister's letter over and over, many times after his brother's death, until he knew it almost by heart. He could almost hear his sister's voice.

Hi folks, Isabel started out. I know it's about time I wrote, but I'm so damn lazy about writing. It's been ages, and I've got lots of news. First, the picture of Sara and Becky is great. They're so beautiful! It's almost incredible how big Sara is, she looks so grown up for a three year old. Becky, as I've said, is so beautiful, it looks like she's inherited more of the Jewish side than the Mexican.

Since I haven't written, I'll start off from the time y'all left. First, I went to see that Jewish specialist who gave me a thorough checkup. He's just a wonderful man, in his fifties, I'd say and very sympathetic, and he assured me that there's nothing physically wrong with me. After we'd talked at length, he told me how a woman's menstrual cycle is affected strongly by a woman's emotions. I had a very hard emotional strain when María Luisa was born, and that's why my cycle was having trouble regulating. He said he could give me some pills, but he'd rather I didn't take anything. He said before long when I was completely settled, the cycle would straighten out all by itself. He suggested that if I'd been working before the baby came and if I enjoyed working, that if at all possible, for me to return again to work.

Vince and I discussed it and we decided to start looking for someone who could take care of María Luisa. I had just about given up because all the ones I interviewed I didn't like for some reason or other. Vince said I'd never find anyone cause I was so particular, when this lady came and said she was interested in working for me. She's about forty seven, and raised eight children of her own, with five still at home and in school. I liked her right away. She'd never worked for anyone before, she said, but she felt she could do it. I started her August first, while I was here, so I could train her for two weeks. She's great!

She does all my work, takes care of María Luisa, and even has supper ready for me when I come home from school. María Luisa is used to her and is growing. We're so proud of her. She has a tooth and a half and says da da. When she first said da da we were so excited and happy. She isn't crawling yet, but seems on the verge of starting anytime now. I think when she does I will go coo coo. She's crazy about Stephanie and Rick, especially Stephanie though. Whenever she sees Stephanie, she's all aglow, for most of the attention comes from Stephanie. She gets on the floor with her and props her up on her legs and María Luisa just loves it. The funny thing is, María Luisa isn't even spoiled, even with all the attention we give her. She plays well by herself, and we only carry her at times. She's just a wonderful baby, and we love her very much.

Stephanie made it for cheerleader and I took María Luisa to see her yell at our first Jr. High game. The pep squad all wanted to carry her, so she went from hand to hand with everybody making a big fuss over her. She just expects that and takes it as her due. It's funny, she must be thinking she's pretty special to get so much attention. It makes me laugh.

When I took her to see Rickie play baseball, all the kids in the stands came down when I arrived with her, and we were both surrounded by kids, all wanting to see and hold her.

So my cycle is regular, Stephanie made cheerleader, Rickie got the gold award for highest point boy in his age group in the field races, and we're all settled now.

You know, I can look back to December when María Luisa was born, and remember how upset and worried I was, and if anyone had told me that this too will pass, I don't think that I would have believed it. Now, I can't imagine how I could have been so upset, when God has a way of making everything all right, in due time. Just look at Alex. He was and has been so ill, and each time he pulls through. I've been down several times to see him and he's doing all right now. I called Mother yesterday, and she said he was going to be dismissed from the hospital on Tuesday the 28th if all goes well. He is so tired, pobrecito, of being in the hospital and you can't blame him of course. When I say that he's all right, I mean he's holding his own. Confidentially, I just don't know if he'll get well completely. I don't think so.

He told me he couldn't even walk now, and I told him once he started eating well, he would start walking again. He is so thin, weighs only 129 lbs. At one time he weighed almost 200 lbs. I was so shocked when I first saw him and I didn't think I could bear it. Now, of course, I have found the strength, and the last time I went, I fed him his food at the hospital. I thought I'd break down and cry in front of him, but I didn't. He and Dolores were married by the priest the night he was so sick, and they didn't think he would pull through, but he did.

That was the night that he spoke to you on the telephone. Since then, he's been doing pretty good. I hope and pray that he gets well, but, I think his liver is too far gone. Maybe not. It would really be a miracle if he pulled through completely. When I see him, sick, thin, and just lying there, I remember when we were all young, and he was so handsome and tall and so much fun. Remember how people used to say he looked like a movie star? I stop to think how our lives are so different, and I wonder just when he started changing so much. I think it was just after his terrible accident, when he was paralyzed. How different he would have been if it hadn't happened. Dolores has been wonderful throughout her ordeal. She goes to the hospital every day and to work also. How she can endure it is beyond me. She's a very special person! Alex couldn't have found another like her in a million years. Let's hope and pray he recovers!

I think I've covered everything. I'm busy at school all day long, but I enjoy it. Now I work only at the Jr. High and Stephanie and Rickie are both here so I can keep an eye on them. Stephanie was elected to Student Council so she's happy. She's a very popular girl and we're proud of her. I have to keep tight reigns on her, so she won't get too far away, too soon. But everybody likes her in school, boys and girls alike, and I don't want it going to her head. Ha! Ha! Our school colors are red and white, so María Luisa got a pair of red pants and a white top. I took her to the beauty shop and she got a pixie hair cut. Stephanie says she's only 9 months old and she's already been to the beauty shop. She'll be spoiled! Stephanie received the little gift and sends thanks. I'll close for now so I can go cook supper. Hope you like the pictures.

Love,
Bessie, Vince, Stephanie, Rickie and María Luisa

Parts of the letter passed through his mind like unforgettable refrains from a beautiful poem. He could almost hear his sister's voice. *So ill . . . each time he pulls through . . . Mother said he was going to be dismissed soon. . . . Confidentially, I just don't know . . . couldn't even walk . . . so thin . . . 129 lbs. I was so shocked . . . I fed him . . . thought I'd break down and cry . . . That was the night he spoke to you on the telephone . . . I wonder when . . . after his terrible accident. . . . How different . . . if it hadn't happened . . .*

Coming down the aisle, from the front of the airplane, a young mother was leading her child to the bathroom. Miguel swished the ice around in his glass, brought it to his lips and savored the whiskey. Even before Alejandro's last telephone call to Miguel his brother's death was announced in a dream.

On Thursday afternoon, June 3, more than five months before Alejandro died, Miguel woke up with a terrible hangover. He reached over for his unfinished whiskey, tasted it and decided he couldn't drink it without ice. After putting fresh ice in his drink he sat down at his work table and sketchily recorded two dreams in his notebook. One dream was very bizarre. It had occurred two days earlier. The other dream occurred during the nap from which he had just awakened that day, and it prophesied the death of his brother, whom he had seen on the last visit to Texas only a few months previously, during the spring quarter break.

Years later, Miguel regretted that the notes he made of these two dreams were so sketchy. He had noted only that the ambiguous setting of the first dream reminded him of a Piranesilike architectural structure. It may have been a brownstone building or a hotel, he wrote. Whatever, the building was surrounded by tenement buildings like those that one sees when one arrives in Chicago by train from the south. The dream was very complex. Notes. Sadistic sexual gratifications. Mutilation of bodies. I am about to make love to a girl, but I feel threatened. Several men are standing around. Cinematic close-ups. Naked bodies. Lovemaking. Close-ups of arms and legs.

That was all that he wrote about the first dream. In the second dream his brother Alejandro arrived at Miguel's house in Claremont, Illinois. He brought suitcases, Miguel wrote, as if he had planned to stay for a long visit.

—I only have one month to live, Mike, my brother said. I needa write a last will and testament. Will you help me?

Later we are driving away so that we can speak in privacy. I have no idea where we are going. Then the scene changes. We are driving to our parents' home in East Austin, Texas. Inexplicably, I have the impression that we are still in Claremont. My brother decides to spend the night. On the next day I will drive him to his home. Alejandro is crying, and saying that he does not want to die. *Why me? I don't want to die!*

Two months later, in August, the telephone rang. Miguel picked it up.

—Hello, Miguel answered. His brother's voice spoke immediately.

—Hey, Brother! Hiya doin'?

—Alejandro! Fine, and you?

—Me? I'm just fine, too. I've been thinking of coming up there to visit with you. Got an extra bed? Yeah! I'm fine. Just fine, sporty. . . . Just got back from seein' tha doctor. Ha! Ha! Have I got a story to tell you! He tells me I'm dyin' and the

115

prognosis—hey! How 'bout this educated language? Prognosis . . . the man says . . . is three more years if I'm a good boy. Man, like I'm almost thirty-five! And I'm gonna make it to forty. Damn tootin' I will! He don't know what he's talkin' about. You know me. You cain't beat my will to live. I go when I decide to go. Yeah! Ha! ha!

Miguel could tell that his brother had been drinking. He could always tell, because Miguel had been observing himself closely. He knew and he could tell about others.

During the past few years Alejandro had begun to speak of death. On a few occasions he admitted having thoughts about suicide, which made Miguel feel helpless. What could he say? Was his brother being serious? Or was it just the drinking? His brother's laughter was not genuine. Miguel recognized his brother's self-protective laughter, with which his brother tried to protect people he loved, the same laughter with which he always made light of his unbearable sorrows.

His brother was born with the gift of laughter and with a marvelous sense of humor. When they were children and adolescents no one could ever stay mad at Alejandro for long. He knew just how to make people laugh, and now their youngest brother, Eduardo, was like him too. He envied their gift of laughter. Alejandro was talkative. Mariachi music was playing in the background.

—I got me an extension cord for the phone now, Mike. Cain't walk no more. Right side is gone, gone, man! But it's okay, Alejandro said. Then he laughed sadly again. It's okay, Mike, I'm fine, man. Don't you worry 'bout me. Hear?

During a few moments of silence, the mariachi music could be heard in the background. Then Alejandro spoke again.

—Hey, Brother! Are you still there?

—Yes, Alejandro. I'm here. I'm listening. Miguel did not know what to say.

—You ain't talkin' much. I'm all right, honest. Don't you go worryin' yourself about me. Man!

Then there was a longer, awkward silence. Miguel did not know what to say. He felt helpless, just as he had felt with his brother so many times during the past several years. The lyrics of the Mexican corrido in the background expressed indescribable sadness. Amalia Mendoza's voice. . . .

—Cain't walk no more, Mike. Did you know?

—Since when, Alejandro? You were walking a few months ago, not very well, but you managed.

—It's happened since you were here. It was already pretty bad, but it's worse now. The extension cord's so I don't have to get up to use or answer the phone. Even had to buy me a hospital bedpan, and they wanna put me in a goddamn wheelchair. I can still drive though, but I gotta put the car in drive, with my left hand, that is. There ain't gonna be no stick shift for me no more.

Alejandro laughed desperately again. He coughed. After the coughing stopped Alejandro tried to be cheerful.

—Hey! Did you hear? Your little brother's done bought himself a great big, new Buick, brand new, and another house. Everybody in the family is on the way up, doing well. Soon you'll be doing well too, hermano. You're the one in the family with all the brains!

Alejandro was playful, but in the context of his imminent death, his playfulness had the opposite effect on Miguel than Alejandro intended. Later, Miguel realized that his brother had wanted to be the one to tell him personally that he was dying. Even when he was announcing his own death, Alejandro was laughing, trying to lessen his brother's grief. In the next few months Alejandro would go into the hospital for intensive care several times.

At the time of that telephone call to his brother, Alejandro still believed that his intense will to live would permit him to reach the age of forty. During the last two or three years of his life, knowing that he was moving towards his death, Alejandro was able to prolong his life by sheer volition. Sheer volition, in fact, was responsible for the miracle of walking again, when the doctors did not even believe he would live through the night. There was nothing to lose, the doctors said, so they asked for permission to operate. Alejandro always hated the huge scar at the back of his neck.

During another moment of awkward silence, Miguel again heard the mariachi music in the background. *Sólo Dios que me vio en mi amargura supo darme consuelo. . . .*

—Hell, Mike, how come you wanted . . . He heard his brother take a deep breath and sigh. How come you wanted . . . to be so far away? Hell . . . never mind. You just do what you please, you're gonna do that anyhow. Ha! ha! But you got my permission. Hell, you'll make it yet. *Tú bien sabes que si ando borracho*. . . . You're almost thirty-six. You'll make it . . . Mike. . . .

Alejandro blew his nose and cleared his throat. He was crying. In the background, the music, *quisiera ser como tú . . . que no sientes las penas, quisiera ser como tú, sin sangre en las venas . . . pero la buena suerte no es para mí*. . . . Then Alejandro laughed again. —No, don't mind me, Mike. I'm jokin'! . . . You know me, always jokin' around. I cain't stop laughin' and my side is splittin'! Then Alejandro became a little serious. He spoke affectionately. —I worry about you, Brother. You better stop hittin' that booze, you hear? It ain't good for you.

That day, they talked a lot about old times. They exchanged affectionate memories of one another and the old days. While they talked Miguel imagined his brother as a boy. That was the way he always remembered Alejandro. Because of travel, because of his wanderings far from Texas, Miguel realized at his brother's funeral that he had known only the child and the boy. He never really knew his brother as a man. Miguel drifted away from his family for years when he was so disappointed in himself. He wanted to be far away where they could not see the life he was leading. In the years after his brother's death, Alejandro's favorite mariachi music, the lyrics of the corridos and the rich melancholy voices of the singers made Miguel wonder about the last few years, the last terrible months and days of his brother's life. On the telephone that day, Miguel and Alejandro reminisced about how close the two brothers and their sister Isabel used to be. They talked about the old days and about what a dreamy and imaginative child Alejandro had been. Unfortunately his first grade teacher, Miss Pilgrim, did not appreciate these qualities.

Miss Mary Pilgrim failed Alejandro in the first grade because he had the gift of laughter, because he was imaginative and curious, because his cheerful temperament led him to expect that going to school and learning would be something enjoyable. Miss Pilgrim failed him and she would never know the irreparable harm that she inflicted on this particular bright, laughing child. Alejandro was never able to live down this irrevocable humiliation, and from time to time as an adult, Alejandro would mention it. Miguel would always remember his brother's words from a conversation they once had. *If you ever become a teacher, Mike . . . don't flunk nobody. Never. Hear?*

Miguel became a professor, and over the years he kept the promise to his brother. Now, aboard the PSA 737, the murmur of conversation among his fellow passengers drifted in and out of consciousness.

Alejandro haunted Miguel after his death as he had in life. Towards the end of the university's fall quarter, death had intruded into the hectic pace of university graduate study, and the trip to Texas to attend the funeral suspended Miguel's duties and activities as student and teaching assistant for a few days.

A week after his brother's death Miguel plunged into his work again, preparing lectures for his course on existential literature, grading student term papers, writing his own term papers for the graduate seminars that he was taking, and during the rest of the time, he was again working in the library, pulling dozens of books at a time from the stacks to prepare himself for the Ph.D. qualifying examinations only five months away. He was reading books dealing with the histories of several modern national literatures, books on art and film; making notes on critical estimates of novelists, poets and playwrights, and their major works. He was reading Joyce, Proust and Mann; Baudelaire, Lautréamont, Huysmans; Faulkner and Fuentes. He was reading Robbe-Grillet, Beckett, Ionesco, Genêt and many others; Paz, Valéry, Borges, Gorostiza, Villaurrutia, Huidobro. At that time he developed an interest in literary influences. He became fascinated with the influence of Poe and Faulkner in France and Latin America, and Whitman too, in Latin America; and with the pervasive influence of French symbolism and surrealism across the twentieth century in all the arts. He learned to systematize his studying and to read rapidly once he discovered the major scholarly sources. The extent of repetition and overlapping of material in scholarly books helped him to organize and retain large amounts of information. He learned the value of the books' tables of contents, the introductions, selected chapters or paragraphs, such as the first one or two and the last paragraphs of special chapters. The index of books was extremely helpful because it listed the most important critics and scholars, the major concepts and themes, and the critical topics, in alphabetical order. Repetitions in scholarly works identified areas that deserved emphasis or special attention. Literary terms created in his mind structured frameworks and conceptual configurations of international literary works on which to build.

No matter how busy Miguel stayed he could not put his brother out of his mind. A few days after his brother died, for example, Miguel was reading Henri Lemaître's *La poésie depuis Baudelaire*. As he got to the paragraph that describes the relationship of theory to poetic creation . . . *jamais sans doute la théorie poétique n'a tenu une telle place dans la préoccupation du poète* . . . the words began to dance before his eyes. They meant nothing no matter how many times he read them over, and his thoughts turned to the funeral home and to the small chapel where his brother's coffin had stood. He could see his mother sitting not too far away from the coffin and people coming up to her to express condolences. Each time a person walked up to her she would cry. After a little while she would settle down again. Or out of the pages from other books the image of his brother's and Dolores' home would rise before his mind's eye, and in memory, he would wander through the living room of their home, where after Alejandro's funeral he had seen the medical paraphernalia of aged or physically disabled people, a wheelchair, a bedpan, a portable urinal, a walker, medicine bottles, the long telephone extension cord that he needed when he could no longer walk to the telephone; and the overflowing ashtrays, his favorite big armchair, the stereo receiver and record player, the records. Los Rivereños, Amalia Mendoza, José Alfredo Jiménez, Joe Turner, Ray Charles. All of these objects created a portrait in Miguel's mind of Alejandro in his last days, when his nervous and his circulatory systems broke down and he lost his voluntary muscular control. At the end Alejandro was almost totally paralyzed.

Alejandro at twenty, tall, handsome, powerful arms and legs, disarming smile. A zest for life. All the future ahead of him. Less than fifteen years later his life was over. Dolores' voice. *He suffered so much towards the end, Mike. He wanted me to buy a gun, and he became so angry when I wouldn't do it. I just couldn't.* . . .

Alejandro's death removed a heavy load from the shoulders of the living. In the Claremont University Library, Miguel closed the covers of a book by Herbert Muller on modern fiction, and he felt sad that his brother thought that his life was lived in vain. But was it really? No, Miguel said to himself, I cannot allow myself to think that his life was lived in vain. Because Alejandro lived. A short, tragic life to be sure, but it was one

120

that permitted him to know joy, to bring cheerfulness and humor into others' lives, and he lived a lifetime in New Mexico, where he knew the ephemeral beauty of love. In death Alejandro became transformed. Alejandro became more familiar to everyone who had taken him and his life for granted. The large eight-by-ten photograph of Alejandro was given a special place in all the homes of his brothers, his sister, his mother and father. In the following years, four nephews, two of them bearing a remarkable resemblance to Alejandro, were named after him; in these little tocayos Alejandro lives on.

As the plane moved towards Oakland, Miguel thought about all the years when memories of his brother's terrible accident and his death followed him about. At times a sense of guilt compounded the awareness of his own shortcomings, his terrible nature and the way that he withheld love. In his own mind he felt that in some ways he contributed, unknowingly perhaps, to his brother's sorrowful life. Alejandro's image, his voice, cherished images of the child Alejandro, the boy, his laughter, made Miguel wonder. Who was the man that he never got to know? Alejandro's story coming together bit by bit, fragment by fragment. The first death in the immediate family. So close in childhood that after they read the story of the Corsican brothers, they claimed to know when the other was hurt or in danger *I was selling papers on Sixth Street Mike when you cut your foot on that broken Coke bottle in the creek I felt it* . . . brother of flesh and blood, hermano.

Over the years the airplane passenger had pondered many times the meaning of his own life. How many people have suffered because of me? To whom have I brought grief? Why can't I be like other people? Have I wasted my life? Where is my life going? Did I betray my calling, my family, my wife, my children? Can any artist make amends for what happened in the past? How?

He looked toward the front of the airplane. As he took a small drink of whiskey he felt remorse about the quarrels with his wife. *Oh, honey! You are impossible to live with! It's a living hell. And yet . . . now and then, like on that morning after we made love, when we remembered our wedding day . . . Why can't you be kind and gentle like that more often . . . like you were in the beginning?*

# III

NATALIE tucked her head affectionately into Miguel's neck and shoulder, pulled the covers over their naked bodies, and she moved closer to her husband. He knew from these affectionate gestures that something was on her mind. Conscious of wanting to remember what Natalie said in their tender moments together, he was warmed by the closeness of this woman who had given him two daughters. Even though the older of their two daughters was barely in her teens, Natalie was already thinking of the day when they would go away to college and get married. Natalie always worried about invented or future events. If she had nothing to worry about, that worried her.

—The other day, she began, when I started to think about Sara and that in a few years she'll be getting married, I thought about how I cried and cried on the day we got married. On the night before our wedding . . .

—Roberto and I spent the night at a hotel.

—My mother was very upset with me. I just couldn't control the crying, and I remember that I cried the next morning too, before you and Roberto came to the house.

—Your mother told me I could still change my mind. It's not too late, she said. You don't have to go through with it.

—She did?

—Don't you remember? You were right there when she said it.

—No, I don't remember that.

—Do you remember that they thought you were pregnant because we decided so suddenly to get married?

—Yes, and we could've had a larger wedding if we had waited.

—Never mind large weddings, ours was a lovely wedding, honey. Do you remember your mother and your aunt both trying to run the show? People talking at once. I got upset and Roberto kept telling me not to take it so seriously. It's a cultural thing with Jewish people, Miguel. You have to get used to it. One moment they're arguing and fighting, and the next moment they are hugging and kissing. Don't let it get you down. Anyway, that's what he said. But it's true of Mexicans and Italians and Irish, too. I know that now. But for me, as you know, it's impossible to show tenderness and affection for a long time after a quarrel. That's just the way I am. Yes, I remember. Your mother and your aunt, each wanting to play the piano and disagreeing about where to place the flower arrangement.

—And for a whole hour just before the ceremony, while I was upstairs . . . I couldn't control my crying . . . and my mother was so angry. . . . I kept thinking how red my eyes were gonna be, and my mother kept saying, Look! You're a grown woman about to get married! Stop acting like a child. You're gonna look a sight when you walk down those stairs. But I just couldn't stop crying.

—I was standing in the living room. . . . Roberto, our best man, was standing next to me; the Rabbi was in front of us. Roberto and I had our backs to the stairs from which you would come. We were facing the fireplace. Around us everyone was waiting for you to walk down the stairs. I could see the top landing of the stairs in the large mirror above the fireplace. Everyone was waiting, and then . . .

—I don't know how in the world I stopped crying. Every time I thought of how awful I'd look, because of the redness of my eyes . . . or when I'd worry that I might break down and cry during the ceremony . . . I'd start up again . . . and my mother kept losing her patience with me . . .

—in the large mirror, above the fireplace, suddenly there you were. The Rabbi looked over across my right shoulder at you, standing on the landing where the stairs turned toward the living room. . . . I saw you emerge into the mirror, dressed in white, so beautiful, mi vida.

—I was so nervous.

—You were only twenty-three years old.

—It was a nice ceremony and you broke the wineglass. Was it wrapped in a handkerchief?

—I think it was a white cloth napkin.

123

—What did it mean, the breaking of the glass?

—I think it meant that we would also have to share the bitterness of marriage along with the happiness. Did I have to repeat some words in Hebrew?

—Yes, the Rabbi told you to repeat some things. Everyone thought your pronunciation was good. I should've had you give a speech. None of them knew you very well. In fact, they hardly knew you.

—But I did give a little speech, the next day. . . .

—I don't remember. Roberto gave a speech, I remember that. He was so tall and handsome, his hair so beautiful and white. My aunts thought he was so adorable.

—Two Mexicans among all those Jewish people. One from San Francisco and the other from Pflugerville, Texas. He was all the family you and I had in New York after we got married.

—He looked like a movie star.

—He looked like some kind of ambassador or dignitary.

—After the ceremony we went to dinner.

—We sat at the same table with two of your childhood friends. Do you remember?

—No.

—It was Lori and Joan. We sat next to them. Finally it was time for us to leave the guests. It was our first night as man and wife, and everyone laughed when we excused ourselves. Roberto was dancing with your aunt and they both waved. As we were leaving, I whispered teasingly in Lori's ear, would you like to join us in a little marital bliss? And she threw her head back and laughed.

—Did you really ask her?

—Yes.

—That's funny. What did she say?

—You know Lori, she just laughed.

—And the next day we went to a brunch.

—That is when I gave my little speech. Don't you remember that I said how happy I was to be part of the mishbuhah? Everyone did make me feel like part of the family. All our Jewish friends always make me feel welcome.

—Funny, I don't remember. I do remember my grandmother's little speech. She couldn't stop talking, but she'd always start out her speeches by saying "unaccustomed as I am." She really liked you, Miguel.

—I liked her very much, too.

—I wonder if Sara's gonna cry on the day of her wedding. I wonder if Becky will cry. It's so strange to think that in a few years they'll be getting married. They're growing up so fast, and after they're gone there's gonna be just the two of us again, just like in the beginning.

For a long time they stayed in each other's arms. How vulnerable she seemed, and she was full of tenderness and love. He drew her closer to him.

A little while later Natalie pushed the covers away. She said that she would use the shower first.

Miguel stayed in bed, listening to the running water in the shower, dwelling on the image of his wife, the bride standing on the staircase landing, dressed in white, twenty-three years old, in the mirror above the heads of all the family and guests, the sudden hush, the whispers about how lovely, lovely Natalie looked, and Natalie high on the staircase landing, in the mirror, smiling.

Most of the time, he thought, as he listened halfheartedly to the murmur of conversation among his fellow passengers aboard the airplane, it did not take much to make Natalie happy—a little affection, a thoughtful gesture, flowers. Now and then Natalie and he went over the family album, and the photographs brought back recollections of pleasant experiences, happy memories of their life together. Unfortunately, the obsessions of the artist for freedom, to seek new experiences, to stay alive at a peak of intensity, to travel, to love many women, brought grief to Natalie. His obsessions bordered on madness, and he knew that his drinking made him quarrelsome and angry, brought out in him a great capacity for rage, over which in recent years he had learned to exercise better control. But it was always there. He wanted to write honestly about his obsessions, about the terrible side of his nature. . . .

*Oh, Miguel! Why can't you be tender and gentle? Remember when we met in New York, that time when I was in bed with the flu you brought a whole roasted chicken from the delicatessen down the street . . . with corn on the cob and bread rolls . . . you earned barely enough to pay the rent . . . remember when you paid the bus fare for that poor drunken man when we got on the 125th Street bus . . . remember? . . .*

He was in the rocking chair, holding a drink in his hand. Valerie was angry.

—Just look at you! Drunk again. I'm sick and tired of how you spend your time. You start drinking at ten o'clock in the morning, almost every day. By three o'clock you're worthless. You stop working and sit in the rocking chair, with the music blaring so loud people can hear it all the way down the street. You go outside and sit in the backyard, you always gotta have a drink in your hand and you stare at the sky and the trees for hours, doing absolutely nothing. You're home all the time and there's nothing to show for all the hours when nobody's here to bother you. What've you done? Show me! Show me something! Why don't you go to your office where I don't have to see you doing nothing. Don't touch me! Leave me alone! I want to see some work before you touch me again. Find a mistress, I don't care. Just leave me alone. Move out of the house. Oh! This is awful. I can't stand it anymore. You never do anything. You don't clear after meals. You refuse to wash dishes, to cut the grass, to take out the garbage, to replace burned-out light-bulbs, to work at your office. Look! I'm going out. I don't even wanna wear my wedding band anymore. Maybe someone'll think I'm not married and wanna meet me. Why don't you move out? I can't stand to see you drinking every day, looking at the sky and the clouds and the flowers, listening to music, watching TV till you pass out. I'm tired of hearing about your dreams, that you're gonna be famous one day. How? Where are the great works of art? Why don't you paint at night instead of drinking and sitting every night in front of those stupid TV shows? I know. I know you told me you'd never be a good husband. Yes. You told me that too. Yes, yes, yes! I agree. We shouldn't have gotten married. Why don't you move out? Find another woman. Why don't you go away? Perhaps if you leave me some decent person will come into my life. . . . Oh, Lorenzo! What is going to happen with us? Everytime I see you there's a drink in your hand!

I remember a night long ago, Valerie, when our lovemaking was so beautiful that it made us cry . . . You were so sweet and tender that night, and you asked me if we would always be to-gether and I said yes, para siempre, mi amor. That made you happy and you moved closer into my arms . . . There have been many happy moments, days and years for us, my love, because you made them possible. But at times when I do not like myself I think of the grief that I have brought to you and

126

the children . . . And when our lovemaking is beautiful like it was that night I think of coming home other nights, after being with another woman, and one night you wanted to make love after a quarrel and I could not. I closed my eyes and imagined a procession of beautiful girls and young women, nameless and faceless, in short cutoffs, in jeans, belly buttons exposed, their long naked limbs, small buttocks, and small mouth-size breasts that stay hard even when they are reclining, open and inviting love. You cried. You didn't say so, but you thought I had been with another woman. It was either tenure or quarrels. That was long ago, before you began to tell me how horrible I am and that I should find myself a mistress because you could no longer stand for me to touch you. Other times you asked me if I was having an affair and I would say no, because it was just someone that I met, no affair, so I didn't lie. You were patient with me when I couldn't. How can I ever forget? Other times when we would be making love my thoughts would drift and I would think of lovemaking as something miraculous, fundamentally sweet and tender, like a journey to other hemispheres and planets, and in the same line of thought, women are galaxies and constellations of stars and celestial bodies. I used to close my eyes and think, oh how good to come so close to the moment of magic and eternity, to pause and stay there at the edge of the sexual abyss, to hold off until the exquisite agony becomes unbearable, all the while thinking how I might describe the act of love in the novel. And you asked on that lovely night, as you ask customarily, do you love me, dear? and I answered yes as I always answer, and I meant it, mi amor. Sometimes I wonder how you could love me, and when I come home after being with another woman I keep thinking as I am undressing and getting into bed, trying not to wake you, what if she should wake up and want to make love? And it makes me feel bad to think of you kissing the mouth that has just been kissing another, holding the hands that have just caressed another woman . . . and it tears me apart to relish and yet deplore the wild insatiable side of my nature, the parts of me that drive me to seek new, wild and passionate embraces, and I hate the lying. Sometimes I wish that I could tell you everything because you understand these bizarre emotions when we talk about them in other people. . . . Please do not wake up. Please do not ask me to make love with the juices of another still on my body, and if I take a shower you will know for sure. Oh, I cannot help what I am, that I was born to love many women. I don't deserve your love and devotion. Your voice haunts me, dearest wife and mother of our children. In the darkness by your side, in bed, often I relive experiences of our life together.

—You were so good for a while, Lorenzo, after Stephanie was born. Remember how you used to get up with me in the middle of the night, when I was breast-feeding? You used to talk to me every night, to keep me awake. Remember? You always worried that I'd fall asleep and drop her. You said you loved to watch us. Remember the drawings you did of us, honey? The drawings of me when I was pregnant with Stephanie? When I was breast-feeding? Remember how we used to walk down to Washington Square? Remember, honey? Now, when I'm pregnant again, you've started to drink so much. Why, honey? What is it that makes you drink? Are you afraid of responsibility? Does graduate work make you miserable? Are you gonna be prepared for the Ph.D. examinations? Is it the term papers? Just finish them, honey, don't take them so seriously. Oh, Lorenzo, I worry about you. Maybe that's why I had that strange dream last night. I dreamed that I was visiting with my family in New York. My mother was there, and my sister and my brother, with their families. I think my mother asked me about the pregnancy. Stephanie was already born and I was going to have another baby. I couldn't remember who Stephanie's father was. I was wearing a wedding band. Where did it come from? Who is Stephanie's father? I couldn't remember who her father was, what he looked like. I didn't know whose baby I was carrying. I felt awful when my mother asked me. It was as if I had wanted to block out your face. . . . Oh, Larry, honey! What's going to happen to us? Please don't drink so much, honey. . . . Please! Oh! Why are you so obsessed with being alone? Would you be able to get along without us? What would you do without me, Larry?

He regretted the quarrels with his wife, that he made the children cry. He had to be true to his nature. He could not help his obsession with art, his longing to love many women, to be free. Somewhere he read that Tolstoy dreamed that his wife died. A person cannot help what he dreams.

128

He was looking down towards the dip in the undulating highway. Like a movie camera his eyes followed the rise and dip of the highway. He saw the highway rise and dip behind another hill farther away. Not a single car was in sight.

In the distance, Brenda, his wife's friend, dashed happily but clumsily across from the right to the other side of the highway. She fell. His wife ran to Brenda, out to the middle of the highway, near the dip. The two women were both happy about something—good news from Brenda, apparently. Their happiness made them oblivious to being out on the highway. No cars were in sight, but one could come at any moment, over the hill. It was Miguel's most discomforting habit, to anticipate accidents or danger. At highway speed, he was thinking, a driver would not see them in the dip of the highway, or be able to stop his car in time. Miguel had to warn them. He cried out.

—Get off the highway before a car comes!

His voice, however, was inexplicably faint. The two women did not hear him. Inevitably, just as he had feared, several vehicles appeared, one after another over the second distant hill. The danger was compounded in his mind because the scene before his eyes was like part of a film. The approaching vehicles were flattened out as on a motion picture screen. They were moving and yet standing still, swaying slightly to the left and right, like in a picture taken with a zoom lens. Shocked to see the cars coming, the two women froze immediately on the spot. The cars were coming closer and closer.

—Get off the highway! Get off the highway! he screamed in vain. There was nothing he could do.

Out of nowhere several people appeared on the edge of the highway, between him and the two women. Their voices, faint and feeble echoes of his own, carried the warning to his wife and her friend, in vain. Far away Brenda and his wife moved to the line that divided the two highway lanes. The two women probably hoped that the cars would go around them on either side.

In the distance the flattened vehicles began to form two lines that would separate them on either side of the two women. They will be safe, he thought with relief. But without warning, obviously not able to see the women ahead, one driver in the distance began to edge his car out of the left line of cars. Helplessly, Miguel watched this car changing lanes. He stood riveted to the spot, terrified, knowing the inevitable. The two women were frozen with fear; the rushing automobile was changing lanes slowly at an angle that would bring it directly at the women. Unable to endure the sound of any object striking human flesh and bone, he let out a piercing animal scream. *Miguel! Wake up! You're having another bad dream.*

Notebook entry. Last night an awful dream. It disturbed Natalie's sleep. She woke me out of it. After a while I went back to sleep. Several short bad dreams, one right after the other. All of them connected with helplessness. One was about buying a home in terrible condition. Its framework was broken and out of line. The plumbing did not work. The porch and the bathroom reminded me of our dilapidated house on Sabine Street, when I was a boy. Years ago, when I was living in New York, I used to have a recurrent dream about our tin mailbox, which was nailed to a chinaberry tree. In the dream I would come home to visit after many years and the mailbox was always filled with countless yellowing letters, postmarked many years earlier. The dream made me feel that I had missed something, that life had passed me by, that I had lost touch with everyone. Cannot remember the other dreams well. Another recurring dream haunted me in New York. I was afraid in the dream of failing an algebra class, of not being able to graduate from high school. In that dream I found myself wandering through empty halls and corridors, going up and down staircases, trying to find the classroom where the final examination was to be given, knowing that I would never pass it because I had not attended classes. I never found the classroom. Other times the dream would be the same, but it would be an English class. Strange. In high school I was an A student in both classes. Now I have terrible dreams about losing my children, about harm coming to them and to Natalie.

The child is running along, headed toward a rope bridge that spans an incredible precipice. She is laughing, oblivious of the danger that crossing the rope bridge presents. Her father cannot keep up with the four-year-old child. His arms are loaded down with books. He should be holding his daughter's hand at this dangerous spot, and he knows it.

He cries out once, twice. Oh, why does she never listen? He calls out to her again, but the child does not listen. She is running and laughing as if she were playing a game with her father.

—*Please*, Becky! *Please*, honey! The bridge is dangerous!

The books are heavy in his arms. His legs are sluggish. He can anticipate what will happen. *Oh, my honey! My baby!* She is on the rope bridge now. It begins to sway dangerously. The little girl is laughing, still running.

—*Ple-e-ease Becky!*

She pays no mind to her father, who by this time should have dropped the books. He sees the inevitable. The rope bridge totters. Little Becky turns around to look at her father. She is laughing, moving backwards, laughing and waving at her father whose terrified face puzzles her. He sees the back of her knees moving towards one of the ropes. She will lose her balance, fall back and tumble down into the precipice.

Frozen to the spot, completely helpless, watching his cheerful four-year-old child about to plunge to her death, he screams out, but he does not drop the books. *Honey! honey! Wake up, you're having another bad dream. . . . Oh my! Just look how you're trembling. You're crying. Why are you crying? It's all right . . . it was just a bad dream.*

The voice of the passenger to Miguel's right interrupted his thoughts.

"Excuse me, can I get by?"

It took a few moments for Miguel to get his bearings. His mind was still on the dream that he had years ago. *Hijitas, I could not bear to lose you.* He shook his head as if to wake himself.

"Yes, yes of course. Just a moment."

He took the empty little whiskey bottle from the plastic tray and placed it inside the pocket behind the seat in front of him. Holding his whiskey glass in his left hand he pushed his tray up, locked it and waited for the woman and the little girl coming down the aisle to pass.

"I really gotta go, Mommy," said the little girl as she passed by Miguel. "How come Daddy wouldn't take me?"

"Because we're both girls, Jennifer, and it's better this way."

"Why, Mommy?"

Miguel moved out of his seat after the woman and the little girl passed by. He remembered his daughters when they were little too, and how he used to tuck them into bed. *Tell us a story,*

*Daddy, please, so we can go right to sleep. . . . Yes-ss, Daddy, ple-e-eas-s-e.* He stood in the aisle to let his fellow passenger out.

"Thank you," the passenger said, lowering his head to step out beyond the overhead compartment. In the aisle the tall man stood up straight and turned toward the rear of the airplane.

Before sitting down, Miguel saw at a glance that almost all the plane seats were taken. A few passengers were reading magazines or newspapers. Some passengers were businessmen travelling with business associates. One could tell by their polyester suits and ties, their attaché cases and gregarious conversation. They were accustomed to conversations with people. A long time ago, for a few years in Texas, in Chicago, and in New York, Miguel had been part of that eight-to-five world, to which he was by nature completely unsuited. The thought of polyester material created in his mind a snapshot image of the United States during the past two decades. The time had flown since he returned from Mexico. The assassination of President Kennedy seemed far away now. The shocking news had spread from mouth to mouth at the Chicago bank where he worked. *The President's been shot! The President's been shot!* Other assassinations followed. Bobby Kennedy. Martin Luther King. The students at Kent State. Rubén Salazar, the Chicano journalist, at the Los Angeles anti-Vietnam War moratorium. Because of his travels, because of his appointment in Chicano Studies, he could see American history with fresh insights, the deplorable and the fascinating sides of each. He saw in a new light, too, his boyhood in the early forties and his young manhood in the fifties. Rapid changes and transformations that took place in the nation passed before his enchanted eyes, the changing fashions in clothing, the development of the automobile industry, the turbulent years of minority social movements; some of the songs of the forties, fifties and sixties were being brought back; the seventies and eighties brought other changes. Yes, the thought of polyester material brought new thoughts and old memories to mind. American history, from 1960 to Watergate and closer to the present, the election of a movie star, a second-rate one at that, to act as President! It was only a few years ago that it dawned on him: I am a witness to a nation, to worlds in transition and transformation! How the past two decades have flown!

At the back of the plane one of the bathrooms became vacant and he saw the woman and the squirming child step inside and close the door. His fellow passenger was waiting near the door to the other bathroom.

Miguel took his seat. He sipped his Canadian Club on the rocks. The ice had not completely melted; smooth whiskey, he thought.

The watch that once belonged to his brother had rather extraordinary evocative powers. A small possession becomes a cherished object, a repository of memories and feelings. It was amazing that only ten minutes had passed since the great steel bird had leaped into the air. In thirty-five or forty minutes the plane would land at Oakland Airport.

The movement of the second hand on the watch had a hypnotic effect on him. It evoked memories of his brother's funeral, of the grey November day and the winter-barren Mexican cemetery at Pflugerville, Texas. The years had fled since then too. Strange to have been conscious since childhood of the passage of time, he thought. Marvelous how travel frees the mind to think about time and the past. What a strange thing too, that some people, like my father, are born to remember. And I?

He closed his eyes. The relatives and friends who attended the funeral were standing in line in front of the gaping hole, waiting for a turn to throw a handful of dirt over the coffin lid. After taking a turn each person stood back. Finally, two men with shovels began to fill up the hole. The clumps of dirt struck and pounded on the coffin lid. Thump. Slam. Slide.

He opened his eyes. The watch reminded Miguel of Alejandro's favorite songs, especially the four Mexican records which Dolores had given him after the funeral, along with the watch. The jacket covers of the four records came vividly to mind. On each of them was Alejandro's name in his own handwriting, Alex C. Velásquez.

The little second hand of the watch skipped three times in a barely perceptible way, regularly, between each second. In seconds the watch conjured up countless images of his brother and the lyrics of his favorite Mexican songs, composed and sung by José Alfredo Jiménez, sung by Amalia Mendoza, Lucha Villa and Los Dos Reales. The voices and the lyrics, accompanied by el Mariachi Vargas de Tecalitlán, related the anguished story of his life. His life was a Mexican corrido, a story of sorrows, memories of better times, regrets, tribulations, of wrong choices made, of destiny's cruelty. *Why me? If only I could live my life over! Lived too fast . . . too fast . . . I burned up my life. . . .*

Alejandro had a beautiful adolescent voice at the age of eleven . . . *There's a tree in-n-n the meadow* . . . Since adolescence he liked songs by Ray Charles and Fats Domino, Joe Turner and B. B. King, and sad Mexican songs which Alejandro used to sing with Isabel, Andrés, Eduardo and friends, at parties when they were teenagers and later, even after his terrible accident. . . . *when I see him, sick . . . thin . . . lying there . . . I remember . . . when we were all young . . . our lives are so different . . . started changing so much . . . his terrible accident . . .* he used to sing.

At the church services the voices of the children in the choir and the song they were singing released a flood of memories connected with Alejandro's adolescent voice, sweetly melodious, deeply moving like that of an opera singer. Long ago, one unusual Texas lady recognized it as a gifted voice. She wanted to pay for singing lessons so that he could become a professional singer. He could very well be another Caruso, she said. *A-ave-e Ma-rí-í-í-í-a-a-a.* . . . It was the song that Alejandro used to sing and the voices flowed from one end of the church to the other, reached deeply into his heart. Miguel's eyes and nose began to sting and burn. He thought that he would be prepared for his brother's funeral, to accept the death as a blessing for Alejandro and for all the family members who suffered with him. They must have thought it strange that Miguel had not cried before now, at the funeral chapel, or on the way to Guadalupe Church where they were now. It was a new church building that replaced the old wooden church where they had made their first communion. Miguel felt Isabel's and Vicente's presence to his right. The stinging sensation in his eyes, in his nose, took him by surprise. The song, the "Ave Maria" and the children's voices made him break down. The deep love for his brother rushed forth in an uncontrollable stream of tears, and Miguel recognized powerful, cleansing emotions and feelings he had not experienced in a long time. It was a calling of the blood, he would realize eventually, and how strangely did the love for his brother occasion a great flow of strength, derived from sharing fully in the grief with Isabel, Vicente, Eduardo, his mother, who all at once turned their lowered eyes toward Miguel as if to welcome him back to the closeness of family and blood.

As the choir was singing the "Ave Maria," other songs of sadness and sorrow were floating about in his head. Ray Charles singing *born to lose . . . I've lived my life . . . in vain . . . all my life . . . I've always been . . . so blue . . . born to lose . . . and now . . . I'm losing you. . . .* The children's voices and the "Ave Maria" summoned up Alejandro's voice on the junior high school public address system. *There's a tree-e-e . . . in the meadow . . . with a stream drifting by . . . and carved upon that tree . . . I see . . . I love you till I die . . . I will always remember. . . .* Adolescent Alejandro's unforgettable voice and smile, his gift of laughter, the immensity of his sorrow, led his mind back to other memories.

At the time of World War II when Miguel and Alejandro were boys their mother used to dress them up as little soldiers, in khaki pants and shirts, including a real soldier's cap for each of them. At school the other children used to ask if they were twins, and they would lie and say yes. In the Mexican homes of their childhood world there were patriotic stars in the windows, to let people know that Mexicans were fighting for their country too, a father, an uncle, an older brother. In those years their mother and father had an old manual Victrola record player. Mexican songs entered his blood then. As he wept, the lyrics of other songs from long ago came back, evocative and beautiful, stirring his heart, bringing back the enchantment of childhood days. *Amapola . . . lindísima Amapola . . .* Yes, they were very poor in the old days, but they had the sky and the sun. *¿Cuál de los dos hermanos? . . .* Because they were poor they used to take off their shoes when they came home from school. *A la guerra ya me llevan madrecita . . . me agarraron en la leva el día de ayer . . . ya no llores, madrecita . . . mi destino fue pelear. . .* How proudly the two boys marched in their soldier's uniforms, making believe they were twins and real soldiers about to go off to war. *¿Cuál de los dos amantes . . . sufre la pena . . . el que se va . . . o el que se queda? El que se queda . . . se queda llorando . . . el que se va se va . . . suspirando . . .* The memories of these songs evoked other childhood recollections, of running barefoot every day, playing cowboys and baseball; the first awakenings to love; selling newspapers in front of the Tally-Ho Restaurant or the Stephen F. Austin Hotel . . .

EXTRA! EXTRA! Re-e-ead-al-l-labout-t-t-eet! AMERICAN FORCES LAND IN FRENCH AFRICA: BRITISH NAVAL, AIR

UNITS ASSISTING THEM: EFFECTIVE SECOND FRONT, ROOSEVELT SAYS. . . . NAZIS NEAR LIBYA . . . BLOW TO KNOCK ITALY OUT OF THE WAR . . . PRESIDENT'S STATE-MENT, Special to the *New York Times* . . . Washington, Nov. 7. In order to forestall an invasion by Germany and Italy, which if successful, would constitute a direct threat to America across the comparatively narrow sea from Western Africa, a powerful American force equipped with adequate weapons of modern warfare and under American command is today landing on the Mediterranean and Atlantic coasts of the French colonies in Africa. EXTRA! EXTRA! Read-d-d allabout-e-et! Selling news-papers in front of the Greenwood Restaurant on Tenth and Congress, the Driscoll Hotel on Seventh Street. MACARTHUR STARTS ALLIED OFFENSIVE IN PACIFIC . . . BERLIN EVACUA-TION REPORTED PLANNED . . . PRIME MINISTER WARNS AXIS ALLIED ATTACKS ARE IMMINENT . . . WAR NEWS SUM-MARIZED. Thursday, July 1, 1943. . . . *New York Times*. Wednes-day, November 8, 1944. ROOSEVELT WINS FOURTH TERM. . . . April 13, 1945. One day classroom activities were interrupted by a voice on the school public address system. *The President of the United States is dead.* Headlines. PRESIDENT ROOSEVELT IS DEAD; TRUMAN TO CONTINUE POLICIES. TRUMAN IS SWORN IN THE WHITE HOUSE . . . Members of Cabinet . . . Cerebral Stroke Brings Death to Nation's Leader . . . . President Roosevelt died yesterday, suddenly and unex-pectedly. . . . August 6, 1945. FIRST ATOMIC BOMB DROPPED ON JAPAN; MISSILE IS EQUAL TO 20,000 TONS; TRUMAN WARNS FOE OF A "RAIN OF RUIN." Day of Atomic Energy Hailed By President. HIROSHIMA IS TARGET. Washington, Aug. 6—*The White House and War Department announced to-day . . . atomic bomb . . . has been dropped . . . one of the scientific landmarks of the century has been passed . . . the age of atomic energy, which can be a tremendous force for the advancement of civilization, as well as for destruction, was at hand. . . .*

Unexpectedly, from somewhere at the back of the church, came a baby's cry, the sweet sound of life. At Mexican funerals and weddings, he had forgotten how customary are the sounds of a baby crying or the voices of children, casting a magic spell over events, warming the heart so naturally, filling the spirit with hope and love, and his thoughts travelled back to songs that brought back memories of when Miguel and Alejandro pretended to be American soldiers going off to war.

*A la guerra ya me llevan, madrecita . . . ahí te quedas . . . sin tu hijito . . . muy solita . . . sabrá Dios si nos volveremos a ver . . . Ahí le entregas este sobre retornado . . . a mi novia . . . que no sabe dónde estoy . . . a otras tierras muy lejanas ya me voy. . . .* How sweetly the voices were singing Alejandro's song, reminding him, too, of being teenagers, going to the first dances, being afraid to ask the girls to dance. *Por tener-r-r . . . la miel amarga de tus besos . . . hoy se tien-n-ne que arrastrar . . . mi dignidad . . . por piedad . . . por compasión . . . no me desprecies . . . no me abandones . . . que la vida, como un perro pa-s-sa-ré. . . . Sin hablarte . . . sin llorar . . . siempre tirado a tus pies. . . .* Drinking a beer to muster up courage to ask the blossoming girls to dance. Songs of love.

*Porque soy como soy se me va tu cariño, porque no hice dinero en el mundo . . . pero sé que en el fondo de tu alma . . . me estás adorando . . .* Dancing closely, cheek to cheek, holding girls closely around the waist, soft undulating forms . . . *I saw the harbor lights . . .* their exquisitely blossoming bodies, fearfully fascinated . . . *they only told me we were parting, the same old harbor lights . . . that once brought you to me. . . .* Songs entered into heart and spirit, gave depth and intensity to mysterious palpitations of the soul, to inexpressibly strange longings, held out promises of future sorrows and ecstasies, not yet decipherable; songs that would return, like now in Guadalupe Church at his brother's funeral services, to move him.

*Those faraway places . . . with the strange-sounding names are cal-l-ling . . . cal-l-ling me . . . I long for the day we shall get under way . . . and look for those castles . . . in Spain. . . .* There it was again, a child's cry. He had taken off his glasses when he began to cry. He turned blurry eyes toward his sister Isabel, who was crying too. She placed her hand on Miguel's hand and squeezed. She knew it was the "Ave Maria" that had moved him to tears. She too remembered the day when Alejandro sang it over the school public address system. He was twelve years old, before his voice changed.

# IV

A STEWARDESS passed by and brushed gently against Miguel's shoulder. She paused, looked back over her shoulder, and apologized with a smile. He smiled to let her know it was all right. He was thinking about the cry of an infant at a wedding, a funeral, or during church services. The cry of a child, to him, was a cry of life indeed, a song to beginnings, a celebration of new life that makes death endurable; it symbolizes the continuity of blood from generation to generation. He imagined the voices of children, their peals of laughter on an elementary school playground, in voice-over, as part of one of many imaginary beginnings for the film to be based on the novel that he could not start. In this beginning the man, for whom he has not even found a fictional name, arrives at his middle-class suburban home. The front door is opening. He walks into the house, passes through the living room, oblivious to his own strange drawings and paintings on the walls, and goes around the breakfast table towards the coffee maker in the kitchen. A few moments later, cup in hand, he retraces his steps which lead him to the entrance of his study by the front door. At the door to his study he halts, brings the steaming cup of coffee to his lips and sips noisily.

He has just returned from taking his daughters to school. His mind is fresh with memories of childhood, evoked by smells of elementary school classrooms, glue and ink, books and newsprint, the wood of tables and desks, chalk and color crayons, and above all, the mingled smells of machine oil and wood shavings and lead which he inhaled deeply at the pencil sharpener. With smells he could make a survey of his life in seconds, it seemed, bring back unfailingly the magic of spring days when he was in the first grade. Childhood memories had

138

come unbidden, had taken him completely by surprise one day, nearly twenty-five years later, when he was standing by the window of his transient hotel room in New York City, sharpening his pencil. After that he was able to bring back that whole childhood year in the first grade simply by smelling a freshly sharpened pencil. The voices and the laughter of elementary school children also affected him in the same way.

At the door to his study he stood momentarily, lost in thought, amazed at how the faces and gestures and mannerisms of school children announce the adults they will become, give a good idea very early of their personality traits as adults, whether they will be serious or mischievous, shy or gentle, solitaries or dreamers, how they will talk and walk when they grow up. Cup in hand the man steps into his study and goes to sit at his extremely cluttered desk. Among papers, books, manila folders, notepads, pieces of paper, five-by-eight cards, small spiral notebooks and other stationery items scattered on his desk there is a large black-bound notebook. It is open to a page that has some writing on it. He turns to a clean page in the notebook, takes up a Parker pen, opens it and begins to write.

Notebook entry. A man has been wanting to write a novel for years. He cannot remember what he has written. Many years ago he began to dream foolishly that his novel might be made into a film. Perhaps he himself would write the film script.

Sitting at his cluttered desk, gazing out of the window, the man daydreams. He wonders what scenes, what visual images the film might begin with. Should a film adaptation be faithful to the novel? If, as some people maintain, the two arts are distinct forms of expression, can film adaptations be faithful to literary works? The man turns away from the beautiful scene outdoors. He looks over his desk at the bookshelves. Between bookshelves the walls of his study are covered with photographs, drawings and paintings.

The main character of the imagined film is a surrealist artist who wants the novel to be about his life. What could be more suitable than to begin with some shots of bulging bookshelves and his cluttered desk? Or, since he is a painter, why not some shots of the garage where he used to draw and paint? The idea is to let his books tell something of the man, before we see him or know his name. Let the personality of the man trying to write a novel emerge from the titles of books that he reads, from the obstacles and the lack of organization which prevent him from true creative work. His desk is cluttered, for example; his garage studio is disorderly. Yes, in the opening shots, during the credits perhaps, the main character of the film is nowhere to be seen. The film could begin effectively with a portrait of the man from which he is physically absent.

Perhaps the opening sequence could begin, while the credits are on the screen, with a subjective shot of his cluttered desk or the garage studio, or alternately, cutting back and forth. Among manila folders, papers, books and newspaper clippings on his cluttered desk the camera could pass inconspicuously across *The Journals of Delacroix*; *Dear Theo*; *Fellini on Fellini*; Michael Meyer's biography of Henrik Ibsen; *Hiroshima, mon amour*; *Axel's Castle*, and *The Romantic Agony*. Then the credits could begin to show the actors' and actresses' names, while the camera moves across bookshelves, passing over works by Malcolm Lowry, Sterne, Baudelaire, Poe, Huysmans, Carpentier, Cortázar, Fuentes, Rilke, Hesse. A cut or dissolve here. Fade in. Subjective shot of the garage, followed by a montage of images. The painter's easel would be holding an unfinished canvas. Both easel and canvas are covered with dust and spiderwebs. An abandoned, dusty masonite palette can rest on a work table. Under the dust it contains large and small globs of oil colors that have dried and hardened. What a terrible waste of good oil paints. Tubes of Windsor Newton oil paints, the best, have been abandoned, left open, so they too have dried up. Stacks of stretched canvases gather dust and spiderwebs. Here and there, the camera could show numerous unfinished paintings on large and small canvases, obviously abandoned.

The camera can pan or track, or cut abruptly from place to place in short shots, to construct a montage of images that create a portrait of the artist. The whole garage is cluttered with rags and empty jars. Some jars are filled with worn painting bristle brushes. Cans of turpentine, bottles of linseed oil and varnish, spray cans of fixative, and brushes are scattered on tabletops and chairs, and among the objects that clutter up the garage studio, two things stand out in addition to the accumulated dust and spiderwebs. Beautifully ornate, richly colored drapery hangs here and there from the rafters, and in parts of the garage, mirrors, big and small, are stacked against worn pieces of furniture, against cardboard boxes, tilted in every direction and at a variety of angles, multiplying to infinity the images of the garage and the fragmented reflections which bounce among the mirrors. This collage of images creates a portrait of an artist who very obviously abandoned his painting long ago. Using several well-composed still photographs, the camera could suggest true works of art to which the artist is blind. Indeed the garage studio and its contents can be turned into a veritable spectacle and shown by the camera from an infinite number of angles and perspectives to which the countless mirrors would contribute immeasurably.

The middle-aged man's lack of artistic originality should be everywhere evident in the garage studio. The artist himself can see through the dust and spiderwebs, in the dusty canvases that he has started and abandoned. . . .

Later. I could not write anymore. I was utterly exhausted. I had to go for a walk, had to get away from this notebook. I also deliberately left my pocket notebook and my pen behind so that I would not be tempted to write. I became overwhelmed by creative inspiration and images. Lost control. The walk did me good.

As I was walking I could hardly catch my breath. I was assaulted by images, but I was too exhausted to write. I do not want to write anything now, I kept telling myself. But the notebook entry that I had left on my desk obsessed me, took possession of me. The idea of a middle-aged man who betrays his calling as an artist, yes, a potentially good idea. The scenes and the setting had come to mind again and again, but only now, on the walk, did I see them clearly. Using an abandoned garage studio to develop the character, an aging artist hoping vainly to write a novel which he cannot begin; what an idea! And the mirrors everywhere repeating to infinity the evidence of his failure. It was certainly worth pursuing, I thought.

The hot sun on my bare arms, on my bare chest conjured up images in my mind of running naked under the clear blue sky. The sun and sky, a brisk wind singing through the leaves of the trees, the perfect quality of this lovely spring day, all of it together, made me tremble with sudden intense physical and spiritual rapture. I had to find a pen and paper.

I quickened my pace and fresh air rushed into my lungs. My lungs expanded and a sudden breathlessness thrilled me through and through. I began to trot, and the use of my body, my legs and arms, made me more joyful. I experienced an expansion of creative powers and a compelling desire to write. At the same time I experienced a heightened awareness of my body's sexual energies, a sense of awakened powers that made my thoughts turn, as I hastened my pace, to the young woman half my age. Some of her words were deeply engraved in my memory . . . *you were just right for me she said you are married and I didn't want to get involved with any man seriously and you agreed that we would not get involved.* . . . Voluptuous images of our love-making and my irresistible impulse to write mutually intensified each other. I stopped at the nearby bookstore and bought a pen. I asked the young man at the cash register for two sheets of paper from the xeroxing machine. Then I stopped at the Neighborhood Cantina, ordered a big glass of tea and I began to write.

The Neighborhood Cantina was crowded, but I hardly looked up from my writing. I wrote in a frenzy, hardly able to catch my breath. Once, as I tried to collect my thoughts, I did look up. In one of the booths a young teenage girl, a little older than Lolita, was writhing in the most provocative manner to the loud rock music that was playing on the stereo system. How young, I thought before I resumed my writing, and how marvelously nature has already developed in her the attributes of woman.

Much later, when I stopped writing I threw my head back and took a deep sigh of relief. Afterward, I walked for nearly two hours, delighted with the two pages I wrote, thinking that many times leaving home without my notebook and going for a walk is not a good idea.

There will be alternating scenes and images of the garage studio and of the middle-aged artist's study, where he will be writing in a notebook at his desk. In voice-over he shall be heard reading the passage where he left off writing in his notebook just before he went on a walk. *The middle-aged man's lack of artistic talent should be everywhere evident.* . . . He makes a few corrections, then adds that the following words should be spoken by a well-known, pompous art critic, Sir Charles Courts, whose artistic conceptions and norms should clash with those of the artist. It is the critic's voice that shall be heard.

. . . in the dusty, abandoned studio, in the scattered unfinished canvases, in the dust and spiderwebs that have accumulated over a long period of time, we have all the evidence we need to see that the artist has betrayed his calling, if indeed he had one, and that he has wasted whatever talent he may have had. Through the dust that covers the unfinished and abandoned canvases one can easily recognize the works of true artists from which the talentless artist has sought inspiration, and which he copied in the most incompetent and outrageous manner. The aborted beginnings of a canvas here and there invite pity for this wretched man, because indeed he had the good taste to appreciate the suggestively erotic females and the bejewelled and colorful patterns of Gustav Klimt. These he explored miserably without success. Behind a huge mirror on one side of the garage, half of it visible, lurks a canvas which is obviously a copy of Delvaux, and reflected in the mirror that mercifully conceals part of that pale imitation of Delvaux, is an atrocious copy of Dalí's Christ suspended on the cross, the one which hangs at the Metropolitan Museum in New York. Two or three unfinished canvases display the oriental qualities of a Monet mixed with Matisse. Absolutely abominable eclecticism. Obviously the middle-aged man had no original ideas of his own. It is embarrassing to find something discernible, in some of the most abominable unfinished paintings anyone could see in his life—something discernible; evidence, I say, to trouble the spirit of those who truly love art, that the miserable failure has looked at the works of Velásquez, Zurbarán, and El Greco, to whose works he has done absolute violence. Among these pathetic objects are canvases that Degas would have started if he had been insane, others, nudes that a drunken Eakins might have attempted in a fit of anger against the Pennsylvania Academy that criticized his work. Some abandoned canvases contain male and female images in erotic positions that only the most perverse imagination could associate with the figures in Rodin's magnificent *Gates of Hell*.

*[Cut. The camera should show the face of the art critic in close-up. There is a smugness about the way that he feigns modesty. He states each word succinctly, weighing their collective effect, as if he were rehearsing words to be turned into a critical review or article about an art exhibition. The art critic continues. Camera cuts back to the spectacle of the studio.]*

It is with profound regret that one has to mention that other canvases are abominable copies and imitations, mercifully abandoned, of works by Edvard Munch, Edward Hopper, Edwin

Dickenson, Max Ernst, George Inness and George Tooker. And one canvas, may the mention of it be forgiven, is based on the style of Tintoretto, and another on that of Caravaggio.

*[Finally, after a flashback showing the middle-aged artist being taken away by two men in white, the film could bring the face of the art critic into close-up. Speaking directly into the camera, modestly lowering his eyes occasionally, he continues speaking. His voice drones on.]*

To this strangely perverse eclecticism of the wretched artist, several mirrors in his garage studio give added bizarre dimensions. Because the mirrors cast reflections back and forth, multiplying fragmented scenes in some cases many times over, because the quality of the abandoned garage studio was that of an abandoned theatre, covered over with dust and spiderwebs, because the wretched artist's presence is so unmistakably and conspicuously felt in his absence, one receives the unavoidable impression that there was in that garage studio the setting and the scenes, which only a gifted person—I say this modestly— can possibly see, multiplied to almost infinity by the mirrors, multiplied additionally if one moves around the garage studio, for a series of truly original works that would escape the sphere of painting, draw on the resources of theatre and film and photography, and indeed cross the boundaries of all the arts to create an image, like a hall of mirrors, a Meninaslike self-portrait as it were, but of a madman, a portrait of a deranged mind, and of the twentieth century.

One expects to see at any moment a flashback of the aging artist coming into the scene. *[Cut. The art critic's monologue is finished. The artist arrives at his studio for some spectacular scenes.]* He does, and in front of his bewildered eyes, he sees for the last time just before he goes mad, the broken fragments of his deranged image in the numerous mirrors, reflecting the disconnected fragments of his wasted life, bouncing them back and forth. Bizarre, broken images. One expects him to be drunk, profoundly morose because he does see in the garage, the story of his whole meaningless, wasted life. In his mind he is convinced now that he did betray his calling as a painter. One expects him to pick up some object, a jar, a hammer, something, and to fling it at the large mirror in which he sees his image, abominable in his own eyes. The mirror will shatter;

the sound of breaking glass will give him perverse pleasure, and there, in hundreds of tiny jagged pieces of glass, he will see the totality of a fragmented life which he will never be able to put together. In an instant of total lucid awareness of his life's failure, he contemplates suicide, as he did long ago, at the age of twenty-eight, when he disappointed everyone who expected so much of him.

*[THE SCENE CHANGES to the study. A flashback. The camera is passing over the books on the shelves. In voice-over a man speaks.]*

*You cannot do all those things, my young friend. It is humanly impossible.* The camera stops at Under the Volcano and Dark As the Grave. The voice continues. *Besides, and this is much more important,* the voice says with a pronounced Spanish accent, *the authors you love*—the camera passes across books by Poe, Nerval, Baudelaire, Rimbaud, Lautréamont—*the writers on whom you would base your own writing were madmen; their spirits were dwelling places for the devil, the dark angels and demons that afflict mankind.* The camera pauses on Rilke's books, as the South American voice insists *there is no affirmation of life in their work, no joy, absolutely no joy. ¡Ilustre, por favor!*

*[The credits continue. On the repetition of the word joy the sound track introduces, moments before the camera cuts to change the scene, the joyful voices and laughter of children. Cut. Long shot of an elementary school exterior. Cut, back to the study. In voice-over, a child's voice sings.* There's a tree-e-e in the meadow, with a stream drifting by.... *At his desk the man looks at his watch. Cut. The film begins with a scene of an elementary school playground. Children are running and playing, laughing and talking.]*

He was looking at his watch. The slow, regular movement of the little, fragile second hand had a hypnotic effect on him, to which he yielded willingly, surrendering control over the working of his mind, while the PSA 737 continued its journey towards Oakland Airport. The movement of the little second hand made him ponder old questions, whether inevitably most people regret the choices they make and that dictate the direction that their lives take. Do they ask, what if I had made another choice? Where am I going? Where is my life going?

What if I could live it all over again? Why was I not strong enough to remain alone?

"I wonder what'at pore fellow'd do if he hadda go to the john. He shore couldn't make it. Ha! ha!"

Once in a dream, he had the distinct impression of suddenly waking up with an unusual sense of relief, which he could neither explain or understand. He was walking. He looked at his watch, uneasily, eleven forty. At twelve he was scheduled to present a paper at a conference, a paper he did not have with him. He was not dressed for a professional conference, nor did he know where it was to take place. He was lost, and did not know where he was going. It puzzled him to have lost track of the time. He was not accustomed to being irresponsible.

Earlier, he remembered, someone had given him a ride to a party. The automobile had been crowded with people whom he did not know. He was perplexed because some of them knew him. It was usually like that. He tended to forget the names of people he met. Shortly after arriving at the party some people who were in the car found the host's liquor cabinet, and they began to pull out large bottles of liquor. At that time, not wanting to drink, he decided to walk home.

It had not occurred to him to ask someone for a ride, because he had completely forgotten the conference paper. Walking along he looked at his watch to see what time it was. His paper was scheduled for presentation in nineteen minutes. He was too far away from the party to walk back and ask for a ride. Besides, the other guests would probably be gone. His only hope was that someone from the party would drive along the same way, catch up with him, pick him up and drive him to the conference.

He was sweaty and unclean, however. Damn these polyester shirts that make me smell. I cannot even wear one for an hour. I need to shower and change. If someone picked me up there would not be time to go home for a shower and to make myself presentable.

He was puzzled about his surroundings. Nervously he looked at the watch again. In eighteen minutes he was scheduled to present the scholarly paper on the other side of town, a good distance away. He was distressed by the thought of arriving late, no matter what the event might be, but especially one

146

at which he was a participant. He could not remember the topic of his lecture. He was unprepared.

The empty streets at this time of night reminded him of places where he had lived, of the city where he grew up, which was usually like a ghost town after dark and especially on Sundays during the daytime. My car is nearby, he remembered vaguely, parked on one of these streets. But which street?

He walked some distance for what seemed like a long time, but it was only eleven forty-one on his watch. Unexpectedly, he suffered a pain in his bowels. Where in the hell am I going to find a restroom at this time of night, with everything closed? The pain was excruciating. He endured the pain, and it lessened.

Luckily he found an outdoor bathroom in time, but there was no toilet paper.

Later, as he was driving home he almost crashed into Preston Goldstein's car.

—Hey! Why don't you watch it? You almost crashed into our car. Are you drunk?

—Yes, Martha added excitedly from the driver's seat. Preston, don't let him get away with it. Remember that he hasn't been very nice to me, and . . . and . . .

—Fine, Martha, I'll handle it, he said with complete composure.

As Preston and Martha were getting out of the car Miguel's wife arrived. Without greeting Preston and Martha, she began to scold Miguel severely.

—How could you have forgotten the time? And this commitment? What was your lecture to be about?

—I-I-I d-d-don-n't r-remem-mber . . .

—Give me the name of the woman who is chairing the session, she said with annoyance. I'll just have to call her and tell her you just can't be there. My God! Why do you smell so awful? You must get home and take a shower immediately. Drive your own car home. I wouldn't be able to bear driving with you in the same car. And this meeting. . . . You're so irresponsible! Can't you ever do things right? If you can't keep commitments, don't make them. . . .

You have fears of missing a plane, a class, an appointment, a professional commitment. Because of your nature and the choices it dictates you do not know where your life is going. For years after you quit graduate school you had a recurrent bad dream.

You are wandering through the halls of Stephen F. Austin High School, looking for Miss Bushnell's classroom on the day of the algebra class final examination. You must pass the examination in order to graduate. As you plod through what seems like a labyrinth, drift aimlessly through the maze of empty halls, up and down staircases that lead nowhere, turning now down this hall and now another, lost, making your way like a blind man towards other parts of the empty building, you wonder where all the people are. You have a premonition that you will fail the examination. Since the first class meeting you did not attend classes, because you could never find the classroom.

Where is it? Vaguely you recall, the classroom was next to this staircase. No, it was down this hall and up the stairs, through the upper level of the auditorium, at the west side of the building.

You arrive finally at the end of a long corridor that leads to an area that opens on to three classrooms. But no one is there. The final examination to graduate from high school was scheduled in another building, on the preceding day. You are a failure. You are going nowhere.

He was sitting inside a crowded bus, on the right side, next to a heavy black man, near the entrance. By stretching his neck a little he could see the bus driver, also a black man. The bus was crowded, but he was mainly aware of the bus driver and dimly of the fat woman, who just a moment earlier was a heavy black man. She is sitting to his right; her soft, fleshy body is pressing against his.

He had almost missed this bus at the stop, but he whistled. The bus driver had heard the whistle, stopped the bus and waited for him. He ran and hastily boarded the bus, a little out of breath.

Once inside the bus he became almost immediately aware of not knowing its destination. It was simply the first bus to come along. He took it because it was going south, towards San Antonio, but he forgot where he wanted to go. Perhaps he was going to a class or to give a lecture. Now he would be late. Yes, he was going to give a lecture. But he forgot the name of the school and the street on which it was located. How could he ask for directions?

The bus was cruising smoothly away from the city, through and far beyond wooded residential areas that recently had started to develop. One undeveloped residential area reminded him of Woodstock, where once he and his wife could have purchased a beautiful home, with a studio loft that had a skylight. The bus was leaving behind the bejewelled city. Down below as in a valley and far away now, the city was glittering brightly with its countless strings of lights. At last the bus passed out of the wooded residential area and plunged into the true darkness of night. Save for the road ahead, illuminated by the bus headlights, the darkness was total.

He had not paid his fare. He had wanted to find a seat first and then to pay. At this moment, reaching for his wallet, he found it was not in his pocket. Could he have left it somewhere, or lost it? Where? He imagined the shape, the flatness and the almost shiny black color of his leather wallet. He tried to reconstruct earlier events, before getting on the bus. His complete lapse of memory frightened him.

There he was on the bus, without money, going he knew not where, severely critical of himself for his irresponsibility, and grieved by a tremendous sense of helplessness. When he tried to look out of the window, it had changed into a mirror. Out there in the total darkness every window was a mirror. Surprisingly, no one noticed that he did not pay the fare. He worried nevertheless how he might explain politely his not having any money.

In his mind, he planned the courteous phrases he would use, the right tone that would appeal to the bus driver's sense of fairness. The bus driver would surely recognize him as an educated person. He would be able to tell by the way that he spoke, that he was a man of culture and learning. He did not want to be perceived as an ordinary or hypocritical person who was unwilling or feigning not to be able to pay his fare. He, who hardly ever cared about what people thought about him, worried about it now. His own self-consciousness on the bus troubled and stunned him.

Unsuccessfully he tried once more to remember earlier events of the day. It seemed that he was standing in front of a dresser, asking Julio, a graduate student, for pencil and paper. He never wanted to be without pencil and paper because he was always writing down his thoughts. Some of his best thoughts came to him when he was without them, like in the morning when he took his shower. Julio had given him a pencil that needed sharpening, or which displeased him for some reason. Julio had also given him a piece of paper, about the size of a bank deposit slip. It had geometric markings and computer numbers that were machine-printed in a faded blue ink. He was annoyed because the paper was not blank. He was at his aunt's house earlier, before getting on the bus. He told her that he had not had breakfast or lunch. Other memories were unclear. Some time before seeing his aunt, he was serving coffee at an outdoor stand where he worked. He had spoken with a girl. He asked her if she wanted sugar and cream.

—There is sugar here, she said, and he saw her take a little sugar package from the saucer.

—Would you like some cream? he asked.

—No, just sugar is fine, she said.

That was all he could remember. The bus continued on, its headlights cutting through the darkness. Through the rear window of the bus the great city was no longer visible. All the windows were mirrors, except at the front. Ahead, the two-lane road stretched on, illuminated by the headlights of the bus, and all around, impenetrable through the dark window-mirrors, was total darkness. Wherever he should be, at some unknown hour previously arranged, he would not be there. He had made another irresponsible decision which raised serious doubts in his mind whether his scholarly career could still be salvaged.

Every year, Lorenzo Correa fell farther and farther behind in his scholarly research. He lost track of the main scholars in his discipline. He did not keep up with new scholarly research. He stopped attending the annual meetings of the National Association of Scholars in the Arts. He became isolated professionally, one of the department's "deadwood," an unproductive scholar. He found the whole process of academic peer evaluations fascinating and instructive.

One day, when Giuseppe was talking with Jeff Scott in the hall, he saw Lorenzo walk into the departmental office. The departmental letter on Lorenzo's tenure evaluation had been forwarded recently to the dean.

—Have you noticed, Giuseppe asked, how strangely Correa looks at you when the subject of his tenure comes up? He hangs on every word I tell him. Does he do the same with you? No. Well, he does with me. His ears cock up. You can almost see his mind working, twisting everything I say around to his benefit. At the departmental meetings he's always writing into those little notepads. What the hell is he writing, anyway? In my oral summary of the departmental evaluation, I told him a major criticism of the department was that his publications reflect no clear concept of modernism. He wanted me to tell him what modernism is! Frankly, I told him, I don't know. I'm not a modernist. As chairman I simply report the judgments of colleagues in your area of specialization. In the opinion of colleagues, also, your research makes no significant contribution to the field, your knowledge of comparative arts methodology is inadequate, and your concept of modernism is hazy. Some colleagues express an inability to judge your Chicano studies research. Well, you know all this, Jeff, why go on? But I know what's wrong with Correa. He doesn't know how to accept valid constructive criticism from his colleagues.

Miguel heard the voice of the little girl, now returning with her mother from the bathroom.

"Are we almost there, Mommy?"

"Yes, Jennifer. It won't be long now. We're almost there."

He was struck by the remarkable resemblance of the little girl to her mother. As far back as he could remember, the resemblances between children or young people and their parents attracted his attention. Before his eyes the marvelous transformation took place. The little girl aged in an second, became the double of her mother.

The transformation made him think of how rapidly the years fly by, and that there was hardly a moment of his waking hours when the pages of his novel did not intrude into his thoughts. Writing had eaten up the years. In the middle of committee meetings his thoughts would carry him away to scenes and memories of childhood and his travels. Or he might be reading a memo from the dean or the vice chancellor and he would think about pages that he had written describing journeys to his home and childhood neighborhood in Texas. The voices of his mother and father repeatedly reminded him of his origins and of the hardships of Mexicans in Texas. They had told him many stories about events and experiences that took place before he was born and during the years when his mother and father were young. Among the library stacks the titles of books on the shelves evoked his graduate student days or reminded him of his brother's funeral. Suddenly, in the middle of a conversation with a colleague about affirmative action or merit evaluations, his mind would drift away, to plans, notes and outlines for writing a novel about his tenure process. The idea had come *one day, when walking through the university parking lot on the way to his car, it dawned on him that his joint appointment in Chicano Studies and Comparative Arts had completely changed the direction of his life. . . .*

Everything reminded him of something else. He would not be able to explain, however, if someone were to ask him why the memories and recollections made him want to write. A leisurely walk across campus, watching lovely young girls, would bring back memories of coming to Ríoseco University. At last he was a professor. Drinking wine and carrying on a conversation at the Campus Cantina would take him back to pleasant undergraduate days at the University of Texas, and to sunny afternoons at Scholtze's Beer Garden on San Jacinto Avenue. Filling out the Faculty Request For Books and Supplies for the next quarter courses was a joyful task. It impressed on his mind the fullness of his association with the world of books and learning, the pleasures of teaching at a university. Over the years, unfortunately, the novel took him away from his family. He drifted away time and again from conversations with his wife and children at the dinner table, to dwell in the past, to return in imagination to years before he met his wife, and to their early years together. Writing year in and year out, he lost sight of how quickly his two little girls were growing up.

This journey to Oakland was making him take cognizance of the enormity of his writing project. He granted that wanting to write a novel had become an obsession. He reflected on his inclination to turn the most trivial experiences into art. He brooded over the difficulty of keeping his mind on one thing at a time. Over many years the novel had become a kaleidoscope of images, memories, thoughts and voices, madly turning in his mind, multiplying its configurations, haunting him endlessly, holding out to him the hope of one day seeing his name in print. During the past four or five years he filled nearly a score of large notebooks, dozens and dozens of pocket notebooks and little note pads. The chapters of a novel had proliferated. The ponderous material had become unmanageable. Writing finally took precedence during these years over all other duties and responsibilities, as father, husband, scholar, teacher. A strange sensation began to take hold of him, that he was going to bed each night, and the next morning when he awakened, months and years had passed during the night.

Happily, to his astonishment, his mind began, independently of his attention, to set aside the numerous tasks required by university and family life. On walks, but especially while he slept, his mind continued the task of writing the novel. During sleep, in dream after dream, effortlessly, his mind gave shape and structure to chapters of the novel. By the end of this journey he would realize that the novel was not one but many.

# V

A YOUNG WOMAN WALKED out of the apartment building
where she lives. It was lunchtime and the sidewalks were begin-
ning to fill with people coming out of tall business office build-
ings. He was walking. The buildings, the pedestrians and the
activity, the sidewalks and the streets reminded him of Chicago
and New York at lunchtime. He heard his name.

—Professor Velásquez! Professor Velásquez!

The pretty young woman was waving to him and she began
to walk at a brisk pace towards him, looking very small against
the tall buildings behind her. She was wearing a light, trans-
parent blouse and skirt that gave her a floating, dreamlike
quality. He was imagining how this scene would look if it were
filmed, perhaps in slow motion. He was embarrassed because
he did not recognize the young woman or remember her name.
Then she was at his side, smiling and hugging him as if she
knew him very well, pressing her firm, womanly body against
his. The softness of her flesh was accentuated by the thin, al-
most gauzelike material of her blouse and skirt. He embraced
her nervously because he did not recognize her. His hands
went around her small waist nevertheless, and then down and
over the buttocks, first one and then the other, as if he were
her lover. She did not object. Perhaps they were once lovers.

—I was in your class in the fifties, she said with a smile. My
name is Sylvia Esquivel. Do you remember me?

—Sylvia. Yes, of course I remember, he lied. But in the fif-
ties! he exclaimed, thinking that it was impossible for this
young woman to have been a college student more than
twenty-five years ago. Why, you could not even have been born
then. You cannot be older than twenty-one or twenty-two.

—I'm over thirty! she declared with annoyance.

Pushing him away, she was about to turn and walk away angrily. He could not understand why she would be so upset. There was nothing about her to suggest that she was as old as she claimed. How could he calm her down? Perhaps if I invite her to lunch, but I had lunch early to avoid the crowded lines of the noon hour. Besides, I have so much work to do, documenting Sixth Street for my novel. I am already behind schedule. Where do the mornings go? Before I realize it, it is noon, and I have done almost no work, and sometimes none at all. Why am I always hounded by guilt whenever I spend time with people? It is horrible. I detest the guilt when I am enjoying the company of people.

Now he was faced with a dilemma. He wanted to invite her to lunch and to make love afterwards. I wonder how much time she has. Will there be enough time for both? On the other hand my plans to work on the novel all afternoon have already been made. He was reluctant to change his plans. But I would like to make love. Damn the time!

A woman next to them was standing in a line. She had dark, almost black, curly hair, and long black eyelashes and strikingly dark eyes.

—Shall I hold your place in line while you talk things over? she asked. She must have read his thoughts.

—That is very thoughtful of you, he said. And without knowing what the line was for, he added, yes, thank you.

As they were walking along, he began to apologize for having offended the lovely young woman who had accidently crossed his path. He began to sense that the physical attraction was mutual. He searched her face for evidence of her years. Although he could not believe her age he persuaded her that he did. She calmed down finally.

Walking arm in arm, like sweethearts in a scene from a film, they approached a playground. She was a very desirable young woman, and he could not resist embracing and kissing her passionately. He was ashamed that he could not put the selfish thoughts about time or the guilt about not working out of his mind. She responded to his passion and returned his kisses hungrily.

Oh! What a blessing, he thought, to have run into this lovely woman accidentally like this. It has been so very long since I have felt desire, so long since I have held a woman in my arms. He cherished the tenderness in his heart.

When they reached a park they found a spot on the grass to sit down. By this time she was eager to make love. She began to unbutton and proceeded to remove her blouse and her brassiere. He filled his mouth with one of her firm, small breasts. She ran her hands through his hair and brought his mouth forcefully against her breast. He relished the soft pounding breast inside his mouth. But he felt inhibited by the presence of school children who were playing not too far away on a playground. The young woman, on the other hand, was oblivious to everything except the desire to make love. He was too self-conscious about undressing and making love on the playground. Damn my inhibited nature! It would not be fair to make love in front of these children. Her skirt was almost totally transparent. She raised her skirt, reached for her panties, and began to pull them down, slowly revealing her beautiful naked thighs. Her hands were clutching, squeezing wildly at him, at his hair, his shoulders, his arms. Gently, she pushed him away. Delirious with desire, she dropped slowly on her back. He was fully dressed. She was ready.

Damn! If only I had the courage to make love here on this very spot, he thought.

—Not here, he said. Those children will see us.

The children were playing near a fence, innocently.

—Where? Where, then? she asked.

—It is too far to my place, he said.

He was lying, first of all because he felt that he had to be on his way soon. He had just finished lunch and had too much work to do. He felt guilty about not working. And secondly, he could not bring her home for the simple reason that he promised his wife he would never bring a woman to their home. And thirdly, he did not want to take up too much of her lunch hour. That would be unfair to her.

He knew selfishly, however, that regardless of her present eagerness, if they did not make love at that moment, it would never happen. There probably would not be a second time. We are after all, he thought, not far from her apartment building. But what if it should be my bad luck that her apartment building's policy is not to permit visitors? And yet, she is after all an adult. How could a lunch hour visit be forbidden?

—Why don't we go to your apartment?

—Oh, yes. Let's hurry, she replied.

She was very eager to make love. Her thin, gauzelike skirt was curled around her waist. Otherwise she was completely

156

naked and lovely. He was still worried that she might change her mind, so before allowing her to dress, a selfish thought crossed his mind. He must do everything possible to ensure that she would not change her mind. He kissed her passionately and caressed the inside of her legs. He cupped one of her breasts with his hand. Then again he filled his mouth with her breast, this time the other one. He could not stop worrying that she would lose her desire, or change her mind in the two or three minutes that it would take to get to her apartment. Her ruffled skirt, light and transparent, lay loosely draped around her waist. Her lovely bare legs, the naked flesh, her wetness, the faint intoxicating scent of her body, all filled him with voluptuous desire. He tasted her soft moist flesh with a hungry mouth and tongue.

Around the corners of her eyes and at the edges of her lips he noticed now, as he coolly observed the effects on the young woman of his deliberate lovemaking preliminaries, the beginning of a few little wrinkles. So, she really is in her thirties, he thought.

He could not help wondering, as he consciously went about the business of increasing her desire, how he might describe this scene in his novel, or how it could be presented in a film. He saw the film images clearly in his mind's eye. On the screen, in a medium shot, a selfish, inhibited man, fully dressed, is busily engaged at the task of increasing the desire of a young woman whose skirt is loosely draped around her waist. She is almost completely naked and ready to make love. He hovers over her, kissing and touching parts of her body that cause her to turn and twist. Close-up shots. She closes her eyes, arches her eyebrows, opens her eyes, rolls them, opens her mouth, gasps, inhales deeply, holds her breath, shudders. The camera tracks back slowly. The older man and the young woman are at a park, lying on the grass. She is breathing heavily, through her mouth. Her eyes open and roll and shut. He, a liar, is composed, methodically titillating the woman, observing her with cool detachment, looking forward to making love at her apartment, and planning with one part of his mind how he will write about this rapturous afternoon and include it in his cinematic novel. In his mind the film is already made. He is the man in the scene and simultaneously he is the observer who is watching himself with detachment. He reads on the face of his double an expression of worry and concern, inhibition and helplessness.

157

Cinematic images. Long shots of the playground, with the high rise buildings in the background—erect phallic things thrusting upward. In the middle ground, the children, and in the foreground, the couple. Long shots alternating and colliding with medium shots and extreme close-ups, cropped images of the man and the young woman, of her near nakedness. Her body is a temple, a sanctuary, at which he cannot worship. Close-up of the older man's face. He opens his dejected eyes. He is in bed, waking up, woefully lamenting that it was only a dream.

If you had to do it again, Lorenzo, would you marry Valerie Feinberg? Or would you choose to follow the path on which you were travelling, to be pursued by vultures and winged beasts sitting on your bathroom sink, waiting to bid you goodnight, at whatever time of day you might pass out, and to laugh at you with wild menacing eyes? That choice, you know, would have meant an early grave. You would not be on this airplane today, remembering that your dreaming mind was warning you.

Not long ago Lorenzo was at an elegant, crowded bar, much like the fashionable bars on Pecan Street and around the University in Austin, Texas. It was like many others in certain areas of San Francisco, too, and on the east and west sides of Manhattan. He was talking with an attractive blonde who had made it very clear that she was interested in him. She had tried very tactfully, in his opinion, to get him to ask her for a date. Politely, he avoided doing so. He did not want to make a hasty decision. After all, he had just met her. Besides, he preferred a Mediterranean-looking woman, someone with dark skin, a lovely Mexican woman perhaps. Lately, he had developed an intense fascination with dark-skinned women.

—I gotta go join my group now, she said. I think they're ready to go.

She lingered a little, wanting very likely to give him an opportunity to suggest meeting again. But he did not seize the opportunity, and when her friends stood up from their table to leave, she started to walk away.

—It's been nice talking, she said.

—It's been my pleasure, he said.

He fell into the customary kind of a daze that seizes him at large social gatherings, when he has difficulty remembering the names of people he has not seen in a long time, or when a conversation becomes trivial. When she said good-bye, he waved his hand and watched the woman join two men and another woman. She was attractive, and he began to regret that he had not taken her name and telephone number. He felt stupid. Her date was a tall, thin young man who was now tucking his shirttails inside his trousers. He stood and loomed high above the table. Since he was a teenager Lorenzo always marvelled at the gringo's good will and absence of jealousy. The lanky young man was not at all possessive of the lovely blonde woman.

The moment the four people disappeared through the front door a very attractive dark-skinned young woman came and sat down in the chair next to Lorenzo's at the bar. She had been watching Lorenzo for a while. He was still regretting that he did not even get the blonde woman's telephone number. But now an awareness of the dark-skinned woman sitting next to him pushed these thoughts aside. Hers was evidently and enthusiastically a sexual interest. She was a beautiful woman of indeterminate ancestry, in her middle twenties, perhaps younger. He was much more fascinated with this attractive dark girl than he had been with the blonde. He was pleased that the dark girl immediately set aside the customary games that take place between men and women.

—You probably think I'm Jamaican, she said. She had noticed that he was trying to determine her ancestry. People always try to guess, she added.

He had been, in fact, studying the dark girl's features. She was right. Polynesian features perhaps, he thought. Mexican? Indian and African? Very Mediterranean, Caribbean, Iranian. She watched his eyes making a careful affectionate examination of her features.

—I am Nicaragüense, she said. Then she extended her arm and took his hand. Ven conmigo.

He loved the distinct flavor of her Nicaraguan Spanish accent. Come with me, she repeated, this time in English, but without saying where. He allowed her to lead him to the service area of the bar, to the right of where they had been sitting.

Lorenzo did not wish to seem eager, so he paused at the service area of the bar. A man and a woman were taking orders for drinks. They were standing in front of a large punch bowl with sangría. Slices of oranges and pineapple and strawberries were floating among the ice. Next to the punch bowl were a few dishes with sliced limes, strawberries and pineapple. He began to think of inviting the dark young woman to dinner, even though he was not very hungry. There was also a large dish with slices of meat that had been cut from thick, meaty barbecued ribs at the service area, and next to it, some good Mexican salsa picante. He was not a big eater. A few slices of meat will do, he thought. No need to go out to dinner.

The dark young woman was not interested in food, but Lorenzo was too stupid to understand. Despite his stupidity she led him to a bed which was located directly in front of the service area of the bar. She quickly undressed and got into bed, under the sheet. He undressed too, but he did not remove his shorts, and he did not feel desire.

Lorenzo was determined not to give the impression that all he wanted was to make love. He wanted the beautiful dark woman to know that he was not one of those men who are just interested in sex.

There was no question in Lorenzo's mind that the beautiful dark woman wanted to make love. She moved her firm naked body up to his. She cuddled up against him, pressed her full naked breasts against his shoulder, wrapped her legs around him, scratched his leg with her wiry tangle of pubic hair. The soft flesh, moist and open, made him think of it as a pair of lips kissing his bare leg. Her hand reached inside his shorts, but his body did not respond. He continued chattering about things in which she had not the slightest interest.

—Men lie to women, he said, especially married men. Married men lie sometimes that they are about to be divorced. They say awful things about their wives. I have never been able to lie. I am married, but six years ago when my wife and I were about to get divorced, we decided, because of economic reasons, and of course, because we have four sons, to stay together. Since then we have been the best of friends, and she encourages me to find a mistress. But I don't care for casual sex. I need to get to know a woman before I want sex. It doesn't mean anything otherwise. Don't you agree?

She simply nodded and continued to seek pleasure from his sexually slumbering body.

He was lying. Furthermore, she was not at all interested in what he was saying. She took his hand and brought it between her legs. Her strong and beautiful body responded to his hand and to his finger while he continued to chatter on. Her soft open flesh became profusely wet.

Here, he thought, is a woman such as I have longed very much to meet, one who does not care for playing games, one who feels desire and wants to get to the heart of the matter, and yet, despite her obvious main interest, why am I chattering on and on? He was conscious of mixed feelings.

—Some men who are married will tell women that they have an understanding with their wives. Of course they are lying. But I am not.

She was not listening to anything that he said. Lorenzo, probably tired of his own chattering, now began to think about making love, and turning his attention to that now, he became ready. At this point, however, the beautiful dark young woman excused herself. She got out of bed. She had a beautiful body.

—I must go to the bathroom, she said. Then she turned and walked away.

—Then it will be my turn, he said, looking forward now to lovemaking after going to the bathroom. The naked young woman disappeared from sight when she stepped through the door of the ladies' bathroom. The bathroom was in a little hall next to the service area of the bar, in front of the bed and slightly to the right. Her dark bronze beauty made him think of Gauguin paintings.

While she was in the bathroom another woman came and sat down on the edge of the bed, next to Lorenzo. He decided not to remove his shorts until after going to the bathroom. Under the sheet, he felt the warmth of the woman's body next to his. He was ready for love. The woman's lovely hand was warm against his body, and he imagined taking her hand, raising the sheet, bringing the woman's hand to place it between his legs, feeling the long graceful fingers sweetly caressing him into rapturous ecstasy. The mere thought gave him pleasure. He was unsure of himself, however. He hesitated. Somehow he knew that this warm-blooded woman was the dark woman's roommate.

When the dark woman returned, she was no longer naked. She had put on her panties, and over them was a garment that held up her stockings, attached to her legs, inexplicably, with little rectangular strips of white tape. Standing near the bed, she leaned over and began to raise the pantyhose over her stockings and panties.

161

Lorenzo felt very disappointed because he had been look-
ing forward to making love when she returned, after his going
to the bathroom. The dark young woman was no longer inter-
ested in sex. ¡Pendejo!

—But I thought after we went to the bathroom we would
make love, he said. I wanted to talk, to get to know you first, so
you wouldn't think all I want is sex. Women don't like men to
take sex for granted. They resent me if I express an interest in
sex right away. A woman wants to be treated like a person,
first. I love sex, but women still feel that men take advantage
of them that way. That is not all I want.

He did not tell her that his ability to control his desire had
come only in recent years. He had lied to the dark young
woman, in fact, and he chattered because he felt no desire at
first. But now he wanted to make love. He was conscious again
of the warmth of the other woman's body next to his. She was
still sitting on the bed next to him while he watched the beau-
tiful dark woman getting dressed.

—Look, the attractive dark woman said. I was interested in
sex. That was all. You appealed to me. I didn't want any hang-
ups or involvements. Just beautiful sex. We probably won't ever
run into each other again. Sorry.

—But I wanted to talk first. To get acquainted. Most
women. . . .

—Not me, she interrupted. All I wanted was to fuck.
There's always time to talk afterwards. Fuck and then talk.
That's the way I like it. When I'm hot I can't concentrate on
talk. I don't like any unnecessary conversation. Anyway, talk is
always better after a good fuck. I hate to play games. Besides,
men can't be honest until after they have sex with a woman.
It's a male shortcoming. I like the honesty after sex, when a
man is next to you with that limp thing waiting quietly to come
alive again. I love the way you can talk openly after sex. You
really get to know each other then, without hang-ups. You
learn a lot about life from sexual relations. Sex is better than
any book for learning about life, about the world, about things.
Look, why don't you wise up?

Lorenzo was astonished to hear a woman expressing the
philosophy of his younger days, when he used to be visited by
intense, exquisite agonies, by voluptuous desires of the flesh.

Damn! It's the story of my life. Whenever I am patient, to
show a woman that sex to me is sweet and beautiful and

162

sacred, that is precisely when the woman turns out to want only sex, like I used to when I was a young man. Then, when I am aggressive and bold, that is when the woman tells me to "cool it," as the saying goes. All you want is a fuck, these women say. Find someone else, Buster. You goddamn fucking Latino macho bastard.

It was the story of Lorenzo's life. If he expressed an immediate interest in a woman, clearly and honestly, it was wrong. If he was patient, that too was wrong, and perhaps stupid.

At the end of this dream he awakened momentarily, with an erection. He touched his erect member, which comforted him, and he fell right back to sleep.

# VI

THE FELLOW PASSENGER returned and stood in the aisle, next to Miguel, who took a moment or two to notice the man's presence. He pushed up the plastic tray, stood and moved out into the aisle to let his fellow passenger pass to his seat. Then he sat back down. He had barely touched his whiskey. Once again, he lowered the plastic tray and set the plastic glass on it. He took a cigarette without removing the pack from his shirt pocket. Slowly he brought it to his lips and lit it.

Great chunks of his life were passing through his mind. He remembered dreams well because he wrote them down. He wondered what they meant. From time to time he would want nothing more than to get away and relax. Sometimes he wanted to forget about books, writing and teaching, committee meetings, research. He wanted to stop thinking about what scholars had written, to set aside their works, and his endless novel. Now and then he became annoyed with his writing habits, to find a little pocket notebook in one hand and a fountain pen in the other. Smoke from his cigarette was floating upwards from the ashtray on his armrest.

NOTES. Down below, great tongues of concrete and asphalt. Super-highways that link the cities of California. Interstate 5 and the Pacific Coast Highway. Great ocean vistas and views of rugged mountains, empty wastelands, and a straight, endless expressway. . . . Thousands of years ago they came across the Bering Strait, the people whom the Europeans would call Indians after the discovery of the New World. Paleolithic man. No toilet paper, no toothbrushes, no toothpaste.

He started a new page of his little notepad. The cigarette smoke irritated his nose, so he put it out and continued to write.

Lorenzo Correa uncrossed his legs and stretched them forward. He could not stretch them all the way because of his black leather briefcase under the seat in front of him. The briefcase contained three large notebooks and two bulging manila folders, in addition to some unfinished articles, long ago abandoned. The notebooks provided a running record of his evaluation for tenure and its effects on his personal life. The folders contained other memoranda and documents pertaining to his tenure review. In addition to working on the scholarly articles, he was planning to go over the notebooks and documents during his stay at Berkeley. For nearly four years he had been making notes, writing chapters for a novel about his tenure evaluation and his joint appointment, about the university, the Chicano studies program, and American education. This trip would give him a chance to reconsider this project. He looked forward to being on the Berkeley campus on the first day of fall quarter classes.

He continued to write in his pocket notepad.


His thoughts drifted to recent dreams. Because of too many responsibilities at the university he had not written them down. Try as he might, he could not recall them. He remembered many restless nights and awakenings at four in the morning from recent times, being unable to get back to sleep until five or five thirty, when the automatic sprinklers would come on and lull him back to sleep. Shortly thereafter the alarm clocks in his daughters' rooms would awaken him momentarily at six. He was touched by the first sounds of his daughter Stephanie in the kitchen, making her own breakfast since she was eight or nine years old. She was always up before Suzie, the night child who had trouble waking up in the morning. While they were getting ready for school he would go back to sleep until a quarter to seven, and wait for one of the bathrooms to be free.

A commotion at the front of the airplane distracted Lorenzo Correa. Several men and women were standing in the aisle. Their faces expressed shock and indignation.

"Oh, my God!"

"What tha hell's goin' on?"

"Throw 'im off the plane."

"How the hell did they let 'im on the plane in that condition in the first place?"

The attractive stewardess who was pushing the liquor cart rushed past Lorenzo on her way to the front of the airplane, where a cluster of several annoyed passengers had formed. Others were glancing over the backs of their seats. All the way to the rear of the plane passengers in the aisle seats were leaning out to see what was going on. Across the plane other people, curious about the commotion, were beginning to stand up.

"I wonder what's going on up front," someone said.

Everyone was curious. The passengers were murmuring. Finally, the explanation for the commotion drifted back. The helpless alcoholic had urinated in his pants. Two stewardesses were trying to restore order among the passengers.

At that moment, Miguel Velásquez wondered where in the novel he would be able to insert the aging alcoholic's misfortune, which he had just imagined. He wanted to introduce some imaginary excitement into this plane journey, to make his trip fictional. The conversation of two fellow passengers about whether the poor man would be able to make it to the bathroom had given him the idea. He thought also of introducing the narrator of the novel into this imaginary episode.

Chère lectrice, et vous aussi, hypocrite lecteur. The author invented me, of that I am sure you will be aware, to help him tell the story of his life. To date he has been unable to find a name for his autobiographical character. Perhaps the writer will make the character a filmmaker, a painter or a sculptor, to minimize the autobiographical element. Maybe an architect.

Poor fellow. His modesty prevents him from being truthful about who he is, about his destiny. Sometimes he suffers from delusions of grandeur. For years he has been writing about a fictional character, to whom he attributes experiences he has never had, invented memories of the future, predictions of the past. In any case, he summoned me to intrude in this way, like we narrators did in the good old conventional novels. By the way, he wrote the narrator's preface, not I. I don't know if you have already come across it, or if it is ahead. Oh well, the wretched fellow is ready to continue. . . .

Miguel was saddened about the elderly alcoholic. The thought did not comfort him much that he could have imagined something worse than urinating on a plane, or anywhere for that matter. What about diarrhea? What if a helpless alcoholic defecated in his pants, in public, on the street, in a restaurant? What if he were far from a shower and a clean change of clothing?

At the corner of Thirteenth Street and Avenue of the Americas the pain in his bowels became excruciating. He was only a block away from the apartment. He was almost running, but he had to stop occasionally to control the need. He closed his eyes and squirmed with pain. It was like a bad dream. He started walking again, but he had to stop a few more times. It was nearly two in the morning, but out of the corner of his eye he saw three people approaching on the sidewalk. He squirmed with pain, then he hastened his pace. There were no people or cars on the streets, except for the three people. He would not be sure later on whether they saw him. He was alone. He could not bear the excruciating pain any longer, then came relief, and the hot liquid was running down his legs, inside his pants. In the apartment Valerie took off his soiled shoes and trousers. She took them out into the hall and dropped them into the incinerator. He could not be sure if the doorman had seen him, or if he had left a trail in the hall to the elevator. She ordered him to take a shower.

—What a shame! That was such a nice, brand new pair of shoes.

Valerie is screaming. *Let me out! Let me out! Stop this car. If you wanna kill yourself do it, but let me out! You drank almost the whole bottle of scotch!* . . . Lorenzo is drunk, speeding recklessly down the Champs Elysées, weaving dangerously in and out among the heavy traffic of automobiles. He screams at her. *Shut up! Shut up!*

He closed his fist and smashed it against the windshield of the 1967 Volkswagen. The glass shattered. Two days before they boarded a ship back to the States. On the ship bikini-clad American and European girls. Unbearable, exquisite agony. Terrible attraction of the great Atlantic Ocean . . . *Why do you do this to yourself, Larry? Why, honey? What a terrible way for our European trip to end, in the first year of our marriage.* The trip that began with picking up the Volkswagen in Paris and driving south to Madrid, in late September, past Chartres and Orléans, Poitiers and Bordeaux, when the grapes of the great vineyards were beautiful and ripe, on into Bayonne, and into Irún,

Spain, past Burgos where they had a delicious brunch at a small family café, and on toward Madrid, was over. They would always remember the memorable picnics with ham and cheese, pâté de fois, fresh-baked crusty baguettes, and wine as they drove across southern France. Across the border, on Spanish soil, Lorenzo and Valerie stopped at the edge of the Atlantic, where the newlyweds embraced and kissed. He wished that he were a poet to describe the inexpressibly strange longings produced by the contemplation of the ocean. He thought he understood how Columbus, the madman with a dream, must have felt. Perhaps one day he would be able to describe the arrival in Spain of a Mexican from Texas and his Jewish bride from New York.

Years later Lorenzo is travelling again, alone on a bus from New York to Chicago; alone on an airplane back to New York City; alone on an airplane to Mexico; making several trips, alone, to Austin, Texas and to Berkeley, California, alone as he was destined to be. *So*, his brother says, *you're gonna get divorced? And tell me, is it true? I mean . . . I hope you don't mind a personal question; after all, you're my brother. Okay if I ask you? Okay, well, is it true that you're an alcoholic?*

He stopped writing, set his pen on the tray, raised the glass of whiskey to his mouth and took a small drink. *Well, tell me honey, what did the doctor say? Did you admit your drinking problem? . . . Mommy, is Daddy an alcoholic?*

When he completed the examination the doctor told him that he could get dressed. He did so, slowly, waiting patiently for the doctor to collect his final thoughts.

—As I was saying, the symptoms of alcoholism are many and they are varied. Symptoms indicate that something is happening to a person's body system. Some symptoms are psychological, but they have a physical basis. Sweating, bad breath, frequent need to urinate or to eliminate the bowels, for example, are physical symptoms, but you can certainly imagine that if any of these are present a person's self-confidence is bound to be low. What's that? Yes, even in dreams, it would seem to me. We can come back to that. Imagine now, in your profession, how you might feel if you had to present a paper at a scholarly meeting for example, with several people in attendance or even at a faculty meeting, and you were worried about going to the bathroom. You can see my point . . . What's that? Yes, there's also in many cases a diminution of interest in sex, and that differs among men. As I told you, your physical examination and the tests don't show any physical damage. Nothing in the liver, but then, nothing usually shows up till it's very advanced. Nothing in the urine, count is okay, slight enlargement of the prostate gland, but that's natural at your age, let's see, you're how old? Yes, I was right. Nothing to worry about now, but that accounts for incomplete elimination of the bladder, the drip after urinating. Yes, I know, but meanwhile, you don't need prostate surgery, it'll be awhile. And as for . . . what's that? Yes, people who are workaholics tend to lose their sex drive, too. A lot of energy does go into writing a book, which may comfort you. Surprising as it may seem, studies show reduced sexual activity among writers when they're in the middle of a writing project. Some studies of artists suggest that the procreative drive and creativity both have their source in the genitals. We can't go into that, of course. It's a scientific area of investigation, but many of the findings are unreliable or conjectural. Maybe you know, in your own personal case, if it's true or not. But let's face it, if you don't use it, as the saying goes, you lose it. Don't expect in later years to recover it. That's why some people . . . if I may say so . . . watch-er-r-r . . . thos-s-se-ah you know, those movies. Know what I mean? Do you and your wife? No, well, watching those movies has helped some people, and affairs too, but don't get me wrong, I'm not suggesting that you have an affair. I'm just pointing out that the newness often brings back . . . well, you know. . . . That's just the way things are. Getting back to alcoholism, some of the questions one can ask if they're answered honestly can lead a person to be truthful with himself. You gotta decide for yourself. For example, does drinking have an affect on your work? If a person misses work, or gets behind, these indicate danger signs, even symptoms. Some alcoholics, however, perform very well, so even this question may not always bring about an admittance of alcoholism. Quarreling, drinking alone early in the morning or at a regular time of day, drinking when there's pressure at work, or at home, blackouts and loss of memory, being in a hurry to down the first drink at a party, or drinking before going to a party, drinking at a party after everyone else has stopped, when they're having dessert and coffee, drinking at home after a party, things like that are generally recognizable symptoms, and alcoholics usually become very angry when family and friends discuss it. No, you don't need to tell me if any of these apply to you. You have to answer to yourself, not to me. If you wish treatment I can, as your family doctor, recommend it. But I do not diagnose alcoholism. There's other questions, if you're interested, that doctors ask patients who are concerned about drinking. Does the patient have the shakes in the morning? Is there a loss of appetite? Hangovers? Bad breath? Does he see things that aren't there? Doctors recommend to people who are worried about alcoholism, but who don't feel they're ready for treatment, to turn to the first page of the telephone directory. There's a listing there, "AA," Alcoholics Anonymous. That's where a person can get help. We also have a clinic. I mean, most hospitals do provide treatment. We do. It's up to you.

His mind alternated between other memories and the commotion at the front of the airplane. Over the years he had seen many men like the elderly alcoholic, legions of them, helpless men drifting by on the street with glazed and vacant, sightless eyes that do not see objects or people. In each of them he saw what could happen. He was thankful for having Valerie, and a friend like Al Caballero. Books, too. He was thankful for books. *How about it, Larry? Will you come along? You're an artist, no experience is lost on an artist. You once told me that your great teacher at U. T. taught you that, eh man, and you said your own experience has confirmed it.* Poor men, those who pee in their pants or worse still. . . . Do they feel embarrassed? Till when? *I finally admitted it. Larry, we're like brothers, I just want you to know what one of these meetings is like . . . might even see people you know and would never expect to see there. How about it? Just to keep me company.* Al finally persuaded him to attend an Alcoholics Anonymous meeting, many years ago, in New York, *for the sake of the experience, Larry.*

After all these years, he could not remember where the Alcoholics Anonymous session took place. He could not remember who was there, only that he was surprised to see people from his apartment building, face to face, eye to eye. Important actors and actresses and writers were there too. His neighbors were also surprised to see him there. Silently, they seemed to share a secret. *They think I'm one of them.*

170

He had observed and listened, without being one of them. Aboard the PSA 737, he could not remember details. But he had a general sense of what the meeting was like. *Perhaps if I go to a meeting in this part of the country, maybe that would bring it back.* There was a main speaker, I think, or a person who was in charge. He could not remember clearly. It was a large place, like an auditorium, and crowded with men and women. They all seemed to have something in common, it was something about their eyes. *Come on, stand up and say it with me,* said the man who was standing in front of a lectern and speaking into a microphone, and everyone stood up, including himself. *I am an alcoholic. Once more, say it and mean it,* and the volume of the voices rose. *I am an alcoholic . . . I am an alcoholic.* Al was saying it, but not he. From time to time he glanced over at Al and smiled, but Al did not press him to join in. He never did. Then the speaker called on the crowd, he remembered vaguely, and invited people to come up to tell their stories . . . *I am an alcoholic . . .* and people went up and they told stories about failures in business, marital violence, broken marriages and families, thwarted hopes, shattered dreams, disappointments, automobile accidents, wasted talents, betraying a calling, broken hearts, and about AA having given them the chance to start over, a chance to live again. They needed one another, but he did not need, would never need, a dependency on others. He was thirty-three years old. Already a solitary, he did not need others. . . . *Tell us, how long has it been since you had a drink? Don't be embarrassed. One day at a time.*

A man with glazed eyes began to stagger up to the lectern. He moved with difficulty, courageously. The crowd cheered him all the way. In front of the lectern, he gazed upward with delirious eyes, then at the crowd, and he spoke into the microphone. *I'm an alcoholic . . . I had a drink . . . five minutes . . . before I came to this meeting. . . . I'm drunk, drunk, drunk, I need help . . . help me, help me, help me, please help me!* The people in the audience gave the man a loud round of applause and when he was walking back to his place, tears in his eyes, people embraced him left and right.

Al turned and glanced at him, as if trying to assess Lorenzo's reaction. Lorenzo was thinking that he was not like them. One day he would remember attending this Alcoholics Anonymous meeting. He was drunk, but he was not one of them.

171

Over the years he discovered that certain circumstances and personal states of mind were more conducive than others to stimulating him to write. Sitting in his favorite rocking chair and drinking, for example, while he listened to classical or Mexican music, playing the records at a high volume, or sitting in the sunshine in the backyard of his middle-class suburban home, going to lunch at restaurants frequented by people who worked from eight to five, where he prepared the first lectures for his classes several years ago, driving around unfamiliar neighborhoods, stopping at cocktail lounges during happy hour, eavesdropping on people's conversations, watching people from a distance, turning his eyes into zoom lenses to observe a young woman or the spectacle of the crowd—all placed him in circumstances that stimulated him creatively.

In his young manhood, as an undergraduate, he lived among beatniks and among people whose lives were irregular and unconventional, who drank and frequented bars and cafés where they talked about Camus and Dostoyevski. During the sixties, he knew misfits in Chicago and New York who talked about Lawrence Durrell and Hemingway, and he knew a few hippies and flower children, too.

Despite the irregularities of his life he was convinced that his real work was tenacious, scrupulous and energetic. He wrote almost every day, even wrote and edited in his dreams. Paradoxically, some of his best writing came almost unfailingly, after days of excesses that others would call wasted. At such times he would write in a fury, doing in three hours, he would persuade himself, a week's work that he could not force himself to do. In his youth he began to relish the word "madman."

In addition to Valerie many people were concerned about his drinking. Years ago, Lorenzo reassured his good friend, Alfredo Caballero, not to worry.

—It's okay, Al. Don't worry about me, man. Yes, I know, I have always appreciated that about you. You never lectured me. In any case, you need not worry. I have control over my boozing. Yes, I go on my little binges from time to time, but I am in control. Honestly. Because I have learned to fear and to respect booze.

There were mornings in those days, however, when Lorenzo would tell himself that he did not need a drink. Yet he would find himself, almost instinctively, in front of the liquor cabinet, after three or four good hours of work. Sometimes he went simply to get a glass for some juice, in the next cabinet, and he would automatically open the liquor cabinet, and there was his hand reaching out for the bottle. *A little drink or two will not matter.* When he wanted, Lorenzo was very proficient at self-deception. It was true, nevertheless, that over the years, through conscious work habits and methods, including boozing, he had learned to tap buried memories, feelings and experiences, and to reach deep levels of unconscious sources of inspiration. During the years of excesses he found comfort in the knowledge that some of the writers whom he most admired had been hard drinkers. O'Neill, Faulkner, Fitzgerald, Thomas Wolfe, Rulfo; and, above them all, was the master of the booze visions, the magnificent borracho. The art of each of them, particularly of the gran borracho, had benefitted from booze. Lorenzo wondered if one day he too might write a book about his fantasies, nightmares, visions and spectacles conjured up by booze or wine, or by guilt and rage . . . *do you see things that aren't there?*

# VII

MANY YEARS AGO in New York, Alfredo Castellano saw them. The shrieking wild-eyed creatures visited his room in the hospital where he almost died. Beverly Feldman, the woman with whom he had been living, wrote to Lorenzo and Valerie. The letter from New York arrived one day at the couple's Blasco de Garay address, in Madrid, Spain.

Dear Friends, Larry and Valerie, the letter began. I write you with a heavy heart because Al has gone back to Liz, but with a happy one because he has a chance to overcome his great problem—the bottle—and perhaps clear up some others that have made the bottle so essential to him.

This man is so dear and good and bright, so lovable in every way. It has been a beautiful life and I'm not sorry about anything. I don't understand everything yet, and I will write you when I know more. The doctor in charge of his case has told me not to try to get in touch with him, see him or send any message. Liz is at the hospital screening his calls, anyway, but I thought I could send a cryptic message. However, I guess I'll have to go by what the doctor says. In time, when Al is better, he will get in touch with me. He told one of his graduate students to give me this message.

Let me tell you what happened as best I can reconstruct it and you see what you can make of it.

We had a quarrel one evening (it was due to drinking—he never gets violent but he goads and goads and I said something nasty) and next morning he was still angry and said he was leaving and would be gone for a couple of days. I apologized for being nasty and said I hoped he would come back, and that I loved him. He said, "It may not be my decision to make." I did not know what to make of that, whether I wouldn't want him back or what. At any rate, the second morning he called and said he would be home around seven. Meantime, I had given a good deal of thought to his drinking and had discussed it with Anita Landau, a psychologist who has known him since his Iowa days and who is the soul of discretion as well as a good scientist. She went through about 12 steps that might be taken, very carefully and thoroughly with me in relation to Al's personality.

He returned that night, but there was someone here who didn't leave and we all had dinner and made chit-chat. Next morning I told him I loved him very much but didn't see how I could marry him while he had this addiction (which, unfortunately, it seems to be in his case—strange how some can take or leave it and others depend on it). I also said I would be glad to stay with him forever, drinking or no, but to marry him was another thing.

Frankly, I can't remember whether it was before or after this talk, but we went to the lawyer and made the final payment on the divorce. Liz had agreed to go to Mexico. Of course, the two days he spent away from me were with Liz, but the agreement was supposedly still good even after he had seen her.

Anyway, the morning I had the talk with him about his drinking I mentioned Anita's 12 suggestions and added a few of my own and he said, "You are the only person who could ever have said those things without making me angry." He agreed that he did need help and I said I would do everything I could to help him.

The first step was to get a physical checkup. I made an appointment with my doctor for him. That week we had no quarrels. He didn't stop drinking (I hardly expected he would right off the bat) but he ate more, particularly early in the day, and he took plenty of vitamins.

On Thursday of that week, there was a conference in Toronto, Canada, which Don Bennett had invited Al to. He wanted me to go also, but of course I couldn't go until Friday after work. We had a ball there, he met a lot of old friends and new ones and it was great.

On the Friday before he left, I had a session with my headshrinker about Al. He was not terribly encouraging about psychiatry in cases of alcoholism, but said there had been some successes. He felt that Al, being a psychologist (they're always at war with psychiatrists) and so sort of hung up on his Mexican heritage, would be better off with a psychiatrist who was a good deal older than him and one who was not American.

I'm not telling this in order, you can see what kind of a state of mind I'm in—like confused. While he was up in Riverdale, Liz apparently found out my number and name, so the same Sunday we had the talk about his problem, the phone rang: "Is this Beverly Feldman? Washington is calling Dr. Castellano." He answered and the other person hung up. He told me to get on the other extension and see if it was the same voice, and dialed Liz. She came through loud and clear, without waiting to hear who was calling: "Al, I love you, darling." The phone rang and I answered it and she hung up the whole afternoon long. Finally I asked if she couldn't be stopped and he went to the phone and said something and the nuisance calls stopped. Al told me once that he used to get calls all the time when he and Liz began to see each other. She was married then, and her husband used to call him at all hours.

Okay, now we're back from Toronto and have had a lovely weekend and he has an appointment with my M.D. in the morning. He gets up and gets dressed and I presume he goes, for in the evening he tells me all about his talk with Dr. Santini, and that he's physically okay, except for blood and urine tests which we'll get the results of soon.

Tuesday morning, a blizzard. Snow piled high on the streets. Freezing weather. I decide not to go to work because I have a typewriter here and can work at home. The phone rings—a woman, for Al. He talks a short time and hangs up. Then he says, "That was Liz. I don't want her calling any more. I want you to have the number changed." He got dressed and said he was going to a therapist suggested by a professor who had beaten the alcohol problem. I said I was very proud. He went off into the snowstorm and I haven't seen or heard from him again.

I did nothing that night except call the hospitals and check the police to see if he had been injured in the storm. It was really bad out.

Wednesday night I called Riverdale and asked if he was in and was told he was not. Another girl called and was told that he was not in, that he and Liz were getting a divorce, that she had not seen him for a month. Next day Al's lawyer tried to get Liz's lawyer. He hedged and said he'd call back, called back and said Liz had a strep throat, couldn't talk, but that she never wanted to see him again, and so on, and so on.

Thursday evening I had a male friend call Riverdale and say he was Boyd McCandless (whose voice I didn't think Liz would recognize but was pretty sure Al would talk to). Al came to the phone. My friend said, "Of course you know I am not Boyd McCandless, but I am a friend of Beverly, and she is most concerned about you." Al replied, "Tell them I am going to the hospital as soon as there is a bed available."

Well, it was unbelievable that he could be gone so long, and know that I knew where he was, and that he would still not get in touch with me somehow. So on Sunday I called up Liz, asked how he was, and she said he had made up his mind to go to the hospital and be cured and that was what she had prayed for and that he was going back to her and everything was going to be wonderful. I told her I had also hoped and prayed that he would be cured and that she didn't want anything for him that I didn't want also. I asked her what she wanted me to do about his things that were here. She said she would let me know. Perhaps I shouldn't have asked her that, but I did, and if he needs them in the hospital I'm glad to let him have them. They are only *things*, after all. I felt that if he was well enough to talk to the fellow he thought to be Boyd McCandless, he could talk to me too. False reasoning. In this frame of mind, I also had the lock changed next day, thinking he isn't going to bounce back between here and Riverdale, he has to make up his mind and I am going to have a damn good explanation before he comes in again. Wrong, wrong, wrong. You see, I didn't believe Liz (don't now) and thought they were just giving excuses.

Finally it dawned on me to call Dr. Santini. With all the lies that had been told the lawyer and everyone, I began to doubt that Al had ever gone to him at all. He was not there, but the nurse told me that Al had indeed been there, and that the arrangements to put him into Roosevelt Hospital had been made through my doctor. I take it that Al has had some sort of nervous collapse. On Tuesday I have an appointment with Dr. S., and it is just possible that he can clear up some of this.

The night I talked to Dr. Santini's nurse and learned that Al was going into Roosevelt the same day, Liz called. A friend answered and Liz said, "I have a message for Beverly from Al." Naturally I rushed to the phone, so relieved to get a message or a call from him—but it was only Liz saying she would pick up his belongings on Saturday, that Al was so happy to be back with her, that he wanted to forget all the things that had happened and that they would have the same lovely, happy constructive life they had had before he left.

Well, I have an idea from the way his friends have received me just how lovely, happy and constructive that life was, even if I discount what Al has told me. One of his graduate students came by to return some books and I repeated this to him and he said, "That is a crock of shit and you know it."

Liz called twice again, once wanting to pick up the things on her way back from the hospital and I said they weren't ready, which was true and she was sweeter than honey which she always is to me except that every sweet word is hurting so bad, and I answer her real ladylike at all times (except I did call her Mrs. Erlich once or twice because that's the way she's listed in the phone book). The second time she called about picking up the things on Saturday I said, "You don't want to see me and I don't want to see you. I will not be here when you come but the elevator man will help you with them. If you want to know what I look like, I'm an overweight woman of 47." When it came right down to the nitty-gritty she didn't come here either but sent a taxi for them. I hope I don't have to talk to her again, at least until I have talked to Al.

Well, that's about all I know right now. I will talk to Dr. Santini on Tuesday and he may help some. The doctor who is taking care of Al is Vladimir Mitrovich. He is definitely not American, which is good in view of my shrink's advice, but he is not older than Al, which is too bad. Al has always had a great respect for older men. He says respect for elders is very important in Mexican culture. Also this Dr. Mitrovich on the phone was quite unsympathetic to me (as if I had caused all the trouble). I have written him today to say I will abide by his instructions but that if Al ever needs to talk to me or see me I will, and that returning his things and having the lock changed was not a matter of rejection but expedience, and that I love him very much and want more than anything for him to be well. For Lord's sake it's not a matter of who's the best woman but what's best for him. On the other hand, Liz has definitely moved in and taken hold, which she has a perfect legal right to do—but would not have had in a couple of weeks.

How do you figure it? What did she say to him on the phone that morning that sent him off? Does he really love her?

Was the idea of divorce so repulsive? Is he protecting me? Is he in such a financial bind that he can only go along with her? Is she blackmailing him, bribing him, threatening me?

Is she a clever enough actress to hoodwink the headshrinkers that she is the all-forgiving earth mother who alone can help him? Would competent medical men believe that Al has been on a 5-month lost weekend, when he has missed class only twice, given a lecture at Adelphi and another at Columbia, and advised any number of graduate students, and he even went through living hell trying to get the committee changed for one girl who had been turned down on her 2nd doctoral exams. "This is a man who thinks with his heart . . . but this is a man who tries."

Dear friends, I have been too full of myself in this letter. You are the best friends he has. Write to him, cable him, call him. He is at Roosevelt Hospital, Tower 10, 59th and 9th Ave. Call him and charge it to me (212–TR5–1212)—the number you can reach him at is 212–265–8741. It will mean so much to him. Your letters were so important to him, he read them over and over. Yet I couldn't turn over anything to Liz that had my name in it because I don't know her, don't trust her, I have them all here and will try to sneak them in through a reliable friend some day soon.

You are so much farther away from him than I am, yet you can get through and I cannot. Please try. And if it should be that I am never to see him again, I would still want to see you two, many and many times, not to cry on your shoulders but just because you are what you are. Love, Beverly.

Shortly after Lorenzo and Valerie returned from Europe their good friend described in his own words one of the hallucinations that he had when he was being treated. Lorenzo would never forget his words. Over the years, some parts of Al's account stood out sharply in his mind, and some of the images that he described became transformed in memory.

One of the first nights when I was in the hospital, Alfredo said, something suddenly woke me up. Jesus! I was shaking, shaking badly with delirium tremens. I think it was just before dawn *in the waning hours of the night, very early.* I remember looking from my hospital bed and seeing myself standing by the window, trembling. I can only liken my experience to a vision, or perhaps to some of those heightened perceptions one has sometimes after smoking a joint. It was like being three people,

Jesus! *in the waning hours of the night* because I could see myself in bed, see myself by the window *the seer, the seen and the seeing all one and the same.* Something awakened me, I'm trying to remember, something that brought about a strange, eerie hallucination, caused by the delirium tremens, I know now. Something I heard, or imagined I heard, woke me up. I heard a man's scream, an automobile horn, screeching tires, a thud, the siren of an ambulance, *a prolonged, excruciating human cry, a loud, shrieking automobile horn, the dull, hollow sound of steel smashing into human flesh and bone, the screeching tires, and the wail, like a sorrowful lament of an ambulance siren.* I remember being in bed and at the same time standing by the hospital window, and looking down at the scene of an accident . . . *looking down upon a great murmuring crowd* . . . at a lot of people. There was a pool of blood on the street, close to the curb. Now I recognized the street, on Broadway, near the 72nd Street entrance to the IRT-Broadway subway station . . . *wail, like . . . a sorrowful lament . . . pool of blood . . . murmuring crowd.*

God! Jesus! It was crazy, Larry. From the hospital bed, I was seeing myself standing by the window, seeing below, on the street . . . *the dazzling white chalk outline glowing strangely round the body of a young dead Puerto Rican man* . . . a boy . . . his corpse was there, lying on the street. You've seen it, Larry. You know how after an accident the police will make an outline of the body with chalk, except I saw it glow. From my window I was seeing all the people below at the scene of the accident . . . *a circling crowd* . . . and suddenly, down below, there I was too! *I saw myself among the passersby with curious, furtive and terrible glances* . . . Here I was in my hospital room, in bed and at the window. Jesus! But there I was down below, too, and I could see two of me. I was drunk down below, walking slowly to conceal it. Everyone was staring at me, Larry. I remember walking toward the boy's body . . . *coming closer and closer to the corpse.* Then, when I got there it was my own body on the street, with chalk around it . . . *I, enclosed by the glowing chalk outline* . . . surrounded by restless, dark shapes. I screamed but I made no sound. I was terrified. Then my body became the boy again. The policemen were everywhere, pushing people back, directing traffic. *I saw halted cars, saw the ambulance attendants take away the young dead boy whose body's outline glowed eerily and emptily in white chalk upon the asphalt street.* . . . Just a few weeks before I went into the hospital, I had seen the body of a young

180

Puerto Rican boy right after he had been struck and killed by a car. Not very far from his body I saw the bottle of cheap wine he had been drinking. It didn't even break, and it was still half filled. As young as the boy was, he was probably already a wino. Being at the scene of the accident convinced me to get treatment. I was already aware of the need to be treated, because I had begun to use my finger, running it against walls, to steady myself. Jesus, I saw so many people like that boy in San Francisco's Mission District, Larry, when I was a kid.

That night, in my hospital room, after this hallucination, I heard my own piercing scream, and I saw a gargoyle sitting on the bathroom sink. It was laughing and laughing at me with wild, menacing eyes. The doctors thought I was gonna die, Larry. They didn't think I would pull through.

—It's great that you did, hermano, the younger man said. You look very well now. And you've been off the booze now for nearly two years. Marvelous!

The two men were walking south on Fifth Avenue. At Thirteenth Street they paused at the corner.

—Let's walk around Washington Square for a while. Look at the pretty girls.

—Great idea, Lorenzo.

—Yes, Alfredo.

—These names are better than Al and Larry. Right?

—Right.

—Look, Larry, I mean Lorenzo. Look what's playing at this theatre today.

The two Mexicans in New York stopped to look at the matinee announcement and the window displays.

—If you haven't, you should see this movie, Lorenzo. You know French. I read some reviews about this film. It's supposed to be a great film about an impossible love. But the love takes place. The lovers are a Japanese man and a French woman. They're both married. Have you seen it?

The younger man said that he had not, but that he would make it a point to see it someday.

Aboard the PSA on the way to Oakland Lorenzo Correa was awestruck that life often works in marvelously strange and unexpected ways. The film by Resnais and Duras had been prophetic. In the years to come, each man would know a passionate April love in the September season of their respective lives.

The direction of his thoughts brought him back to the recent past, to memories of the young woman half his age who had come in and out of his life. He too had his moments of helplessness, in life, in art and in dreams, because of alcohol. He knew. The young woman helped him to see. She appeared to him as the barefooted Nicolette, beloved of Aucassin, appeared to the dying pilgrim in the desert. Perhaps it would be different from now on.

The presence of a helpless, aging alcoholic on board the airplane made him ponder what his own life would have been and could not have been. He cherished the memories of sweet ephemeral tenderness, of loves that come and go. In this mood of gratitude and compassion he wondered who his aging fellow passenger was, the alcoholic retired professor of American history. What period of American history was his specialty? Did his knowledge of his country's history contribute to his desire to escape into insensibility? The aging alcoholic made Lorenzo wonder why one of his favorite writers drank himself to death. What compels the human spirit to fly from routine, from the drudgery and monotony of everyday life? Why does it seek the heights and the depths? Why must one soar above the common herd from time to time? Did the borracho magnífico ever pee or defecate in his pants? Would that have made him less great? Why do creative men and women have major disorders? How can some among the sensitive ones not understand? One, for example.

How could you, a poet and critic, and a man with a social conscience, have been so far off the mark? You wrote fiction, plays and journalism. It is said of your critical works that they deal mostly with issues and problems of modern literature. You are one of the elders among the poets; your poetry brought you prominence during those magnificent years of experimentation and innovation in all the arts, the twenties and thirties. You were born in London. If I remember correctly, some people attribute to this accident of birth a singular trait about which your work is praised: it has been said that throughout your life you avoided extreme pronouncements. Others see a want of development in your thinking and ideas. Some apply to you the label of romantic—the critics' polite way to disparage. Others see in you an unresolved tension between your sensibility as a poet and your obligations as a citizen. They

182

called you an angry young man of the thirties and say that you criticized the modernists because they avoided politics. You posed, it has been said, "the dilemma of the morally and socially sensitive individual."

For all your sensitivity as a poet and your consciousness as a citizen, how strange that you should be blind to the relationship of life to literature in one extraordinary case. Were you not aware that you were contradicting yourself in your introduction to a great novel by an extraordinary writer who drank? To separate the life of the man from the work of the writer, surely you had to know, does violence to the creator and the work of art. How can anyone appreciate a work of art fully without a knowledge of the artist and his life?

Miguel took another drink and savored the whiskey. How perplexing that the poet-critic would admit that it was a book in which the hero is drunk for three quarters of the time; would grant that the book is perhaps the best account of a "drunk" in fiction (he put "drunk" in quotation marks!); would concede that by the end of the novel the reader knows how a drunk thinks and feels, walks and lies down, and how the drunk experiences not only the befuddledness of drinking but also its moments of translucent clairvoyance and perfected expression—how astonishing, given these acknowledgements, that the critic yet went on to say that the novel has nothing to do with alcohol!

Fundamentally, the critic declared, the novel is no more *about* drinking than King Lear is *about* senility! According to some people, said the underground man, four times four equals five.

That is not what the great writer himself told us! He avowed that he wanted to turn his greatest weakness—he went so far as to tell us that he loathed the borrowed phrase—into his greatest strength. In the very book, with the poet-critic's introduction—Miguel knew the page of the Plume Books edition by heart, page 292—the writer made an inventory, he recreated the hallucinatory spectacle of his hero's—his own—the Consul's life, with a nearly exhaustive list of alcoholic drinks from all over the world, which he had consumed, booze which the writer alias the Consul, and alias Sigbjorn Wilderness, had consumed in a lifetime, and he did it again in another novel, a posthumous one—on page 211. Listen.

Look—the writer wrote to express his character's convictions—I have succeeded, I have transformed, single-handedly, my life-in-death into life, nay what is more I am going to make that life-in-death pay for the future, in hard cash; I have come back to show you that not an hour, not a moment of my drunkenness, my continual death, was not worth it: there is no dross of even the worst of those hours, not a drop of mescal that I have not turned into pure gold, not a drink I have not made sing.

A more insightful writer, also a critic, saw it clearly. He too wrote about the magnificent borracho with compassionate and unsurpassed understanding; he saw that the borracho's art and the booze were inseparable, that he was the lucid master of alcoholic visions and deliriums, a literary Hieronymus Bosch or a Goya. His was the world of cantinas where he drank himself back through his life—this brilliant writer-critic writes—where he became always magnificently and perfectamente borracho, when he felt that it was absolutamente necesario to have a drink, in order to reach the desired condition of splendid incompetence and helplessness.

Yes, solitary one, your books tell us that the cantinas were your favorite playground, your dimly illuminated, candlelit sanctuaries, the shrines where you worshipped booze and contemplated your deranged image in the frightful mirrors behind the bars, above the rows of tequila and mescal and aguardiente; cantinas where you used to listen to the murmur of imaginary conversations during strangely veiled hours of the early morning, day and night; cantinas with strange, mysterious names; cantinas where the heroes of your books return in memory to their childhoods and travels; where they relive the terrible advances of night and remember one-finger musical preludes played in the fearful crease of a woman's body, which only the finger could penetrate; cantinas, where the heroes journey, aboard drunken boats, descend, with brains darkened by alcohol, into regions of hell. Yes, it is true. You described cantinas where there is no o'clock, you recorded extended conversations and quarrels with invisible companions and with empty corners and empty seats; and after that you would pass out, and yet you would remember afterwards what had been said in the presence of your absent self. You described the shrieking, wild-eyed gargoyles on the kitchen sink, the trembling of your hands, the need for just one more drink, just one more to steady the nerves, the limp and useless male thing, the ground rising up to strike you in the face. It is in your books, great one.

Given that it is all there, how can still another man, the biographer of the borracho magnífico, choose to stress the great writer's human imperfections! How dare he, in the preface to a posthumous novel by the monumental borracho, say that we must begin to realize that he was not really a novelist, except by accident! Like the poet-critic who said that the novel had nothing to do with alcohol, the biographer too, makes paradoxical statements about the solitary writer's character.

The magnificent borracho was a genius and unique, the biographer grants, but he was not a writer! The biographer says that he does not know, or rather, he absolves himself by saying that it is difficult to know what to call the writer, the dipsomaniac: diarist, compulsive notetaker, poet *manqué*, alcoholic philosophizing rambler. These, he says, will do for a start.

The writer was a man obsessed by the need to write, his biographer concludes. But the biographer, judging the writer by the nearly two hundred *unpublished* pages for each published one; after telling us that hardly a day in the writer's life from early adolescence to his death passed without his writing something—notes, paragraphs, journals, chapters for work in progress, revisions of earlier works, revisions of revisions, and so on, often in his impossible tiny and illegible handwriting, for what was to be a vast, endless literary work—after all this, the biographer judges the writer on the basis of what he did *not* publish, which he uses for an absolutely splendid interpretation of the writer's character, for which he penalizes the writer additionally, to conclude that the man of whom he writes, on whose literary works the biographer's livelihood partly depends, was obsessed by the need to write, while at the same time he was almost totally unable to write!

Miguel Velásquez frequently wondered what it is that fascinates the literary critics and biographers of writers, poets, painters, playwrights and filmmakers whose final judgment is based on what the artists did *not* do rather than on what they did; who write with extraordinary insight and perception about the artist's life and character, only to penalize the creator for the very traits that make him unique and distinctive among men. Why do they judge the artist on the basis of what he did

185

not do or might or should have done? Why not judge him for what he did or does, or for what he *was* or *is*?

A writer, only by accident! Indeed! Miguel Velásquez leaped frequently to defend those artists who are most misunderstood. What artist is not an accident? What poet or filmmaker is not obsessed with the perfection of his work? What writer has not studied his own sufferings, bringing knowledge from hellish depths that we might learn about other unfamiliar realms of life? That is exactly what the magnificent borracho did. The writers whom the borracho inspired and influenced know it. He was one of many great modern writers, artists, painters, sculptors, filmmakers—the Mexican Tolstoy has said—who raised the curtain on a *new reality*. The borracho and many others reached back to the poetic roots of literature, and through language and structure, he helped to create an artistic convention of reality--a new reality that aspires to an unprecedented, all-embracing comprehensive wholeness.

That is important, and more important still, the solitary writer made an inventory of his grief, his suffering, his introspective visions, his alcoholic hallucinations, the derangement of his senses, and his haunting obsessions; and he paid tribute to the visionaries whose collective artistic tradition inspired him: Dante, Poe, Baudelaire, Rimbaud, Joyce, Proust, Hesse, Wiene, Cocteau. Deep inside, the man wanted—he admitted candidly and courageously—to account to himself at the end.

His literary works attest to the fact that he did not betray his artistic gift with alcohol. The man struggled with alcohol, as the perceptive fellow writer recognized, against galloping cockroaches, against the polygonous Proustian stare of imaginary scorpions, against vultures on the kitchen sink, and against imaginary interrogators. The effects of alcohol on his introspective visions shaped his whole personal vision of life and of the world at large. His life did shape his art; his art cannot be judged apart from the life of the man.

The characters of his novels were earthbound, a fellow writer has said. They were afflicted by passions and guilt. They wander like tortured shadows through veiled scenes, twisted labyrinths, dimly lit cantinas, places in Mexico that are blurred with mist and color; they are haunted by love and sorrow, by memories and regrets, by longings to fulfill the great calling. He did not betray the great gift of art. At the end he succeeded as a writer and his works speak eloquently to this. He succeeded in making exquisite art out of his afflictions.

It is written that at the end, after several attempts, the borracho magnífico successfully cast off the two tyrannies of his life, booze and the pen. On the 27th of June, 1957, one month before his forty-eighth birthday, gin and sodium Amytal took his life. Death by misadventure, according to the doctor who pronounced the writer dead. No one, says his biographer, will ever know precisely what happened that night.

This we do know. He did not betray his calling as an artist.

# *Part Three*

It is the curse of a certain order of mind, that it can never rest satisfied with the consciousness of its ability to do a thing. Still less is it content with doing it. It must both know and show how it was done.

. . . . . . .

If any ambitious man have a fancy to revolutionize . . . the universal world of human thought . . . the opportunity is his. . . . All that he has to do is write and publish a very little book. Its title should be simple . . . *My Heart Laid Bare.* . . . But to write it— there is the rub. No man dare write it. . . . No man could write it, even if he dared. The paper would shrivel and blaze at every touch of the fiery pen.

Edgar Allan Poe, *Marginalia*

# I

Travel, you think, makes you aware of your solitary nature. You are watching the pen move across another little page. Notes. Thoughts of other countries, other places, other skies. Longings to love foreign women. Daydreaming about other loves. Inside an airplane, you think of being at the steering wheel of an automobile. You hear the humming of the heat-inflated steel-belted radial tires. Slight vibrations of the steering wheel. Other journeys converging on the present one. The sense of freedom is exhilarating the moment the plane is in the air; your thoughts run freely the moment the car is on the highway, with you in the driver's seat. Your mind journeys across years and centuries. You seek the anonymity of the stranger wherever you go, among crowds of people. The spectacle of the crowd excites and stimulates you. You find pleasure in being a stranger among strangers. Yes, you emerge now and then from the hermit's life of six or seven years to enjoy the anonymity of a stranger among strangers. Since childhood in Texas, when from your grandfather's garden you used to watch the tiny cars in the near distance going north and south on the old Hutto Highway, you were attracted by the mystery of unknown places. Your curiosity thrilled you, and you were invaded by a feverish longing to be anywhere except where you were, and as a grown man you were driven by an impulse to live where no one knew you and to move away when they did. In the course of your life you met and loved women who never got to know you well. When you travel you remove the mask, become who you really are, forget the false roles of real, everyday life, and on occasion you pretend among strangers to be any of several characters from your favorite novels. It is easier when you travel alone, among strangers, to be true to your nature. You can meet a woman and say truthfully that you are from out of town. You can pretend that you are visiting from New York or Chicago, where you have lived, and be truthful and honest about your exciting experiences in the Near North or Greenwich Village during the sixties. You can talk about the Art Institute or the Metropolitan. You can share memories of how the works of Auguste Rodin in the Metropolitan are associated with the loneliness of the stranger who comes to a big city, the need for companionship; and then you mention casually that you will be in town for a few days, perhaps a week. They look at your left hand and see no ring. Usually they do not ask if you are married. If they do, you answer truthfully. Only once, never again. If they pursue it, you lie. You learned. If a woman accepts the fact of your short visit, a beautiful ephemeral experience becomes possible. You invent a name and a character, a composite creation of your many selves. You become an actor, you talk about your dreams and listen attentively. This is the side of life that never loses its fascination for you. Two strangers, a man and a woman, discovering the eternal world together, sharing tenderness for a brief moment, until you say farewell. That was the kind of life for which you were born, like those people in the songs of Leonard Cohen, that move you to tears when you listen to them during the burning tapers of the night. Sometimes you imitate the character of your novel, insatiably seeking life and stories that strangers tell you.

You lift the pen away from the notepad to reflect on the difference between that life which you associate with the passion and liberty of the artist, and the other life of middle-class equanimity and quiet suburban neighborhoods like yours. They are alien to your nature, the middle-class ranch-style homes, water sprinklers turning on the front lawns, you and your neighbors washing cars in the driveway. Every so often jogging men and women pass by, making you wonder what they are thinking. Your friend Lew Pierce has shared his jogger's thoughts with you. Perhaps Lew will write the jogger's novel. You have more than enough material on him for a good chapter in your novel. You even have a fictional name for Lew. Walt Price. Because his father, named Walter, gave his son the cropped form of his name only, and never ceased to remind his son of that deliberate mutilation. Lew Pierce told you so.

This is the middle-class life which you dreaded long ago, thinking that it would destroy the artist in you. You wonder if it has. From time to time, however, you look around at what Natalie has made possible. How middle-class you have become. You do not cease to speculate about what your life would have been otherwise. The restless spirit is still in your nature, wild and tender by turns.

Which of the neighbors have you gotten to know well, only because of Natalie and the children? Not many. And the university. No matter how badly you try to put it out of your mind, you cannot help asking yourself if it should have a place in your novel. You feel duty-bound to convey something about what has happened to the American language and to education in this country. Neighbors, professors and the fewest of friends. You prefer the hermit's life, but now and then you allow friendly neighbors into your heart, like the air force family that used to live down the street, people from Indiana. A few years ago they invited you and Natalie, Sara and Becky, to little Steven's unforgettable first birthday party. Your mind's eye sees the party in cinematic images.

When you arrived with Natalie, Sara and Becky, the one-year-old had not taken his customary afternoon nap. He was rubbing his eyes. Many other parents and their children were already there. For you it has never been comfortable to be around children. You are frightened by tables and objects with sharp corners. Around children you measure unfailingly the distance between a part of their bodies, a cheek or the forehead, and the sharp corners, if they should trip or fall.

The adults clearly wanted to have a good time. They wanted the older kids to watch the infants and the smallest boys and girls. Friends of the parents were introduced to one another. In the family room countless toys were scattered for the children to play with. A few little disagreements are customary and occured among the little children.

—Hey, stop fighting.

An eighteen-month-old little girl, Amy, wanted to climb into the playpen.

—Here, let me help you, honey.

Then she wanted out. Later, again, in. After a while she tried to climb out again.

—Let's go into the living room and let the children fend for themselves, said David, the father of the birthday child. The adults need to do some talking and serious drinking, he added. In retrospect, you would imagine the scenes in a film. You walked through the living room towards the kitchen. The adults passed by the dining table. It was generously filled with plates and bowls of many kinds of food, a veritable feast! Roast beef, arranged rare to well, ham, spinach, meatballs and sausage in a crockpot, pickles, carrots, peppers, celery sticks, scallions, dips, potato chips, Fritos. Onion rolls, hamburger rolls, whole-wheat bread, rye, small rolls.

Little one-year-old Steven crawled under the table. Camera bulbs flashed.

—Look up, Steven. Hi, Steven! Atta boy! Flash! Play the toy piano.

The proud father's camera flashed. There was wine, beer, and champagne. A while later, the first two adults began to eat.

—I'm glad I haven't eaten all day.

—Me too.

A little boy and a little girl started fighting over a toy.

—All right! There isn't gonna be any fighting.

Some of the mothers were feeding their little children. The proud smiling father of the birthday child brought out white and rose champagne.

—Why don't you eat? the proud mother asked the guests.

—It takes too much to get drunk if you eat, the proud father answered.

After everyone had eaten, Steven cut his birthday cake, awkwardly. Janet, his mother, helped him hold the big knife. More flashing bulbs were followed by the birthday song.

Happy birthday . . . dear Steven . . . happy birthda-a-y-y to you. . . . You touched Janet on the shoulder and pointed slyly to a single big blue phallic candle on the cake.

—Miguel, you're awful! She laughed. You're the only one who noticed the candle, Janet said. It's just like you.

Your daughters were about to take more than one piece of cake.

—Sara, Becky, don't take too much. You told them they could have more later.

—Don't be a killjoy, Dad, Becky said. But a little later, Becky understood. You were right, Dad. I'm stuffed. I shouldn't have eaten so much.

There were pieces and crumbs of cake on the floor. Steven walked in it, sat down in it, ate it from the floor. He raised his grinning face up at the adults. More photographs were taken. The light bulbs flashed one after another.

—Smile, Steven!

The older children were looking after the little ones. The feasting and conversation continued, indoors and out. David opened up the jacuzzi. A few adults disappeared to put on their swimsuits. The children were playing, dangerously near the jacuzzi.

—Be careful, children, one of the mothers said.

How quickly the time passed, and people began to leave.

—Bye! Thanks for having us. It was a feast. Delicious!

—Bye! Marvelous party.

—We must go, too, Natalie said. Sara and Becky pleaded to stay. All right, children, you may stay. But just for a little while.

An hour or so later, Sara was running all the way home, screaming down the street, crying, terror on her face, tears streaming down her cheeks. She dashed into the house.

—Oh, Mom! Oh, Dad! Steven fell into the jacuzzi. He's all blue. I think he's dead. I went in to help Janet with the dishes and stuff. . . . Then . . . then I didn't see him. All the grownups were inside the house. . . . Nobody knew where he was! Where's Steven? I asked. I couldn't see him. Where's Steven? Nobody knew where he was. His dad pulled him out. I ran all the way home. I think he's dead!

Sara was crying uncontrollably. You ran all the way there immediately, in socks, without your glasses, unable to see well. Oh, God! What if he really drowned? Only an hour and a half ago Steven was grinning under the table, the cameras were flashing. You ran straight into David's house, through the living room, through the kitchen and family room. In the backyard by the jacuzzi, Janet was giving the blue child mouth-to-mouth resuscitation. David was standing next to her, helplessly.

—Please call the fire department.

The mother revived the infant. The wet child was in her arms. Dogs were licking the child's vomit, wagging their tails.

The child cried! The child cried!

—Don't blame each other. Please don't blame one another, you said. It looks like he will be all right. The one-year-old was blue. He blinked his eyes.

When the fire engines arrived the neighbors were lined up on the street, watching the firemen as they leaped from the trucks. The dogs began to bark at the firemen. At first the firemen were afraid of the dogs. They stayed in the front yard while the dogs were barking loudly and jumping about excitedly.

—What happened?

—The baby fell into the jacuzzi. His mother gave him mouth-to-mouth resuscitation. Come on. Move away, dogs. Behave!

Then the firemen ran into the house to take over. Dogs were everywhere, jumping and barking.

—Can't find the pulse, one of the firemen said. The baby began to cry. He seems all right, though. Take him to the emergency room of your hospital.

At one long stretch of straight highway, on the way to the air force base hospital, the speedometer was at ninety miles an hour. You were driving your magnificent 1973 General Motors gas-guzzler, once the pride, now the shame of American automobile technology.

—Don't go to sleep, Steven. The child was in his mother's arms. Wake up, Steven.

The mother slapped the child's face gently to keep him awake. She forgot that he had not taken his afternoon nap. You slapped his face a little more forcefully, brought your hand back to the steering wheel.

—That's it, cry. I'm afraid if he goes to sleep he won't wake up. At that moment crying was the most beautiful sound in the world. Steven was very sleepy. Only in retrospect will anyone remember that Steven did not take a nap before his party.

—He's fine, the Polynesian doctor said, in one of the emergency care rooms. In another emergency room an adolescent boy with a broken arm screamed. Steven's eyes opened widely. He's fine, the doctor repeated. Just a little shook up.

When they were about to leave a black man was brought into the emergency room by a white woman. His eyes were covered with a bloody bandage. From under the bandage blood was running down his face. His shirt was blood-spattered.

The next day you and Natalie went to visit the air force couple, and you sat outdoors, by the jacuzzi.

—Yesterday was like a nightmare, Janet said. Then we all woke up and Steven was all right.

—You both saved him, Janet, Natalie said. Dave pulled him out and you gave a mouth-to-mouth resucitation. It is a miracle that he is alive.

—I gave life to him twice, the mother said.

—Yes. You both acted quickly. Natalie and I hope you will not blame each other.

—Greg and I just came in for a minute to change, Dave said awkwardly. God! When I pulled him out . . . I thought it was over. . . . He was so purple. I pushed out the water, I knew enough to do that. . . . Then Janet began mouth-to-mouth. I was thinking, if we lost him, we'll just have to have another child. You gotta include this in your novel, Miguel.

For Sara, too, the experience was unforgettable.

—I'm gonna be a doctor, Mom, Sara said a week after the incident, so I can help babies, and moms and dads, so they will be careful. It happened so fast. Guy!

—Just remember, honey, that it is natural for human beings to remember things in a way that they not blame themselves. It's very understandable. What matters is that the baby is fine. You conducted yourself admirably and maturely. This was your first major crisis as a young adult. My baby, mi corazón, I am so proud of you. If you had not noticed he was missing, who knows?

—I saved his life, Dad.

Four years after Steven's first birthday party, you remember. *Yes, m'hijita. You saved a human life. Daddy is very proud.*

Earlier, Miguel was amusing himself with a story of an incident at another evening party at Giovanni Fortunato's house, to which he was not invited. Soothingly, the even droning of the airplane engine took his mind back to the story which Claude Sorel told him. *Oui, cher ami, Giovanni told me that you and Dimitri would be arriving soon. So, he did not invite you, I see.* He replaced the cap on his fountain pen, put it in his pocket, closed his little notepad and turned it over on the plastic tray. This time he took a large drink from his whiskey glass, held and savored it in his mouth. As he swallowed, he imagined the continuation of a scene from which his mind had strayed earlier.

Guillermo Carvajal approached the group of people who were talking about Miguel's novel. Impeccably dressed in a blue poplin summer suit, wearing a tie, hair neatly combed, he sucked in his stomach, strutted up to them like a peacock, and with a wide smile that displayed the teeth which gave him so much trouble and which caused him to miss so many departmental meetings, Guillermo greeted them all with the American word of which his many years in the United States had made him very fond.

—Hi! he said. Hi, everyone. Lovely party, isn't it?

He clicked his heels, stood at attention and bowed before the smiling group when he said it. Then the Latin American luminary kissed the ladies' hands, one after another, bowing gallantly. They had all returned the greeting except for Jerome Stone, who watched Guillermo going through his ceremonial performance with fascination. He waited so that he could get Guillermo's attention. Then Jerome spoke.

—Hello, Guillermo, hello. We were just talking about you and about Miguel's novel. You've read some juicy parts of Miguel's novel, I understand. Would you care to tell us, in your own words, about it?

—Juicy! he exclaimed with a scandalized expression on his face. Juicy, he repeated, is not the word, my friend. I cannot speak of it in mixed company. No, my friends, not in mixed company.

—We won't mind, Guillermo, said one of the women. Will we, girls?

The other women nodded their heads in agreement.

—Do tell us about Miguel's novel, another woman insisted.

He was pleased by their coaxing. He resisted playfully. They encouraged him further. They could tell by the mischievous look on his face that he was collecting his thoughts, carefully choosing words that would shock the ladies a little, organizing images and allusions to embellish the story they wanted to hear.

—Very well, but remember that I did not wish to speak of those "juicy" things in mixed company.

Some of the people among the group moved to form a circle around Guillermo, who relished the opportunity to tell them an embellished story. He was the center of attention.

From where he stood Jerome Stone could see Claude Sorel, who was just arriving.

The visiting French novelist arrived at the party in his honor with Kenneth MacMillan, the Rimbaud specialist. Ken opened the door and they walked through the great glass door to the large, plush backyard patio. Claude Sorel smiled at people that he recognized and waved to them in a friendly way. He looked toward the largest crowd, standing by the table which was generously filled with hors d'oeuvres. Other people were standing in small groups on the grass. Among them was the group which Guillermo now held as a captive audience.

From where he stood the French novelist commanded a view of the whole scene. He's probably looking for his friends, Jerome surmised, as he waited for Guillermo to begin. But among the guests Claude Sorel did not see the Chicano, or the soft-spoken, kind gentleman from eastern Europe. He did not see the tall young man either—what was the name of the flame-haired Marxist who made him think of Martin Luther nailing his theses to a church door in Wittenberg, in 1517?

At last the chairman saw the French novelist.

—Please excuse me, he said, to a small crowd of people with whom he was speaking. Our guest of honor has arrived.

In a moment he was greeting the guest of honor.

—Ah, vous êtes arrivé, Claude. Quel plaisir! Quel plaisir! Venez, venez. Je crois que vous connaissez presque tout le monde.

The chairman shook the French novelist's hand vigorously and kept chattering and chattering, in French, politely, saying, "et vous connaissez Madame... Mademoiselle... et Monsieur," and others he introduced, referring to them by their first and last names, while the French novelist seemed still to be searching for his two friends.

—Et le Chicano? he asked. And he inquired also about Dimitri, to whom Claude referred affectionately as the "gentleman from eastern Europe."

—A bientôt, à bientôt, Claude. The chairman, who had not invited them, lied.

A short distance away, Guillermo did not want to disappoint his captive audience. There was interest and curiosity about Miguel's novel, but Guillermo was the only one to whom he had read some pages. Miguel read quite a few pages, in fact, about his aging parents in Texas, about his grandfather who fought in the Mexican Revolution, about his experiences in Chicago and New York, about his travels, and about his daughters, Sara and Becky. To Guillermo, Miguel's project was excessive, and he cautioned him repeatedly, but the younger man could not follow reasonable advice. But what stood out in Guillermo's mind was a single page that Miguel once read to him, which described a return trip to Mexico City from Cuernavaca where Miguel's character had spent the day with his beautiful neighbor, Aurelia.

—I never thought, Guillermo lied, that I would ever tell in mixed company about the juicy parts of Miguel's novel. But . . . if that novel ever gets published it will be the most indecent and pornographic novel of the twentieth century. Miguel has read passages to me that are absolutely dripping with the juices of the body. That is not art, I told him. Mi joven compañero, ilustre poeta, I said, that is nothing but sheer pornography. Don't you know, my friend, I told him, that the great writers never take the reader into the bedroom? They never describe all the gory details. The great writers leave something, even all of it, to the imagination of the reader. But no, not Miguel. He takes you right between the woman's legs, like a camera in a pornographic film, or so I hear, because I have never seen such films, and he shows you everything. Everything! He leaves nothing to the imagination! He is, as the Mexicans say, cachondísimo! What? What does it mean, the word? Ah, well, ah . . . it means . . . someone who . . . is known for an excess of sexual passion. Yes, yes. In English, that's it. Horny.

They were all laughing at Guillermo, who was rolling his eyes and talking wildly with his hands.

Guillermo's account had an amusing consequence. Many people at Ríoseco University were eagerly waiting for Miguel to finish and to publish his novel. Guillermo, intentionally or not, became Miguel's best press agent for a novel that sounded better and better as the accounts of it became more varied and embellished. The rumored novel, if it were to be written, would far surpass anything that Miguel was capable of writing.

—I don't understand. If that's so, Edith Steinmann mused aloud, . . . how can the novel be about an older man who can't, you know, and with a twenty-two-year-old girl? Is Miguel pulling our leg? I wonder.

# II

At an evening dinner party given by Preston and Martha Goldstein, a small group of people gathered around Miguel and Natalie. They laughed and giggled when one of them asked Natalie about what Miguel was writing, and if it had any sex. Natalie did not know what to say. She and Miguel were smiling and pleased by the attention.

—Go ahead, Natalie, tell them. It's okay, honey. Tell them about the time we agreed to meet in that East Side bar. You remember.

Natalie was not sure about what to say, so Miguel helped her along by starting the story.

—One time, when Natalie and I lived in New York, we decided to meet at a bar on the East Side. We agreed in advance to pretend that we didn't know one another . . .

—I remember now, Natalie said. Afterwards we laughed so much.

—She arrived after me, Miguel said. She walked into the smoke-filled, crowded bar and she pretended not to know me.

—I walked in and pretended I was looking for a friend. Miguel was sitting in the middle of the bar next to other tables where several men and some couples were sitting.

—I deliberately picked a good spot, he said. And when she walked in several men turned to look in her direction. Well, she was alone, and this good-looking woman was only twenty-three then.

—When I came near Miguel's table he said hi to me. I looked at him and smiled, and I also said hi. Then he asked me if I was looking for sex.

—You should have seen the look on the men's faces when I said that. They were sitting at the table next to mine. They

200

looked at her with wide-eyed disbelief, wondering how she was going to react, I guess. And then they looked at each other, and at her.

—I told Miguel I was looking for a girlfriend, but, I told him. . . . It was so funny, and I managed to keep a straight face, but, I said . . . sex sounds good to me.

—Natalie then asked me what my name was. I told her, and she told me her name. Actually, we exchanged names, fictional ones just for the hell of it. I invited her to have a drink with me.

—I said, no thank you, I'd rather have sex first. We can always have a drink afterwards. If you like, we can go to my apartment. It's not too far from here.

—Splendid, I said. So I got up, and we left the bar together. As we were leaving I took a look at the people who were watching and listening to us, and I winked. I heard one of them exclaim, do you believe that? And another guy said, did that really happen? I can't believe it! When we got out into the street Natalie and I laughed and laughed. We had so much fun in those early days.

—We used to do some crazy things in those days, Natalie said.

The guests at the Goldsteins' party were laughing at the story. Preston Goldstein put his arm around Miguel and gave his neck a friendly, fraternal squeeze.

—And is that in your novel, too, Miguel? he asked.

—Not yet, Miguel answered, but now it will be.

—Did it really happen?

—Yes. No. Maybe.

They all laughed, but they would never know.

—The novel's also about the university, Preston said to the guests. Maybe it'll even be about what it's like for a nice Jewish girl to be married to a Chicano. Not easy, I suppose, Preston started to say, smiling.

—Yes, and we're in it, Martha Goldstein beamed in. He goes around taping conversations with people to include them in his novel. Including us, she added with a smile.

—What are these conversations about? asks one of their guests.

—University life in general, I guess. He's probably gonna include how he and I have been mistaken for each other . . .

—He borrowed our tape of Shawna's bat mizvah the other day when he and Natalie came to see us. Preston and I were telling them about my recent medical treatment . . .

—When Miguel came to Ríoseco, one of the ladies at the library used to call him Dr. Goldstein! And I was . . .

—We told him, Martha interrupted, how we checked out all sorts of medical books and articles, and we even showed him two of the books we read and we gave him two articles, too. Right, Pres?

—That's right. And as I was saying, several years ago I stopped at the Texaco station on Bailey Street, over by Hawkins Drive, behind the University, and the station manager said to me. Dr. Velásquez, what are you doing here again? You just filled up this morning. I knew then that there was a man on this campus who was my double, and a Chicano, at that.

—It's true, come to think of it, you do resemble each other.

—Yeah. A Jew and a Chicano. How about that?

—What is it like, Natalie, being married to a Chicano?

The anguish of wanting to write a novel compounded the dilemmas which tormented him regularly. Writing obsessed and possessed him.

Since his years in New York, the notebooks had proliferated. After New York, three years of graduate work took away irrecoverable time from his wife and children. Later came the appointment at Ríoseco University, where he had to design courses no one had ever taught him, followed by three summers to write the dissertation and by years of pressure to publish that led up to the tenure evaluation. During these several years his artist's spirit rebelled against the inertia of passionless routine. He was a creature of the night. The spectacle of life was essential to the artist. He was drawn to large crowds, strangers, the night life he had known before marriage. Usually he was content to be an anonymous observer, a witness. Slowly, he changed, became more a hermit.

Natalie changed also. At first, whenever he was going out at night there would be terrible scenes. They would quarrel and he would storm out of the house. She could not understand his temperamental moods. She used to ask if he was having affairs. But over the years she began to understand. It was sad to see him staring out of the window or lost in thought, pacing restlessly about. He was like a caged animal whose instinct is to run wild. Then she would say that perhaps he needed a night out. Maybe you need a mistress, she would tease. Eventually she stopped asking where he had been the night before, or whom he saw. Irrevocable patterns of married life began to congeal.

He kept notebooks. The years passed, the notebooks proliferated, but there was never a novel. Writing, he learned, is a lonely, solitary activity. No one could encourage or discourage him. At times he was anguished by self-doubts. What if it should turn out to be the greatest mistake of my life? Self-doubts were attended by guilt about not being a good husband or a good father. Had he fulfilled his own prediction? He was a solitary even in his own home.

—Daddy! Why are you always working at your desk?

—Come on, Dad. . . . Please play a little game with us.

—You never do anything with us, Miguel.

Countless memories from the past, from places he had known and visited, assaulted his thoughts. People whose images and voices haunted him clamored for places in his novel. In his imagination, he relived many journeys and travels. When he walked, his body, his legs, his feet remembered. The hard concrete beneath his feet evoked the streets of Mexico City, Chicago, New York, Paris, Madrid, Amsterdam, Austin, Texas, and many other cities. He could not get his brother's funeral, his mother and father, his grandfather or the Mexican Cemetery in Pflugerville out of his mind. He had all the characters, the themes, the settings and scenes for a novel. They invaded his thoughts almost all the time. At dinnertime especially, he would sit with Natalie and Sara and Becky at the table, lost in his own thoughts. Unexpectedly, one of them would talk to him or ask something, and he would realize that her lips were moving, but he did not hear what she was saying.

One of many incidents grieved him with particular force. Becky was five years old. It occurred during a period of time when he was always tired. He was working on his dissertation at the time, spending long hours in the library. The scholarly work in itself was a pleasure. It brought him knowledge on which he would continue to build as a scholar. But he could not suspend his inquisitive nature. The search for knowledge that had nothing to do with the dissertation led him joyously to new discoveries and expanded his learning. Much of that knowledge was not pertinent to scholarly research expected of him at Ríoseco University. He was also writing in his notebooks all the time. To relax, he would come home and fix himself a drink or two. The drinking compounded the exhaustion.

At first Natalie and the children used to greet him at the door, with hugs and kisses, wanting lovingly to tell him about their day, to hear how his day had gone. He was tired and grumpy.

—Please wait until after I have a drink, he would grumble.

One day, after working for several hours at the library, he came home terribly exhausted. By then they no longer greeted him cheerfully at the door. He fixed himself a good stiff whiskey and went out onto the patio. He took the newspaper with him and his pocket notebook. It was one of those exquisitely long spring days, close to summer, when the sun stays high in the sky until late in the day, when the sky is majestic and the varied greens of the plants and the leaves of trees are beautifully crisp and speckled with sunlight. On days like this he had known immense loneliness in the past. Something was troubling his thoughts that day. He had to get it out in writing. Wearily he sat down at the picnic table, took a good stiff drink, and began to write.

I am sitting outdoors on the patio. So very tired after a long day at the library. Right now I have doubts about today's work, about the value of everything connected with scholarship and literature. I am completely exhausted and utterly depressed by printed words, by endless pages xeroxed from countless journals and periodicals and books; by words of articles which I have been ripping out for years from newspapers and magazines to which I subscribe—all of it, accumulating year after year—words, words, words, which I will probably never look at again, which are supposed to help me develop the background of a novel I will never write, articles I will never go back to. My own words proliferating in worthless notebooks; typed on hundreds of sheets of paper, on five-by-eight cards; written in little pocket notebooks, in large black-bound notebooks; and articles started and abandoned; and the unmanageable novel. Oh! The exhaustion with words!

Damn this newspaper on my lap. I don't want to read another word. Enough of words! And yet I am writing. Why don't I put this fucking pen down? I am sick and tired of reading and rereading my own words until the letters start to dance before my eyes and lose their meaning.

I wish I could relax, enjoy the trees in this backyard, the branches that meet and the patterns they form where they interlock. I just want to enjoy the beautiful shape of a single leaf, from a tree or a split-leaf plant, the beautiful colors of the plants. One of them has light green leaves speckled with yellow. There is something serene about this backyard scene that is inaccessible to my spirit. The different kinds of ivy on the ground and covering the redwood fence, the varied plants in pots, the sky and the shadows made by trees and bushes on a concrete wall create a mood of tranquility that I am unable to enjoy. I want my heart to be enchanted by the miracle of a leaf that has recently emerged, folded and intact, from the stem of its predecessor on a great split-leaf plant. It is beginning to unfold. A new frail-green leaf.

Just as I was finishing the preceding sentence, little Becky came and stood next to me. Sweet, five-year-old Becky. I am weary, tired. Becky was saying something, but I did not listen. Her voice was soft and sweet.

—Dad . . . Dad . . .

M'hijita, so lovely, so polite. I paused and looked up from what I was writing. I will never forget her child's voice.

—Can you play a little game with me, Dad? Please please, Dad . . .

Wearily I responded.

—I am tired, my honey. Hijita preciosa, mi vida. Weary of words, I thought. I did not stop writing while she was standing here. I spoke, but my attention was divided, talking and writing. Tired of words and yet writing!

—I am very tired, my honey. Can't you see that Daddy is busy writing, my little sweetheart, mi corazón? Please leave me alone, honey . . . and I might have added, with these stupid words that will never bring back the precious, lost moments we could have shared. Oh, my baby!

Becky always understands when she sees me writing. She hesitates to interrupt me. I have told her that I am a writer.

I will never forget this incident, the heart-rending image of my little baby, mi corazoncito, or my immense grief. Slowly, very disappointed, my little Becky turned and began to walk away. At that very moment a bird began to sing cheerfully in the neighbor's backyard, in one of the trees, and I looked up from my pocket notebook. My little girl was skipping cheerfully away, full of love and understanding for her father, as usual. I broke down and wept like a child.

Years later, she may not remember this disappointment out of countless others, but this image of my little five-year-old daughter turning and disappearing through the garage door will weigh heavily on my heart forever. Oh, my baby! ¡Hijita preciosa!

There are many things for which Miguel cannot forgive himself. He could not be like other men. Was his family always to suffer? He was most severe with himself when he judged his actions and life by the norms of other men. On the way to Oakland Airport, he remembers the remorse of that day.

My baby, hijita preciosa. Why didn't I take you in my arms that day? Why didn't I play a little game with you? You will never be five years old again. One day I will wake up and your precious childhood will have passed. If the bad dreams were interpreted, they would surely say Miguel has lost his daughters' childhood. Shame! While he was writing away his life he let their childhood slip away. His writing comes at a terrible price.

One night when he was putting the children to bed, his older daughter, Sara, began to cry. She was seven years old.

—Daddy! Daddy! You're getting old! Your beard is getting white.... You're going to be a grandfather before I grow up.... Oh, Daddy! I don't want to grow old! I'm afraid to die! Daddy! Daddy! Give me magic so I won't grow up and be old!

They are real, the fears of childhood. What can a father say? How can he respond to his child's fear of death? How to comfort her? Then he realized that Sara had already supplied him with the answer. All she wanted was magic. Magic to stay a child, to keep from growing up, to keep her from old age and dying. Her fears inspired a fatherly imagination and gentleness. He held her as he always held her since she was born. Sara always calmed down in her father's arms. Miguel spoke in a gentle, comforting way.

—Yes, m'hijita, mi corazón. I will give you magic. Here, I will put it under your pillow. But this magic can only be used by a fifteen-year-old. When you're fifteen, you can use the magic, and if you still want to be a baby then, the magic will work. Now go to sleep, my precious baby, hermosa.

Her cheeks were wet and salty. That night Miguel was deeply touched by his daughter's belief in magic. The lie worked. He held Sara in his arms, kissed her gently and said goodnight. She was relaxed. Then he went over to Becky's bed, held her and kissed her, too. They were both sleepy.

—Buenas noches, mis hijas preciosas. Hasta mañana, he said. He turned out the light and walked out of their bedroom.

Oh, my children, you are mirrors, he often thought, and I do not like the image of myself reflected there. I cannot help how I am. Natalie, too, is a mirror. *We hardly make love anymore, Miguel. Are you having an affair?* Obsessed with school work, with the novel, he was irritable and quarrelsome. He wanted to be alone. He drank to relax. The drinking made him more irritable and quarrelsome. How can people make love after a quarrel? And the tenure process? How can a man make love when he dreads the possibility that he will not be able to support his family?

A passenger two or three rows behind Miguel laughed loudly, and his laughter scattered the memories of many years.

# III

ABOARD THE AIRPLANE, he completely lost track of the time. Before long the plane would be arriving at Oakland Airport. . . . *How's your novel coming along? . . . When are you gonna finish it? . . . Am I in your novel, Miguel?* The word that colleagues used against one another echoed in his mind. Should he have been a productive scholar instead? *There's a lotta deadwood in this department. Some colleagues haven't published an article since they got tenure. . . .* Giovanni Fortunato waved his arms wildly and turned up his visigothic green eyes in despair. *Hell!* he exclaimed, *this is not a department of deadwood. It's nothing more, nothing less than a petrified forest!*

Miguel could see the spoken words arranging themselves on paper; he could hear them in voice-over coming together into clusters of thoughts and ideas, obeying the logic of consciousness and involuntary memory. The voices of people from his life, past and present, were clamouring for a place in his novel. The people wanted to be characters. He imagined the words and phrases becoming sentences and paragraphs and chapters. But he could not get beyond the notebooks to bring his project to completion. Nevertheless, he continued to make plans for future books, outlines of chapters, inventories of ideas and thoughts, character sketches, notes, without knowing where to begin. He had still to find a name for his fictional character. Unsummoned, the voices came, and with them came the memories and experiences of a lifetime, changing their configurations, rearranging themselves from year to year, inexplicably, because after all they were the same memories and images repeating themselves, yet changing, perhaps because he was not one man but many, a different man each year. Was Guillermo right, that what he wanted to do was impossible for

one man? Were the notebooks to tell the life story of a failure?
Did he betray his calling?

His attention turned to his own constant complaining that
busywork robbed him of creative energy. He was tired of la-
menting that too many demands on his waning energies pre-
vented him from carrying out his true work as an artist.

Notebook entry, April 20. Too many tasks at once: a manila
folder full of unanswered correspondence, letters of recom-
mendation for students, committee meetings, preparations for
classes, meetings with graduate students, abandoned research
articles, reading and editing and planning memoranda, er-
rands, family obligations, reminders that fill the calendar, un-
used tape recordings of conversations. Impossible to fit them
into the busy daily schedule that spills over into the weekends.

Other things drain me emotionally. Hypocritical people at
the university, enmity among colleagues, dissimulation and hy-
pocrisy, refined and polite malice, the mentality of crooked
used car salesmen and politicians. In their minds the university
is a place of business, a political arena in which power struggles
take place, not an institution of higher learning. Publish or
perish means plagiarize your own works. Change the title of
your article, publish it five times with different titles. Change
them around on your word processor. No one will know. Go to
conferences, outline the talks that others give, combine them,
make one or two articles, publish them first. Ron Artmann
warned me. *The academy is very different when you see it from the
inside, amigo . . . be gentle as you go along . . . don't become like
them. . . .* I cannot help it. My great capacity for hatred grieves
me. I want them to know. They can tell when I look at them.
They can tell when I do not. They can tell when I do not greet
them. They no longer extend their hands for a handshake. My
looks express contempt. *A veces se levantaba Papá . . . muy eno-
jado . . . quién sabe por qué . . . y se bajaba el sombrero sobre los ojos y
no le daba los ojos a nadie. . . .* I am a man of rage. I avoid peo-
ple who bring out in me a despicable capacity for hatred. I
mutter obscenities under my breath. I turn into a vile animal. I
snarl.

Today I wrote a few pages in a rage. They are about a fat Chi-
cano who looks like a tadpole. Fat Dan Vásquez derives per-
verse pleasure from not flushing the toilet after he finishes his

business. In years no one has enraged me like he has, and even though those pages could set Chicano literature back several years, I shall probably include them in my novel. I wish I could use his real name. One day I will tell the fat son of a bitch to his face that he is the biggest asshole I have met in my entire life. As I make this notebook entry his fictional name becomes clear. I will call him Cacarizo Tepocate.

April 26. During the last two months I had many dreams, but I lacked the energy to write them down. Impossible to keep up with them all. Then, after many lost dreams, there were none for what seemed an unbearably long time. The absence of dreams made my heart sink all the past week. It was dreadful not to dream, especially when my control over the dreaming had risen remarkably, to the point that I could will the dreams to come, return and continue, even if I awakened, when I went back to sleep.

The lucidity of my dreams was extraordinary. I knew that I was dreaming, in my dreams! I became acutely conscious of writing the very dreams I was having. In some dreams I awakened while I was dreaming, to write them down. When I really woke up I was disappointed. The writing had been only a part of the dream. In countless dreams, I dreamed that I woke up, aware while I was dreaming that I was not awake, rehearsing the events of dreams within dreams to help me remember them when I really awakened.

My dreaming mind moved beyond mental rehearsals of the dreams. It has taken over writing parts of the novel while I sleep. My mind compresses dreams into written outlines and abbreviated notes. These amazing notes outline and enumerate, clearly and succinctly, the images, settings, events, characters, voices and dialogues of my dreams within dreams. My dreaming mind taps powers which I do not consciously have, to organize and recall. The notes enable me to write the dreams down, after I awaken, as if I had actually written them down. While I am dreaming I am lucidly conscious of mind powers. At first, it was disappointing to wake up and not find the notes on the night stand, as I had dreamed they would be. My ability to remember the dreamed outlines and notes was rapidly improving, making it possible to recall entire dreams in detail.

In a striking, almost miraculous way, the dreams offer other versions of chapters which I have written during my waking hours. These dream narratives are structured by the unconscious mind. They are artistically organized and esthetically pleasing. A while back I began to study my dreams as I study films and works of literature, novels, plays and poems. The dreams sharpened my understanding of many novels and films.

Many dreams reflect my interest in film. Images of pages of my manuscript, in my own handwriting or typed, appear on a picture screen, in close-up shots, with my left hand holding down a page, the right hand making corrections, crossing out words, substituting others, making additions in the margins and between the double-spaced lines. In dreams, close-up shots of my own typed material are edited and corrected. The type is recognizably that of my typewriter. The pages contain words and lengthy phrases inserted between the lines and on the margins, in my unmistakable handwriting, to be added into the text. Upside-down bows above lines and symbols to insert between words instruct an imaginary typist who will retype the manuscript where words and phrases are to be added. Some pages are marked with changes to make the predicate consistent with a plural or a singular subject, others to establish parallel structure in a sentence. There is a noticeable absence of contractions; the manuscript pages imply an old-fashioned respect for auxiliary verbs.

These increasingly numerous dreams are about what I do every day: write, read, edit, correct, delete, rewrite, compress, insert, reread, rewrite. On and on, hours and hours a day. The dreams are mirrors of my daily waking life. They reflect my obsession with writing, my fanatic veneration for correct English grammar as it used to be taught in American schools long ago.

Dreams have given me the power to suspend myself in a state between waking and sleeping, so that my mind remains conscious of being awake and dreaming, simultaneously. In bed I close my eyes without falling asleep and will myself to dream; I remain awake, dreaming simultaneously, wakefully watching myself dreaming. The dreams are teaching me something about writing. Watching myself dreaming that I am dreaming. Another occupation and method from which to learn how to write.

The temporary absence of dreams bordered on unbearable anguish like that produced by the overwhelming lethargy that used to render me incapable of writing from time to time. After countless dreamless nights, and many more since I wrote my dreams down, finally, two nights ago, the dreams began again. Two nights in a row I wandered through strange landscapes, dazzled by uncommon scenes that changed frequently and unexpectedly, puzzled by mysterious, indecipherable events. It became my regular custom to keep a notebook and pen on the night stand by the bed.

I am standing in the long, dimly-lit hallway of the wooden barracks once used by soldiers during World War II, and which later housed the art department at the university where I studied as an undergraduate. Paintings in many post-World War II styles hang on the walls. Abstract, non-objective and abstract expressionist paintings on huge canvases overshadow smaller, modest surrealist works and drawings done from the model. Even though my brother is nowhere to be seen I sense his presence. Just a moment ago he was here.

Gregory Chan, one of my best students, surprised me when he tapped me on the shoulder. He telephoned me the night before, to thank me for a letter of recommendation which I wrote in support of his application for a University fellowship. He said that he did not receive that particular fellowship, but he was eligible for another fellowship, which he did receive in the amount of five hundred dollars. I congratulated him.

In the dimly-lit hallway we spoke about his progress in school. Gregory told me that he came from out of town to take a midterm examination on the following morning. I invited him to dinner with my family.

—My wife will be preparing lasagna this evening. Would you care to join us?

—All right! he responded, in that singsong fashion that has become popular among young people in recent years.

Remembering that I had spent the night with friends less than a week ago I thought of inviting him to spend the night, but I hesitated. Perhaps my wife had other plans. So I said nothing about staying over. Besides, Lew Pierce would be staying with us for several days. He would arrive in two weeks.

Then the scene changed to my childhood neighborhood. At home, through the front screen door, Gregory and I saw my father arrive, from work perhaps. My father, an octogenarian, was walking very strangely. Slowly, he moved from left to right across the dirt front yard. He was wearing an old, shabby, dark suit, almost black. Because Gregory introduced me to his father at the end of last spring I was pleased by the opportunity to have him meet my father, whom I love very dearly.

—Come, Gregory. I would like for you to meet my father.

—All right! he exclaimed, again in his typical way.

I pushed the screen door open and Gregory followed me out. We stood on the small wooden porch for a moment. Then we walked down the three small steps. Walking toward my father I felt a great longing to embrace him. We always embrace. But his slow, strange walk and the dazed, sleepy-eyed look on his face disturbed me, because my father is strong and energetic despite his years. He seemed small and helpless, in a way that I had never seen him. I embraced him, and the old man's strong, hard body impressed me. My father is always demonstratively affectionate. It puzzled me that he did not return my embrace, or speak. His strong arms remained rigid and pressed against his body.

He seemed to be in a trance. I stopped hugging him and moved slightly away from him to look at his face. His lips were puckered. They extended far out and almost formed a bird's beak. He was beginning to look like a bird. It worried me that my father was imitating the bird again!

Over my father's right shoulder, about eight or ten feet away, the huge bird that my father was imitating appeared. My father's puckered lips made him resemble the bird and his shabby black suit made my father look like a penguin, too.

The enormous bird had a white body and dark wings. No doubt, I thought, it is one of those sea birds called an albatross, the winged voyager of which a great French poet has said, *comme il est gauche et veule!* . . . *naguère si beau, qu'il est comique et laid!* Prince of the clouds, the poet called the awkward, clumsy, comic and ugly albatross.

The ungainly bird seemed to be threatening my father. Inexplicably I was afraid that the bird was going to take possession of his body.

Then, right in front of my eyes a transformation began to take place. The clumsy albatross slowly became lovely and graceful. The curve of the line that went from below the beak to the breast took on a delicate and graceful quality. The swelling white softness of the round white breast awakened desire in me for the soft breasts and belly of a beautiful woman.

Without knowing why, I was nevertheless alarmed for my father. The bird had to be killed. I walked toward the large beautiful albatross, grabbed the neck with one hand, and with the other I seized one of the huge wings. My intention was to raise the albatross high in the air and to smash its head over and over against the concrete, as I once saw a Greek fisherman smashing a baby octopus on concrete, at a small village on the Corinthian Gulf. But when I tried to raise it into the air it resisted. Its incredible strength and weight were too much for me. The bird's left wing, which was free, began to open and shut. The wingspread of the huge bird had to be more than ten feet. Surprisingly, the enormous bird never attacked me. The bird simply resisted me and tried to free itself from my grip.

Once as we struggled I placed my weight on the albatross in a way that brought its head and the beak to rest upon the concrete. I was wearing boots with thick leather heels. Here was my opportunity to smash the beak against the concrete with the heel of my boot. It was a cold-blooded thought. I shifted the weight of my body to the left leg and raised my right leg to bring the heel of my boot down on the beak. But the bird quickly arched up its lovely, swanlike neck and moved its head away from the concrete floor.

In imagination, however, the brutal act of violence was committed. My boot smashed and shattered the bird's beak. Something had snapped in my brain. Jagged fragments of the broken beak scattered across the concrete. A horrible rage had set my brain afire.

Coming so close to breaking the great bird's beak caused me extreme mental suffering. I must avoid people who bring out this horrible hatred and rage. Relieved not to have shattered the bird's beak, I was terrified nevertheless.

Despite pangs of remorse I was still trying to kill the huge bird, struggling with it near the edge of a cliff that dropped precipitously over huge rocks and boulders and down into the sea. Still, the albatross did not attack me. It resisted peacefully all my efforts to kill it. Nor did the bird try to get away, even now as I held it above my head at the edge of the precipice. No living being could survive the great fall down over the jagged rocks and boulders and into the sea. But what about the albatross? If I hurled it down over the edge of the cliff the huge bird would drop a few feet and fly away to safety. Why hurl it, then? I held on to it.

Without warning the scene changed to a huge concrete dam. The transformation of the albatross was complete. A huge, strikingly beautiful woman was suspended in the air, between two thick steel bars of a safety rail, and I was pressing hard against her shoulders, near the neck, trying to push her over the edge of the concrete dam into an infinite space of nothingness. With powerful strength the beautiful woman resisted and rose against the pressure of my arms to push her down. Finally, her superhuman powers overcame my strength and she was free.

The beautiful woman slowly arched her back. Her great, lovely wings unfolded and spread out in front of my dazzled eyes. She rose high above me, triumphantly, majestically, like the Christ figure on the cross in a painting by Salvador Dalí. She was of a radiant beauty before which I stood in awe and admiration. Her huge outspread wings were of an extraordinary loveliness. Behind her, as she was rising, getting smaller and smaller, only the immensity of the sky. Whoever she might be, whatever she represented, she triumphed over me. Some hidden sense led me to a conviction that she was the most infinitely gentle creature in the world.

Then she spoke for the first time in a haunting, chantlike voice. It came from far away, from another world perhaps, another planet, or from another life. *I am the symbol of life that has no beginning or end; life that must fulfill its own destiny; life that is fated and will be; life that wills its own continuation; life over which there can be no earthly domination.*

I woke up in a theatre. I had fallen asleep when Gregory and I were watching a film that I directed and in which I was one of the principal actors. In fact, I played the main male role.

—She was much stronger than you all through the story, Gregory said, without even fighting back or attacking you. This perspective is all wrong, Gregory added. Women shouldn't be depicted being stronger than men.

What he said bothered me. I cannot say why, but Gregory made me feel defensive. I remembered that just a few days earlier I wrote in one of my pocket notebooks that when a man lets his wife control the checkbook, he relinquishes control over everything in his life. With this thought in mind I responded to Gregory defensively, hoping that I could persuade him to see things in a different light.

215

—Maybe you feel that this perspective is wrong, Gregory, because in our society we are accustomed to male perspectives, in which we men appear dominant. We are not accustomed to seeing things from the perspective of women. Some men are quite vulnerable and gentle, like women.

—Yeah! Yeah. I see, Gregory replied. All right! he added emphatically.

She tossed and turned in bed in a state between sleeping and waking. Her husband next to her was sleeping soundly. She had been awakened by the ruffled scratching sound which the ball-point pen made when he got up in the middle of the night to write down his dreams. She was sleepy. At least he did not turn on the light. That was thoughtful. Again the squeaky pen was scratching on the little notepad that he kept on the night stand. He is asleep, she thought drowsily. I must be dreaming that he is writing.

The next morning she wondered if she had been awake or if she dreamed that she heard her husband writing down his dreams. Or was I just a part of his dream?

The majestic winged woman. What does she symbolize in this dream? Life? What is the meaning of the dream? Is the woman a symbol of art? Of human kindness and love? What does her statement mean? Does it refer to some kind of resemblance? A kinship among human beings or among artists? Blood relationships? How does life fulfill its own destiny? By dying, followed by nothingness? Or followed by a moment of rest upon the wind, as the gentle Lebanese poet said, and then by birth and life again, in the womb of another woman? I do not know.

The majestic woman's statement was remarkably similar to something my father said. Can it have a bearing on this dream? He impressed me one day when we were talking about family resemblances and heredity. He was full of memories about his father that day, and despite being in his eighties he still speaks of abuelo Miguel with the love and veneration of the child he used to be. The beauty of my father's words and his wisdom moved me deeply. Perhaps I will never be able to translate his words appropriately into English. English, in this case, can only approximate what my father said in Spanish.

—Sí, hijo, my father said, ¡la sangre hace su deber!

216

When I translate my father's words something delicate and inexpressible is lost. It requires the entire statement of the majestic woman to translate my father's single statement. Blood obeys its own will? Carries out or fulfills its own destiny? Was the dream establishing a connection between blood and art, suggesting a mystical genetic inheritance?

Is my impulse to write an inheritance of the blood? Perhaps there was something of this to the albatross dream. I may never know, but this I do know. I have pondered my father's words many times and my remarkable resemblance to my grandfather. I am struck by the marvels of heredity that bring about in successive generations the same configurations of genetically inherited characteristics and that make doubles of parents and their offspring, and of grandfathers and grandsons. I know, too, that he wanted to be a writer, and that my father has also wanted to write a book about his life.

One day my father told me that after my grandfather learned to read he began to question all philosophical ideas and religious dogma. This too raises unanswerable questions. He became like a man gone crazy, my father said. He read too much. *Sí, hijo, es peligroso leer tanto. Uno se puede volver loco.*

# IV

A FEW DAYS AFTER THE DREAM Miguel Velásquez visited his friend Guillermo Carvajal. The older man was a little sad because he had just returned from taking his son, a junior in high school, to the bus station.

—It made me sad, Miguel, to see him go off to spend the summer with his mother in San Diego. Next year, when school starts, he'll come back to live with me. He's graduating next year, you know. Children grow up so fast. Well, you are learning that now, ¿verdad?

—Yes, Guillermo, and you are a good man for feeling sad. Sadness makes us aware of our deep feelings and that is good. But let me change the subject. Perhaps it will cheer you up, for the moment. In any case you will miss your son, no doubt about it. Why, all you have to do is walk into his room and you will find something that reminds you of him. Or in the kitchen, if he did the dishes or dried them, just the way he stacked them or the way he left the towel on the rack. Perhaps some things annoyed you while he was living with you, but they bring him to mind.

—You are right, mi amigo. The bathroom, for example, was always a mess. But tell me, how are you going to change the subject?

—I want to tell you about two dreams that I had recently. One is about a huge albatross that turns into a magnificent woman, and the other is about a horse whose nose is broken by a speeding train. Let me know what you think.

—Very well, but how's your whiskey?

—Todavía está bien, ilustre.

—All right, then, mine is okay, too. Now, tell me.

218

Guillermo listened attentively, without interrupting Miguel. Gradually, he became less sad and even began to smile over some of the details of Miguel's dreams. Guillermo sipped from his whiskey and stared at the ceiling as if to see the scenes Miguel was describing.

—Well, Guillermo, Miguel asked when he finished telling them, what do you think of these dreams?

—The majestic woman is probably your wife, ilustre, Guillermo responded almost abruptly. Yes, she could very well be. The majestic woman symbolizes goodness, which you and I know is a dominant trait of your wife. She is la esposa perfecta, I tell you. Joven poeta, without her your life would have been entirely different, and shorter. Yes, ah, but your glass is empty. I must fix you another whiskey. But in a minute. Well, in fact the majestic woman might even represent a core of goodness in your own soul, to which you do violence sometimes, my young friend. No matter how vile and abominable you think yourself to be, no matter how much you say that you despise yourself, I think that basically you must be aware of a fundamental goodness in your nature. I myself have seen it, the way that you show your love for Natalie and your daughters. Natalie has helped to preserve that goodness in you. By preserving your life, she has prolonged your goodness, which is there, no doubt about it. Believe me. A sense of guilt, which abounds in you, is not the attribute of an inherently evil person, and it is a sense which sometimes vanishes from people in whom life has crushed all sense of decency and killed the capacity to love. What you said about sadness is also true about guilt. And as far as the battered horse goes, ilustre amigo, it is probably a symbol of lost virility. The horse is a symbol of sexual power in most cases. The shriveled horse probably symbolizes a penis that doesn't . . . well you know, and the dream expresses fear of impotence. Perhaps you mean it when you say jokingly that it doesn't get up anymore.

Guillermo smiled, arched his eyebrows and waited for a response from Miguel, but the younger man only returned the smile.

—The horse symbolizes your magnificent depravities, my friend. The train, well, it symbolizes an attack on your lust, ha! ha! Hard to believe in a man almost twenty years younger, and there is tremendous guilt in that dream. See, my friend, you are being irresponsible when you don't publish. The horse is also your career. Whatever, the train represents something harmful you are doing to yourself, I think. The dreaming mind works in strange ways. Your dreams, joven poeta, are trying to tell you something, probably about your dissipated life, mi estimado.

Guillermo laughed mischievously.

—And the bird, I think that is your wife. In the beginning, in the part about your father, she may be your mother. Who knows, maybe you sense that she dominates or threatens your father or your father's life, only you would know. Your mother may not realize it. But in your case, my young friend, the albatross is your wife, who inhibits you. She prevents you from indulging yourself, shall we say, in your magnificent depravities.

Guillermo paused and laughed again in a friendly way. Miguel did not interrupt. Then Guillermo continued.

—Lovely Natalie stands in the way of your voluptuous pleasures, my friend, and maybe the train symbolizes the guilt in yourself that prevents you from. . . . Well, it seems obvious to me, ilustre compañero, noble poeta. Yes, obvious indeed, my magnificently degenerate friend.

Then Guillermo walked over to his stereo set.

—Now, let's listen to some Lizst, he said. We will have another whiskey, my friend. Ah! Isn't it wonderful to relax? You should visit more often. We need to relax. Ah! Listen. There is the music of the magnificent Hungarian who did not know his own language. Did you know that? No. Well, I will tell you about Lizst. But first, another whiskey.


Miguel lifted the plastic glass to his lips and listened vaguely to the murmur of the other passengers' conversations. A few years ago during an after-dinner nap when he had too much whiskey he overheard his daughter, Sara, talking with Natalie. *Is Daddy an alcoholic, Mommie? How can you tell if a person is an alcoholic?.* He took a small drink from the plastic cup, which still had some ice in it. His wife did not respond immediately that day. Is he an alcoholic? Why does he always have a drink in his hand? How could she answer? How can I tell Sara that her father is an alcoholic? She chose to avoid the first question. *Well, an alcoholic is a person who has to drink. It's . . . an illness. If an alcoholic doesn't drink his whole body starts to shake, and he feels* pain. *That's why he can't control his drinking. Eventually the alcohol gets to the liver and the person could die if he doesn't stop.* . . . He was dozing, fighting sleep to hear what his wife was saying. He wanted to hear what his daughter would say. *Mommie, is Daddy an alcoholic? Is he going to die?*

Other memories. Vividly remembered incidents, but cloaked in the veiled and shadowy visions of alcohol, like the Thanksgiving dinner several years ago. Little Becky, four years old, five perhaps . . . walking into the dining room . . . little Becky, laughing . . . holding a loaded Colt .45 automatic pistol . . . bright-eyed, holding it by the handle . . . he, seeing her through a wine-glow haziness. . . . Immediately, when they see her, the terror spreads from one end of the dinner table to the other. . . . Everyone except Natalie's uncle is unable to move, he speaks softly in a low voice . . . he is pushing his chair back . . . getting up slowly from his chair, while Becky points the weapon smiling . . . he is a World War II veteran, instinctively calm . . . Stan is saying something like . . . *well, sweetheart . . .* in a soft voice betraying no alarm . . . *oh, look what you have brought to Uncle Stan . . . thank you, honey . . . here . . . give it to Uncle Stan* . . . walking slowly towards little Becky who is pointing the loaded gun toward the dinner table . . . now at Aunt Helene, now at Natalie, now at Miguel. What is he saying? . . . his voice barely audible, as if coming from far away . . . Uncle Stan is walking slowly towards little Becky who is holding the pistol, pointing it . . . she is smiling . . . then she hands it to Uncle Stan. . . . Wineglow. . . . It is over. . . . Everyone is relieved. Little Becky is smiling, standing there, proud of herself for bringing Uncle Stan's pistol to him. She had gone into their bedroom, found the weapon under the bed, where he keeps it, he said, in case someone tries to break in.

For a long time the terror over what could have happened lingered over the great dinner table. The incident had left them with pounding hearts. It had weakened their knees. Shivers were running up and down their spines. After the incident they watched little Becky running off to play with her older sister, Sara, six, perhaps seven years old.

Like a man waking up from a dream he sat back in his seat, raised up his face and breathed a sigh of relief. His journeys, always forward into the past.

You were following in their footsteps. One was found babbling on the streets of Baltimore on the day that he died; and about the other, it is recorded that on the night when he hanged himself, he borrowed just enough money to spend the cold wintry night at a cheap hotel or rooming house.

Earlier that night he had been with friends, drinking wine at a café. Perhaps he drank too much. He was sad and knew not what he might make of his life. Later, out in the street, the wind ripped into him as he turned a corner. He wrapped the scarf tightly around his neck to keep out the wind, then he lowered and tucked in his head, and he pulled up the collar of his overcoat. The temperature was freezing, about 18 degrees. *Qui será là? . . . j'écoute, j'écoute. Hélas! Personne n'est là. . . . J'écoute. Le vent? Peut-être c'est le vent. Seulement le vent . . . personne. . . .*

The dreamer is shivering from the cold, rapping at the door of the rooming house. In one of his pockets he has the few coins which he borrowed to pay for one night's lodgings on this cold January wintry night.

The woman listens again. *Sacré bleu! Comme il fait froid cette nuit. . . .* It is only the wind, she thinks. The rapping on the door has stopped. She listens and hears nothing. *Peut-être je rêvais.*

The next morning they will find the dreamer. Hanging. They will find the coins in one pocket and a manuscript in the other pocket of his coat. The manuscript is the other half of *Aurélia.*

You were chasing their shadows, Lorenzo, wandering drunkenly down the darkened streets of Baltimore, looking for the place where they found the lucid man babbling; staggering down the streets of Les Halles to where the author of *Aurélia* hanged himself; chasing the shadow of the dandy who said he translated Poe into French because they were so alike. Will someone chase your forlorn shadow, retrace your steps in many cities of the world?

Without the conception of his nameless character being clear in his mind, Miguel Velásquez was envious of him at times. He identified with his character up to a point. For example, at this moment when the plane was cruising smoothly towards Oakland Airport, attentive to the murmur of conversations among his fellow passengers, gazing around the airplane interior, pondering his strange inclination towards solitariness, he could easily imagine a foreign-looking character, travelling by airplane, remembering and wanting to write about his own life, like himself on the present journey. But it always happened that the character preferred a life of his own, diverging enviously on many counts from Miguel's dull, orderly, middle-class life; and he rebelled against Miguel as if to prove that a character is more real than the writer, challenging his creator, moreover, to invent scenes and episodes that might rival those of other fictional characters, leading Miguel over and over back to Jorge Luis Borges and his precursors, particularly Poe, of whom it is written that he engendered Baudelaire; who engendered Mallarmé and Rimbaud, Verlaine and Huysmans; who engendered Valéry, who engendered M. Teste, who in turn engendered Octavio Paz and Borges; and the character always led Miguel to others of Poe's progeny, Dostoevsky and Proust, Nabokov and Fuentes, Cortázar and countless others; including Fellini, who might be one of Poe's progeny, but about Fellini it was difficult to say, conceivably his precursors might be Pirandello and Cervantes or Moravia. In this way Miguel's fictional character, who would be nameless for a few more minutes of the present journey, was perennially discovering and making a list of his own precursors, to which he added from year to year, until one day when contrary to his father's warnings, because he read too many books, Miguel's character stepped across the threshold of madness.

His madness was probably precipitated on the day when he was passing by an artist's materials store. Some mysterious force had made him stop and go in. The former surrealist artist wrote about this unforgettable experience in a notebook which he was keeping at the time. Standing in front of an easel he was seized, he wrote, by a pervasive sense of failure. I have betrayed my calling as an artist. There is still time, however, a few, perhaps ten or fifteen years more of life.

A few days later, he decided to go back to painting. After many years, he stood in front of the door to his garage studio, trying unsuccessfully to remember when he had last seen his studio. He knew what it would be like to stand in front of his own easel again, because the visit to the artist's materials store had brought it back, but he wondered what it would be like to see the paintings again, the ones which he had started and abandoned many years ago.

He opened the door with a trembling hand and stepped down into the darkened garage. A small air vent in the ceiling

223

above the rafters and a small window on the back door were the only sources of natural light, and they created unusual shadows and chiaroscuro effects that impressed the artist. Spiderwebs and dust were everywhere. The abandoned canvases, failed imitations of artists' works that he admired to the point of idolatry, brought back the mysterious song of art. Would he be able to hold a brush? Mirrors everywhere, standing at every conceivable angle, created labyrinths of crisscrossing rays of light and disconnected scenes of the strangely illuminated garage, multiplied and bounced reflections and cropped images of himself among the mirrors. The whole scene assaulted his senses, assailed him with evidence of the futility of his life. He was overpowered by a sense of failure unlike any he had ever known, as if an immensity of failure had accrued from all the million moments of his life when he tasted bits of failure, and now, in a single moment, all of it struck him at once with intense grief and a heavy sense of loss. He walked slowly towards his easel. It was covered over with years of spiderwebs and dust. Slowly he scanned the whole garage studio with eyes becoming accustomed to the darkness, and slowly, without his knowledge he stepped into a place which very strangely and accidentally made parts of his reflections appear simultaneously in all the mirrors, and from where he stood, at the center of all the abandoned and dusty canvases and among the mirrors, he saw, as he gradually shifted the weight of his body from one leg to the other, as when he used to stand at the easel and draw from the naked model, one mirror, shattered completely from top to bottom and from side to side, and there in that shattered mirror, he saw hundreds of tiny jagged fragments of his own multiplied image, in a split second, like when because of the angle of its descent in relation to a viewer, the setting sun suddenly comes aflame in a hundred windows of a distant building in New York or San Francisco; just as he once saw in a dream, hundreds of miniature Kafka pictures on a painting used for the cover of *Time* magazine, the failed artist contemplated with fascination and horror his own fragmented and deranged image in the hundreds of tiny jagged pieces of the broken mirror, like a man who is dying regretfully sees his whole failed life passing in review in disconnected fragments, and he knew instantly that his failures in life and art had led him across the threshold of madness.

# V

THOUGHTS AND MEMORIES that passed through the mind of the foreign-looking passenger since the journey began fulfilled old prophesies, his own. He knew long ago that he would cause distress to himself and others. Some day he would have to choose between art and marriage, between a solitary and a family life, and between a calling and a professional career. His dilemmas were compounded by drinking. As it was, he had an insufferable personality, and he felt sorry for his wife because of all the years she put up with his miserable temperament. These thoughts took him back to the year when he met her in New York and to the first spring and summer of their life together. He made some notes in his pocket notebook.

Film depictions. Two people falling in love. A camera circling around the couple. A lovely woman's smiling face fills a large screen, her long brown hair swirling. Images of the couple in slow motion. Locked hands in close-up. Bright light filtered through flowing transparent gauze, like in Fellini films. Moonlit nights and beautiful sunny days. Shots of the lovers walking hand in hand. Kissing. Montage of images of lovely places to which the newlyweds travel; picnics with wine and cheese on Mediterranean beaches. Scenes. The Pacific Ocean and the crowds at Laguna Beach. Skyline of domed churches seen from the Piazza Monte d'Oro. The couple walking hand in hand through the Parque del Retiro, the Bosque de Chapultepec, or Washington Square in Greenwich Village. The couple running in slow motion. Holding hands. Kissing. He picks her up, turns around. They laugh, embrace and kiss. Close-ups of the couple's faces. Scenes of New York City, Paris,

Rome, Madrid. Visits to the Metropolitan, the Prado, the Uffizi, the Vatican Museum, the Sistine Chapel, the Louvre. Slow motion images superimposed. Swirling collage of images. Flowing transparent gauzes, hair flying, dancing lovers. Joy. A camera circling around them, tracking out. Their theme song, "Strangers in the Night"... exchanging glances.... Long shots. Fade-out, fade-in. Bright, flickering illumination. Close-ups of their mute laughter. Cinematic images of being in love. In voice-over: *How can you marry someone who's not Jewish?... Hi, Valerie... I'm calling about your party. May I bring someone? He's not Jewish... It's all right? Oh, good.... What is he? He's Mexican, from Texas, yes, fine. See you then....* Five minutes of reel and the lovers have been married for years. They quarrel bitterly, make up, kiss, feel passion. They love. *What's it like, Valerie, being married to a Chicano?* Images, nothing but images of dreams.... How brief is happiness with a madman, yet they stayed together, despite the grief. Then come children, the years pass. In voice-over: *Oh, Larry, must you go out again? You were out last night?* Awful scenes when he wants to go out at night.... *Is there someone? Is it someone I know?* Then one day it does not matter. *He will never change.*

How strange that men and women develop patterns of life as responses to the other's interest or lack of attention. She wanted only to love and be loved. In the beginning she used to smother him with love. She wanted to share everything, wanted their lives to be one. She wanted to make him happy, to be by his side, to protect him from his own destructive impulses, and to be happy. He thought only of traveling, of being free to go where he pleased. He dreamed of faraway places and longed to be alone. He wanted no one ever to tell him what to do. He wanted never to inflict himself on another.

In voice-over: *Larry! Oh, Larry! Why do you do this to us? To yourself? Why can't you be happy? Why must you drink so much?* And his wife merged in his mind with his mother, saying *your grandfather made me suffer so much* ... And little Stephanie crying ... *Mommy, why did you marry a man like Daddy?* The very same words that his aunt used to ask his grandmother. *Mamá, ¿por qué te casaste con un hombre como Papá?*

Did you have a choice, Lorenzo, about being the man you became, were always becoming and are? How well you knew your own temperament; you knew that you would never want to resist those intense longings and those exquisitely agonizing appetites, those voluptuous hungers of the flesh! You knew from a very early age that you wanted no one to hold dominion over your life, to stand in the way of the treasures that life holds in store and places in one's path, when one is free to love, to travel on to other countries, other skies, to other galaxies and stars. You wanted no hostages, no wife or children for fate to hold over you, no mirrors of your blood in whom to contemplate your loathsome reflection. You wanted no one ever to tell you what to do or think or feel, even if you chose to destroy yourself, to burn up your life, to depart from this world in blaze and smoke. And knowing all this, it was inevitable that you would bring grief to anyone who might begin to love you. You realized this long ago when you began to disappoint people who had faith in you, in your intelligence and in your art; so to protect the gentle souls who loved and wanted to love you, you would run away, and you kept on running away, like those outcasts who join the circus or the carnival and become clowns or horse-trainers or performers, whose smiles and laughter conceal despair, whose home is a tent or the open air and the sky is the roof over their heads. Long ago your letters to family and friends became less and less frequent, until you almost stopped writing. When you did not know where your life was heading, you assured your family back in Texas that things were going well. You lied so that they would not worry about you. You assured your mother and father that people did not hate Mexicans like they did in Texas when you were young, and that was true enough, because you found yourself among other misfits like yourself, the dropouts and cripples of life. They were bohemians like yourself, weren't they, Lorenzo? Sometimes you betrayed them. They invited you to their pads, to parties, and in return you fornicated with your friends' women . . . Hi, Larry, nice to meet you. This is my old lady. . . . You convinced yourself it was enough to be discreet, and thought no one would ever know . . . bastard, cuckolder! Damn you, motherfucker! . . . sonofabitch! . . . You betrayed friendships and violated many people's codes of honor.

Was there ever a choice, Lorenzo, when your whole being cried out to be just what you were born to be? Your life bordered on madness. You knew long ago that grief would be your constant companion. Bare your heart, abominable man.

You paid a terrible price for writing a novel you cannot even begin. . . . Who knows if you will ever be able to bring it off. You might have been a good scholar. . . . You betrayed your calling. You wasted more than twenty years of your life, explaining to yourself in stupid notebooks why you were born to bring grief to people who love you, explaining why you have disappointed many people, including yourself. . . . You might have been a good husband and a good father. You failed in everything that you undertook . . . your hungers were excessive. It does not help to say that you were born with the hungers of several men. There is nothing but your stupid notebooks to show for the past twenty years and more. And what are they? These notebooks are nothing more than a record of your passions and lust, your obsessions and regrets, your self-contempt and hatred, the violence that you have done to others and to yourself; they are nothing more than the record of a man who was born to bring grief and anguish to loved ones like your grandfather; nothing more than the chronicle of a man who had the capacity to be gentle and tender, who could have given love and comfort to those who have suffered. Now and then you think about your childhood and about your elderly mother and father, the people who brought you into the world. You want to write a novel to let your wife and your children know that despite the past you love them, you feel remorse, you recognize in yourself the once terrible traits of your nature, your former disregard for people's codes of honor, the old eccentric impulses and obsessions which used to plunge you into reckless experiences without concern for others, because you wanted to live out your life feverishly, knowing that there is only one life and that it was your destiny, as you told others, to live it deliriously, without inhibitions, to burn it up, and it may be that you would have succeeded; but then a young woman, half your age, came into your life, for just a short while when you had forgotten how to laugh . . . *travelling lady, stay a while . . . I'm just a station on your way . . . I know I'm not your lover . . . you chose your journey long ago before you came upon my highway . . .* and the travelling lady stayed a while and gave you shelter. . . . You had recognized the multiplicity of your selves long before you found them confirmed when you were thirty years old, in the story of Harry Haller's life, in which you saw yourself vividly, perhaps for the first time, when you began to imitate fictional characters, but you were already surrendering to your own reckless impulses, allowing them to carry you off in countless directions that turned you into the failure you are now, because your heart and your spirit and your nature were gluttonous and voracious, your hungers and longings insatiable, and your nature made you incapable of leading an orderly and ordinary life. You could never stand the regularity, the discipline of a settled life, of being a professional scholar, which Valerie made possible for you, because you could not stand deadlines and appointments, taking out the garbage, cutting the grass, fixing the sprinkler system, going to bed early. You were fascinated with the nocturnal life, and until the time of your tenure evaluation, you were obsessed with feverish longings, the beauty of incandescent flesh, the physical presence of the female body, and you preferred to be the solitary wanderer rather than to be a family man, you were driven away from family and friends by the intensity of your exquisite agonies, tormented by the cries of the great loin tigers of lust. You have always been selfish, and you wanted in your younger years no human limitations or restrictions, to burn like a flame, you wanted fortune to hold no hostages over you. Two years before you met Valerie, another woman sheltered you and gave comfort to you, kept you away from the abyss. She loved you and saved you. *Oh, Larry! Don't do this to yourself . . . you were born with a gift, don't betray it . . . make something of yourself, even if it means going away from me. . . .* Christine, thirty-one years old, and you, twenty-eight. Remember the letter that she wrote to you, that you read in your wretched hotel room after you left Chicago and went to New York, when you were unemployed . . . *Lorenzo . . . I'm carrying your child . . .* You remember how desperately you and Christine made love in her apartment, in Skokie, on the last night that you were together, in the kitchen, standing up, against the wall, in the elevator, in the front seat of her 1956 Buick. You remember crying in her arms, the sudden violent desire, hers and yours; she was insatiable that night, knowing that you were leaving. You remember the explosions of desire, the voluptuous grapplings, and how you used to watch *Candid Camera* at her apartment. . . . *How strange, Larry, that the only time I see you laugh is when we're watching* Candid Camera. . . . It hurt her to know that you were born to love more than one woman. *Why do you look at other women when we are together, Larry?* You have always known that men and women have the capacity to love more than one person, and that no woman would understand you, and perhaps that is why you could never fall in love. You were possessed by inexpressible longings, hungers, possessed by a fever for new experiences, for travel, for knowledge and learning, for art and creation.

It was hard to believe the change that had taken place in yourself when you began to feel no longer young, when the young woman came into your life, the April sun of your September life. *It's madness, Lorenzo*, she said. You wanted to understand why you became numbed to life, why you betrayed your calling, why you brought grief to others. You do care about Valerie and the children. You accepted your nature and your destiny, that made you what you are. You learned to accept the contempt and the consequences brought upon yourself by your feverish impulses, and you chose to be solitary, and still you choose to let the writing make a hermit of you, but you do care and you want them to know. The capacity for rage and hatred is still there, Lorenzo, and you know it. You wanted to be gentle and kind, so you learned to avoid people who bring out your great capacity for rage. And one reason why you write is to exorcise the demons that haunt you, so that you can be gentle. A few years ago you began to wonder if you would ever know love, or passion ever again. You were dulling your senses for years with wine and alcohol and tobacco, falling asleep every night in front of the television set. You began to feel no longer young, that living past fifty would be a dull death in life, that you would never know joy and laughter with a woman. Oh! to feel alive again! And a young woman came into your life.

Suddenly, his mind was assaulted by a chorus of voices. In his mind's eye faces of the speakers passed in procession, looming largely as on a great picture screen, in close-ups, faces of people who pursue him and visit his dreams and thoughts, appearing and disappearing; their voices each in its turn conjuring up thoughts and memories, images and whole scenes, arranging a whole lifetime of daily episodes and events in such a way that they coexist in one instant of time. . . . Dammit, Miguel, when are you gonna finish your novel? . . . You've been talking about it for years, when? . . . Don't make any appointments with him after lunch cause he's always drunk . . . he's an alcoholic, and número dos is a drug addict. . . . Am I in your novel, Miguel? . . . ¡Chingao! Por eso estamos bien jodidos. La raza misma nos jode. . . . You must get away from those morbid writers, Miguel. . . . Your writing must sing, Miguel . . . Don't dwell on depravities and morbidity. . . . What are you gonna write about me, Miguel? . . . What would you say, Larry, if you were to write about me in your novel? . . . You'll never do it, Miguel . . . What you want to do is impossible for one man. You can't put everything into your novel . . . Is there any sex in your novel? . . . . Find a woman who will accuse him of sexual harassment. . . . Don't cry, Miguel, please don't cry, I'll get it up for you, you probably just had one drink too many. . . . the limp balloon is flying through the air. . . . the train broke the horse's nose. . . . Did you read in the newspapers that Miguel Velásquez was accused of sexual harassment? . . . They ruined my whole life, Mike . . . Daddy's a real scrooge. . . . You were so good, Larry, when Stephanie was born. . . . Don't do it to yourself . . . please don't drink so much . . . don't waste your talent. . . . Te gusta mucho el pedo y te gusta la parranda, no vas a llegar a nada . . . Tu abuelo me hizo sufrir mucho, jamás se lo voy a perdonar . . . Why did you marry a man like him, Mommy? . . . Mamá, como llegaste a casarte con un hombre como Papá? . . . You have paid a terrible price, Miguel, for a novel that you may never write . . . Ya verás, hijo, cómo pasa el tiempo. . . . Since childhood, a sense of immensity . . . an inexpressible longing to travel . . . *One ought to wait and gather sense and sweetness a whole life long,* said the gentle poet from Prague *one must see many cities, men and things . . . know the animals . . . feel how the birds fly and know the gesture with which the little flowers open in the morning.* . . . Since childhood, strange, inexplicable longings. . . . Your writing makes me feel so unwanted, I walked around for hours, afraid to come home and bother you. . . . Strange, how I can't remember what you look like when I don't see you for a few days . . . I dreamed I was pregnant again, but I couldn't remember who the father was, I blocked you out from my mind completely . . . what does it mean, Larry? . . . You are vile and abominable, your nostrils flare with lust. . . . You son of a bitch, you've been shacking up with my old lady. . . . Talk to me dirty, say you like to fuck me, say you like my cunt, tell me to lick your cock, tell me to suck you and to swallow your semen. . . . Sorry, but I'm afraid the department was not able to recommend you for tenure. . . . Now that you're a professor you will see many things from the inside, but don't let it get you down, Miguel, try not to be like them. . . . You gotta get some articles out, it's been a long time since you published, our department is full of deadwood. . . . Why do you write, Miguel? . . . To exorcise the demons, to express remorse . . . to speak for the inarticulate . . . to preserve the beauty of a summer day, to describe the immense joy of travel . . . because I must! What do you mean, Lorenzo, when you say that you have loved many women but that you have never fallen in love? . . . Oh, my darling, I cannot marry, I know my nature, life with me would be impossible. An artist must be free . . . no suburban home for me, no swirling water sprinklers, no taking out the garbage or washing dishes, no two-car garage or family dinners at the saddest time of day, no hostages of fortune, no children ever . . . Were you spanked when you were a little boy, Daddy? . . . Get away from me, go out and find yourself a mistress . . . don't touch me . . . oh, why don't you move out? . . . Maybe someone will come into my life. . . . If only I could live my life over again, it would be so different. . . . I told you, Valerie, that I would never be a good husband or a good father . . . Please, Daddy, will you play a game with us. . . . Do you see things that aren't there? . . . armies of cockroaches, vultures on the kitchen sink. . . . Alejandro wanted me to buy him a pistol. . . . Suddenly, Alejandro sat up in his coffin and laughed. . . . ¡Diosito! ¡Ay diosito mío! ¿Por qué te lo llevaste? . . . nosotros tan viejos . . . y él tan joven! . . . I wanna see Miguel fuck up, he can only fuck up. . . . Is he writing about what it's like to be Chicano? . . .

All the material for a novel was stored in his mind. A great deal of it was written down in notebooks. He knew now that his thought processes, his memory, his imagination, and his dreams were endlessly working together, shaping and organizing that material into words, phrases, paragraphs and chapters, over and above his conscious control. In his mind, a lifetime of experiences was arranging itself into clusters of images, ideas, dreams, nightmares, fantasies, longings, reflections, memories. Thinking, dreaming and remembering were structuring those experiences into networks of associations, of perennially haunting images, voices, themes and dreams. They reflected his obsessions, and from them a self-portrait would emerge, with all the warts and moles, his flaws and his shortcomings; he would bare his heart and stand naked for the world to judge him. The thought was somewhat terrifying.

The material for a novel was itself structuring the literary work, much of which was in his head; the novel itself was dictating the style, the narrative forms and techniques. He would have to learn to let the work lead him, let it tell a dramatized story of lives coming together, touching one another, loving and hating; lives wending in and out of other lives, then going separate ways, aging and dying.

The novel would make and leave behind a record of a mind endlessly watching itself thinking, creating, imagining and dreaming. Too much material in his mind all at once, he realized; he had to write it down. He thought of the methods of creativity which he could handle with a measure of success, which he had learned to use consciously. Boozing, making love, being idle, reading good books, listening to music, going back to places where he had lived and travelled, being a passenger on an airplane or a bus or a train. Unwritten material kept growing, from thinking, remembering, imagining and dreaming. Above all, he was inspired by voices from the past, by the spoken words of gentle suffering souls of whose experiences he had firsthand knowledge, and they confirmed in him the desire to be infinitely gentle, despite his flaws; voices of people who wended in and out of his life briefly and who shared with him too few memorable and ephemeral joys. He lamented that these joys were few. In a few years Lorenzo would be fifty, and he realized that he was just beginning to understand. *It's madness, Lorenzo. Too much for one man. Give it up before it's too late. Besides, it is sick exhibitionism. How could you want people to read those scatological pages?*

# VI

HE HAD SEEN HIS FACE IN MIRRORS countless times.
Like now, under recessed spotlights that made him morbidly
and distressfully self-conscious, his hair became a silvery
white, como si hubiese nevado mucho sobre su cabeza, and his
full beard became entirely white like snow, and all that silver
made him think of himself as one of the elders. People compli-
mented him on his silvery hair and his snow-white beard. He
knew that it attracted attention. But now he did not want any
attention.

People kept coming into the restroom. Men and women
were using it without paying any attention to one another or to
him. It was a large restroom and sometimes there were as
many as five men at the urinals, and three or four women in
the stalls. But from the moment that she stepped into the rest-
room one woman was immediately struck by the whiteness of
his hair and beard. From the look on her face one could tell
that she delighted in his white hair and beard and in his dark
complexion under that very special kind of illumination. He
had no trouble imagining his face dramatically lit up like a face
in paintings by Caravaggio and Zurbarán, but what made him
morbidly self-conscious was the embarrassing position in which
he found himself. He was defecating, not inside a stall that
would have made it a private matter, but in a urinal, the far-
thest among several from the door. Not being separated from
the other urinals by a partition, the one on which he was sit-
ting placed him in a position that turned him into the center
of attention. The attractive woman was pointing at him. She
was extremely effusive in her compliments about his white hair
and beard.

234

—Oh! What absolutely lovely white hair, and his beard is so silvery! Isn't that just one of the most attractive older men one could possibly look at?

The heat of his own excrement against his bare buttocks added to his extreme discomfort and he wondered how in the world he would ever flush it down. Meanwhile, the woman's enthusiasm had called attention to him. Several other men and women had walked into the restroom. The arriving men and women and the men at the urinals all turned towards him and fixed their oppressive eyes upon the embarrassed older man.

—Doesn't he look just absolutely handsome, with his silvery white hair and beard? the woman exclaimed, pointing her finger at him. He is just simply adorable!

He did not hear the pilot's garbled voice over the speaker system. His mind was busily at work sifting and arranging the thoughts and memories that were passing through his mind. He recognized a familiar thought that in recent years had entered his mind and which he entertained from time to time, but without really reflecting seriously upon it. The proliferation of his notebooks and the perennial changing of the novel's configuration from year to year had begun to suggest to his mind that perhaps he had undertaken a project which was no longer the same. Was it possible that what he had once wanted to do consciously had now given way to a totally new project? Could it be that "the" novel was not one but two, or three perhaps? Had he taken all too seriously, without conscious knowledge, that passage from Goethe that he read long ago, in which he stated that one should set for himself a vast, interminable project in life, because if one set for himself a task that could be finished, what was one to do with the rest of one's life?

It began to dawn on him that since the tenure evaluation he had lost sight of what he had wanted to write about in the first place. Yes, the thought struck him afresh. Might he have deposited more than one novel in his notebooks? The university experience, yes, had turned him away from stories that his mother and father had told him, away from their experiences. Before long they would be celebrating their fiftieth wedding anniversary, and he would be seeing family and friends of many years to celebrate this joyous occasion, when four generations of his family would come together. The tenure evaluation had taken him away from the novel that he wanted to write, about the travels of a Mexican from Texas to large cities, Mexico City, Chicago, New York; in Europe; and about the memories that travels conjured up, of childhood and family; and about how he met his wife. Realizing this, he thought of how many times he remembered and dreamed about people who were clamoring for a place in his novel, and he was troubled to discover that one of the most difficult things about writing a novel was to find fictional names for the people from his life. Perhaps it was even madness to think that. . . .

They think I'm one of them . . . come on, stand up and say it, and people went up and told stories, but he did not need this dependency on others, he would always be alone . . . *I have come back to show you that not an hour not a moment of my drunkenness my continual death not a drop not a drink I have not made sing* . . . many times he too had crossed the threshold of madness, forbidden pleasures had awakened him to life again, after how many years? . . . I'm not suggesting, the doctor said, that you have an affair, but that sometimes . . . the tree in the front yard was dying and the skies stayed grey all that spring as if to mock me in the September season of my uneventful life, and el Chichón erupted that year and according to the newspapers it polluted the atmosphere. . . *C'est l'amour qui fait qu'on aime . . . c'est l'amour qui fait rêver . . . Dans l'amour il faut des larmes, dans l'amour il faut pleurer* . . . Daddy's so mean, he's a scrooge, oh, I hate him!

One of the neighborhood cats wandered about through the garage, looking for mice as it usually did, up in the rafters, inside and under the storage cabinets. After that it went out and strutted gracefully across the patio. Then it began to pace nervously back and forth on the sidewalk. From its size one could tell that soon it would give birth to a litter of kittens.

He was perturbed by something inexplicably strange. Why should the cat be pacing back and forth nervously about something natural like giving birth? If one could read emotions on cats' faces one would say that this cat was deeply troubled. Why? Animals give birth more naturally than human beings.

A glob of blood began to form at the left side of the cat's mouth. It burst, ran down the cat's jaw and fell to the sidewalk where it made an ugly crimson puddle. Good thing it didn't happen in the garage or on the patio, he thought, having observed the whole scene. I would have had to clean up that mess.

Out of nowhere a voice spoke.

—It is ready to give birth.

He could not tell where the voice came from. The cat's mouth began to swell. The animal was giving birth with its mouth. How strange. A little creature became visible when the cat opened its mouth as if to deposit it. But the cat gripped the newborn creature with its teeth, began to chew and devour the little creature, which was furry, unlike newborn kittens, which are born with almost hairless wet skin. Mother cats immediately wash their babies with the tongue, he knew. This cat, however, was devouring the first of its litter.

Blood dripped from the cat's teeth and at the corners of the mouth. Then it spat out a small piece of fur on the sidewalk. The piece of fur remained on the sidewalk, like the carcass and feathers of a bird that the cat caught during the night.

I wonder if the cat is going to devour all of its litter. How strange that the mother cat was vomiting up its litter instead of giving birth in the natural way. How more bizarre, too, that it would devour the first of its litter.

The gentle side of the man's nature came to the surface. He imagined the mother cat resting calmly after giving birth, lovingly contemplating its litter, affectionately washing her babies with the tongue.

You invent a name and a character, create a composite creation of your many personalities, not one self but several . . . I don't believe all those things you've been telling me about yourself, Lorenzo. I can't believe you have ever been mad. You're so tender . . . not you, Dr. Correa, you never threw ashtrays just to hear the sound of glass shattering . . . a song, Diana Ross singing . . . Together they explored many things which neither of them had known before. The young woman taught him how to laugh again. Sex is dirty, she said, only when it's done right . . . Cariño, amorcito . . . *I can't, Lorenzo . . . when I'm ready, I will let you know, I can't, not yet . . . I wouldn't be able to handle the guilt . . . can't we be just friends? They'll talk about us, they'll say I'm your mistress . . .* We can be discreet, but I understand. I don't want anyone to hurt you. I will be patient . . . ephemeral pleasures are the sweetest of all, cariño; I want to love you until the right man comes along for you . . . *Your eyes travelled over my body*, she wrote, *your hands were affectionate, giving me pleasure, like your lips and your tongue.* And countless voices assaulted him. You cannot do it, Miguel . . . it's too much for one man . . . forget those morbid writers . . . that's not art, that's sheer pornography . . . it will be the most indecent novel of the twentieth century if it ever gets published . . . they used to greet him at the door with hugs and kisses. *Dad, will you play a little game with us?* . . . He needed to go out at night . . . He did not associate the unnatural violence of the mother cat giving birth to its litter of kittens with his own family life. Nor was he able to decipher the insight of the dream into his own nature as it was affecting his personality and the waning relationship with his own older daughter because he was becoming a terrible father, an embittered, hostile, solitary man, a misanthropic hermit . . . and a man of rage. The younger man's dreams made Guillermo laugh and after they drank several more whiskeys Miguel pondered other interpretations while Guillermo offered others. . . . The magnificent winged woman is your conscience, ilustre, your esposa perfecta inhibiting you from exquisite depravities . . . don't feel badly, Miguel, you probably just had too much to drink; we can wait until tomorrow and try again . . . and the horse, well, it is a symbol of virility, probably lost in your case, or at least you pretend with your joking, ha! ha! . . . we'll never know for sure, eh, ilustre? The train is more difficult to interpret, it is like a wild, untamed force that strikes at your virility; maybe it is your conscience disabling you, blunting the edge of your tool, as Petronius put it ha! ha! . . . maybe the train is booze that is destroying your body, perhaps it is your life passing swiftly by, aging you of course, breaking your nose, ha! ha! so you can't use it anymore, the train is your tenure process that made you impotent, it is your youth, your daughters' childhood that has passed, the horse is the calling of art, that you are betraying, your abandoned scholarship . . . glass shattering broken mirrors, fragmented images of your deranged face . . . the train went by at an awful speed, it was life passing you by, carrying away your wife's youth, your own young manhood, your daughters' childhood . . . your writing makes me feel so unwanted . . . it will be all for you, dear, I want nothing more than to be done with it, to discharge the responsibility of my destiny, I'm sorry, mi vida, for everything, I would have wished someone better for

238

you . . . the train is the destructive side of your nature, the violent forces, the rage *oh, Lorenzo, I love when you come in slowly you are so tender* his hard flesh penetrated her soft, moist flesh . . . he paused at the peak of desire and he let out a terrible animal cry and he held the young woman in his arms as if it would be the last time he would ever make love *you cried out like an animal and you became tender, Lorenzo* . . . When I was twenty-six, he said. . . .

Aboard the PSA 737 he remembered telling her.

It was summer. I had just come back from Mexico. One night, I remember it was really hot, I stopped at Scholtze's Beergarten on San Jacinto. I ran into friends. There was an older woman. We were introduced. She was very pleasant, and something clicked between the two of us, silently. I don't even remember the conversation, but I will never forget her. When the place closed she came to my apartment. We had agreed beforehand. Discreetly. I remember that she was a little shy, perhaps embarrassed about the differences in our ages. I don't know. But she accepted my invitation to come to my apartment. Now I understand what she meant.

—You're twenty-six, she said. I'm forty-seven, and I know I'm not young anymore for a woman, but . . . in my body there is a girl.

It was a beautiful, hot summer night. That I remember. And the stars were out that night, shining through the trees. Every time I think of that woman I think of all the women my age with whom I would have liked to make love when we were young. At my apartment she took a little time to become comfortable. She didn't want any more beer. When I held her and kissed her she was like a girl, but she did not resist when I began to unbutton her blouse. She didn't want to take off the brassiere. She said she had had a mastectomy. Well, I was young and it must have made her feel self-conscious. We made love and we talked afterward. I think I fell asleep first, and in the morning when I woke up she was gone. I remember what she told me. I will never forget, especially now, after our experience, cariño.

—I am aware of our ages, she said . . . my age, but in my body there is a girl still. About two weeks ago, my daughter came home early . . . there was a young man, in bed with me. We had just made love . . . my daughter's twenty-one, doesn't understand how I feel as a woman . . . she's so ashamed of me, won't talk to me now. Oh, Mother! she said, how could you? . . . She says she'll never forgive me; she was furious and I don't know why I'm telling you this, my young lover, except that in the morning when you wake up . . . I will be gone, but remember me, and one day when you are my age, perhaps you will understand. Try to remember this summer night and a forty-seven-year-old woman who still had a girl's feelings . . . who feels no longer young but can't help needing love . . . like a girl.

And then she said now let's make love and try not to think badly of me. When I entered her she cried out, and now I know at my age why that night was important to her. And to me. Mind you, I have never forgotten that woman. In my imagination she rode buses and the L train and the subway with me for many a month after that summer, and she comes back to memory from time to time, especially in recent years. She trembled and cried as I have in your arms, God knows; men, too, make love when they feel no longer young as if each time might be the last.

—You too will cry, my young lover, when you are my age, when you meet and love a young woman . . . You will know in the depth of your heart what gratitude means in the heart of one who feels no longer young . . . what it is like to wonder if there will be a next time . . . And you will know what it is like to make love with shame . . . because people say . . . that at a certain age . . . when one is no longer young . . . you are no longer supposed to feel desire.

She told me not to hurry, to hold off for her. She said to pause when I was close, that I could hold off for a long time, and that it would be good for the two of us. I did. I will never forget how she said that she thought she would never again hold a young man in her arms. God! Now I understand. I do. In the morning, as I told you, she was gone, but she left a little note for me. She said she considered our night together a gift, and that one day I would understand what she meant. I do now, because of you, Helena. She said that I would understand if I ever made love with a young woman when I was her age. A single night of love like this, she said, when you're older, will be memorable to you. You will know and understand. She was right, Helena.

Diana Ross was singing. *We won't have tomorrow . . . but . . . we'll have yesterday.*

—Don't worry about me. I know how to lie. Besides, it's none of their business.

—Yes, but they are bound to notice. You must be careful about what you say.

He placed his face on her belly. His lips and tongue licked at her belly and at her moist flesh. After lovemaking he explored her body with affectionate gestures.

—I know what I'll say if someone asks me if we're having an affair. I'll pretend to become very annoyed, and I'll say . . . angrily, what's the matter with you? Are you crazy? He's very nice, but he's twice my age, and he's older than my father!

—You are magnificently depraved and mad, my dearest.

—Two of us, ha ha! Listen. That's the song you seduced me with.

They laughed and kissed.


A few months after she went away she wrote to him.

I can listen to the tape of our music, close my eyes, and I can imagine your body on mine, your lips on my lips, on my neck, my mouth-size breast, as you described it, fully in your mouth, being sucked gently, first one and then the other. And when certain songs start I remember exactly at what point in our lovemaking we were, and when "Primavera" starts you are inside of me como piedra preciosa and I can hear your cries, you sound like a wounded animal when you come, Lorenzo, and it makes me feel good to know of the great powers a woman has over men and that I helped you.


She closed her eyes when he got on top. He entered slowly. Her moist, soft flesh opened up to his hard, erect flesh. He thrust in and out a little at a time until he was inside and they were thrilled by the pressure of bone against bone. Her soft, moist flesh pulsated around his hard flesh; her legs were high and around him and her buttocks rested against his loins. The older man was immensely joyful. Life was palpitating vigorously through his body in great rhythmic tides of desire. The great forces of nature gathered in his loins; waves of passion mounted joyously. A man and a woman fulfilling nature's purpose.

She opened her eyes. The animal expressions on his face were unlike any she had seen. She marvelled that she herself had awakened his passion, that she could sustain it with incredible power, of which he had made her fully aware. His hard flesh was thrusting inside her soft, moist flesh. Several times he paused and then continued on. Finally, he thrust his head back. A great cry broke from his throat, the strange cry of an animal or of primitive man reaching across the centuries. His eyes were shut tightly. He squinted. With each deep thrust he gasped. Each thrust, each gasp engraved indelibly in her mind an acute awareness of her powers as a woman. She was the source of those wild, ecstatic sounds and those exquisite spasms of desire that were filling her body. She had brought this man to delirious peaks of sensual pleasure. The power of woman was in her blood. He sobbed in her arms, and womanly instincts that seemed to have their origin in another life invaded her being and increased her pleasure. The life of the earth was pulsating in and through her. Afterward the man remained inside of her for a long time. He did not have to tell her with words that his tenderness was an expression of infinite gratitude.

He very much preferred the tenderness to his obsessions, demons, ghosts, rage. . . . Why, Miguel? Why this obsession with failure? . . . You'll never make it . . . te gusta mucho el pedo y pos tú sabes te gustan las nalgas un chingo . . . doesn't your husband know how simple it is to get merit increases, two articles a year, and before long . . . I have lived and loved and travelled, a solitary, yes, a dreamer . . . you long to be a citizen of the world, you say, but you cannot get along with your own family, your children . . . they are grown now . . . Why, dear? Why? . . . Because I am one of those cripples of life, crippled by dreams and smashed ambitions and by unfulfilled longings and the hungers of many men in one body in one spirit, crippled by curiosity and insatiable hungers . . . hijo, tienes que escribir lo que te he dicho, la historia de nuestro pueblo, escucha y apunta lo que te voy a decir . . . Perché Guido? Perché? . . . Aha, the doctor said, un altro film senza speranza, eh? Their childhood, Miguel, and your wife's young years and your own young manhood, a terrible price to pay, you have written away your life and theirs . . . that's what the train means . . . Why don't you write something cheerful and uplifting? You gotta get a little humor in it. You should read Jonathan Swift and Kurt Vonnegut . . . It was beginning to break up. Could it be two, perhaps three novels? . . . You must make general, Miguel, just two articles a year, the university is like the military, a full professor is a general, you can do it. . . . Want to hear the latest rumor, Lorenzo? Yes, well they're saying that you've fallen in love with a woman half your age. Is it true? What do you mean, yes and no and maybe? You're so funny. They saw you dancing together. They're asking what did she do to make that old man dance that way. They're saying you were showing off . . . Niña-mujer-hembra, you came into my life when I had begun to feel no longer young . . . the older woman was right . . . clumps of dirt struck the coffin lid, pounded, slamslideslip across the coffin lid . . . little three-year-old Sara on her small tricycle, a prophetic image . . . your grandfather's notebooks would have rivaled la verdadera historia, hijo . . . I was so afraid each time that I would die giving birth . . . pobre cabroncito nos salió prietito . . . I will never be a good husband or father . . . his mother's world of illiteracy . . . el año que viene, Miguel, ya verás como pasa el tiempo . . . Ay Mamá, what if you and Papá had gone to school . . . accustomed to long voyages . . . Why didn't you leave me, Lorenzo? She lied in the letters that she wrote . . . I understand, mi vida, why the children became the center of your world . . . he could hardly bear the sight of so much forbidden loveliness; he shuddered with unbearable exquisite agony great ocean waves crashed angrily against the Italian liner . . . his destiny, his drunken mind deliriously pondered the leap into the ocean . . . one day a burro came into the house and destroyed them . . . no leas tanto, hijo, porque te puedes volver loco . . . Perhaps it was a dream, I thought I was dreaming . . . he relished the renewed connections of his body's rhythms with those of sea tides and waves; he was joyfully conscious of voluptuous palpitations, the strange and marvelous blood power again, radiant passion and infinite tenderness. Ephemeral love without tomorrows . . .

# VII

A LABYRINTH of halls and doorless corridors, empty and strangely illuminated, twisted and turned, led to staircases that went up and down but went nowhere. He was naked, walking briskly through the labyrinth. He did not know where he came from or where he was going. He surmised that he was in one of the university buildings. Conscious of his nakedness, he wondered what happened to his clothes, and he hoped that no one would see him. His pace made his testicles sway from side to side and strike against the inside of his legs. He was not ashamed of his nudity, but who would understand if someone saw him? Not knowing why he was naked, how could he explain to anyone else?

He came to another darkly lit staircase and tried to determine where the source of light came from, but he could not. He took the stairs to the next level, awed by the silence and the immensity of the emptiness. At the top of the next landing an open door led him into a corridor that seemed endless also. It had countless doors on either side. What am I looking for? Where the hell am I?

Far down the hall a door opened slightly. A thin sliver of light struck the floor, broke against the bottom of the wall at the opposite side of the corridor and ran quickly up the wall to about a yard high and immediately stopped. A lighted room means there are people in that room. He forgot his nudity.

The door was so far away down the hall that he thought he would never get there. But after what seemed a long time he reached the slightly open door. He pushed it aside and it opened on to a great conference hall that made him think that perhaps he was in the university club. Sixty or seventy people were there, and they were all staring in the direction of the door, as if they had been expecting his arrival. They were all university people, administrators, colleagues, office secretaries and personnel, students.

The whole scene and the setting seemed obviously staged. Could I have stumbled on the making of a film? Right by the door he saw an easel with a huge empty canvas on it. Maybe they are waiting for an artist to come and do a painting of the group. How else could the easel with the canvas be explained, and the obviously staged postures of the people there? They were like actors playing roles, pretending. Perhaps because they did not express any offense about his nakedness he became oblivious to it. Over to the right, behind the large crowd of people, at the back of the large conference room, was a huge mirror. The crowd of people were obviously there to model for a painter. Come to think of it, I am a painter. True, it has been many years since I finished a painting, nevertheless I am a painter.

Now he looked at the scene before him with the eyes of an artist. He liked the chiaroscuro effects of the recessed flood lighting on the faces and bodies of the men and women. His naked reflection in the distant great mirror, off to the right of the people and partly concealed by the huge canvas in front of which he stood, pleased him. Yes, why not incorporate myself in the painting, like Gustave Courbet did in his painting of the studio? He was even impressed by his own naked image in the huge mirror. Well, why not a male nude? He remembered what his daughter had said the summer when he was doing a series of female nudes. She objected that they were all females. She said that was unfair, and she asked him why he didn't draw male nudes. And because of his daughter, then twelve years old, that was exactly what he did. In the present case, he would be different from Paul Delvaux, who uses female nudes. Yes. He would incorporate his own naked image. After all, nudity is natural to an artist. We are not bound by any laws of morality like ordinary mortals. It is the spectator and not life that art really mirrors.

He had not noticed it before, but just inside the door, to the left of the huge canvas was a pallette on a table. The smell of oil paints and varnish and linseed oil and turpentine made him tremble with a sudden joy. All the colors were freshly set out, and there was a large assortment of bristle brushes, too. He moved closer to the empty canvas on the easel and leaned around it in order to see his reflection in the mirror. He spread his legs and he remembered the day when he walked into the artist's materials store in Berkeley. Gut feelings of his drawing and painting days coursed through his blood. The manner in which he now stood in front of the easel, leaning around it and looking at the scene in front of him, the great spectacle of the crowd, moved him, stirred old memories of his painting days.

Many colleagues from Comparative Arts and from Chicano Studies were there. His eyes surveyed the scene, pausing a little longer on some of the faces than others. Some of the secretaries lowered their eyes when he looked directly at them, just as they did that year when the ladies learned that he was not going to get tenure. The young dean, Dennis Walker, shook his head in disbelief and puffed aristocratically on his pipe. Giovanni Fortunato cast an olympian glance, full of scorn, at him. His visigothic green eyes glared with unusual brightness. Dan Almafuerte brushed his Zapata mustache with the fingers of his tiny left hand. He exposed his small teeth when he smiled maliciously and with unfeigned glee to see Lorenzo in this situation about which Lorenzo was not at all embarrassed. Next to Dan Almafuerte, standing as if to give him moral support, were two men, Henry López and Tepocate Cacarizo. Many other people were regarding him with furtive and terrible glances, as if they were accusing or judging him. Among them, twelve men and women, who were said to be men and women of learning and culture, were gathered together in a manner that suggested a conspiracy. It was rumored on campus that these twelve people were trying to remove the new young chancellor from office because of his commitment to the humanities, and it was conjectured that they and a few Chicanos on campus and from the local barrio community may have contributed to his fatal heart attack. It was all conjecture, however, and only they and their consciences would ever know. The art critic, Sir Charles Courts, was there, arching his eyebrows, blinking his eyes in arrogance. Then he caught sight of her among the large crowd, the young woman who was half his age and with whom, according to unfounded rumors, he had fallen in love. Lovely and youthful, indeed sweet and vulnerable, Helena Valencia was truly out of place among the hostile crowd. She was embarrassed for him, and he felt bad that she should be a witness to this spectacle.

Dan Almafuerte was the first to attack him. In his eagerness to get at Lorenzo, Dan pushed aside brusquely his friend Henry López, and his student, Greg Gonzales.

—See, Dan exclaimed, pointing his finger at Lorenzo, I told you he would fuck up. I knew he would!

—He fucked up! He fucked up! said two of Dan's students almost in unison.

—Yeah, we knew it, added fat Dan Vásquez, who looked enough like Tepocate Cacarizo to be his twin brother. Only an alcoholic would run around like him without any clothes. Just look at him.

—Now we can go after número dos, said Dannie Rodríguez, who used to be one of Lorenzo's favorite students.

The young woman was distressed by the hostility of the Chicanos. She was perplexed that anyone could have as many enemies as Lorenzo did, but she was a new graduate student and did not know what the local Chicano campus politics were. Other people joined in the attack on Lorenzo.

—He's deadwood. He can't even publish one scholarly article a year.

—Liar! He says he's been working on a novel. He's been saying that for years. Where the hell is it?

—He don't even know what modernism is.

—He's been sexually harassing his female students ever since he came to this university. Tells 'em he's got a vasectomy.

Lorenzo could not hear, but he could read the curling, malicious lips of young Greg Gonzales.

—Pinche puto . . . cabrón. Quisiera chingarte la madre.

As if someone had given a signal, the crowd began to move toward Lorenzo. He stood nakedly defiant in front of the empty canvas on which his imagination had painted the spectacle in front of his eyes and which had also already filled with portraits of the people in the large conference room, including his reflection in the mirror in the background. The scene and all the images were engraved in his memory forever. He was too old to be intimidated by anyone. He was too old to play childish games.

—Where the hell's that novel you been talkin' about?

—Yeah! There ain't none.

—It's all talk. He has nothing to say!

—I told you. I told you he was gonna fuck up.

Several people reached out to grab him. One of them kicked him in the groin. He doubled up and moaned in pain. . . . *What is it, honey? Wake up! You're having another bad dream.*

Again, as the PSA 737 drew closer to its destination his obsession with the novel brought back scenes and images of his life, conjured up by voices that followed him whenever he travelled. He marvelled that his mind could make such a large survey of his life, independently of his attention, in seconds. And it was of added astonishment to think that his mind could conjure up in an instant what could take days and months and perhaps years to write. Where to begin? How? . . . You were not a Chicano when you came to Ríoseco University. . . . One day on the way to his car, in the university parking lot, it dawned on him that the joint appointment changed the whole direction of his life . . . When I first came to the university the other secretaries told me, Edith, we're gonna give you the scoop on all the professors and this department . . . and boy! I'll tell you, they did . . . and I'll tell you, it's a real looney bin . . . a zoo! Which of the animals is you? . . . How could he fit all these people into the novel? They were all storytellers. He thought of Roberto Castellano, who was best man at his and Natalie's wedding, who was more like a brother than a friend; and there was José Durán, the Chicano Gauguin, and Gato the parrot who was more like a roommate than a bird to José; Gato always listened politely to José's stories about the way things were going in his life. If that parrot could write, what a novel it would be. And those very nice secretaries, Kathy Hartman and Vickie Jones and Veronica Arthur, from the Academic Senate office; and a few good friends—they had told him some good stories, too. Sara and Preston Goldstein; Gee and John Anderson and their whole family; Doug and Cathy Jones; Lew Pierce, alias Walt Price; and four generations of his own family, and of course, there was also Natalie's family. How many memorable young people, too, students who had passed through his classes? And during those years in Mexico City, Chicago and New York, the fellow dropouts, the misfits and literate outcasts, the cripples of life; and the wonderful women, some whom he saw only once or twice—and it was their voices that came back, over and over, like exquisite passages from favorite novels or poems, plays or films. They all clamoured to become characters of his novel.

248

When it came right down to it he was a witness, a citizen of the Americas because of ancestry and birth, and in a few years the 500th anniversary of the discovery of this continent, the "New World," will be upon us, he thought, and he wanted to contribute to that celebration. He was a solitary who needed the spectacle of life, large crowds of people. He simply chose when to meet people and to talk. He preferred to be a stranger among strangers. He was an eavesdropper, but he cherished the stories that he heard . . . at the departmental office; at the university, from students and secretaries, from colleagues and administrators; in conversations at the Campus Cantina, at Juan Sullivan's El Paso Bar and Cocktail Lounge; and everywhere, when he travelled out of town, to professional conferences or meetings, with strangers at happy hour. There was indeed much to be done. Where to begin?

"In a few minutes," the garbled voice of the pilot began to say, "we'll be landing at Oakland Airport . . . It's a beautiful day; we're about to start our descent . . . ask that you put your seat belts on . . . extinguish all cigarettes . . . "

"Excuse me, sir." Miguel Velásquez heard the stewardess's voice. It jolted him back into the present and made him aware that the PSA 737 would soon be landing. "Are you finished with your drink?"

He raised the plastic cup to his lips and drank the whiskey that remained. He had lost all track of time for the large part of the journey.

"We ask that you please remain seated," the pilot was saying, "until the plane comes to a complete stop."

"Yes, thank you for asking," Miguel answered as he handed the empty cup to the attractive stewardess. He flirted with her again, made a little insignificant conversation. Around him there was a clicking of seat belts and the murmur of people talking. She smiled, too, when she took his cup. Then she turned toward the passengers in the next row of seats ahead of him. Miguel took the seat belt and inserted the flat end into the other and locked it with a click.

The plane circled and tilted its great steel wings as the pilot prepared it for landing. The plane straightened out and began a smooth descent.

A few years after Alejandro's funeral, standing in front of his brother's grave, Miguel remembered the wake at the funeral chapel, the services at Guadalupe Church, the crying of a child lingering in the church interior and across the years. The Mexican cemetery had changed. It contrasted with the way it was when his brother was buried. Then it was rocky and barren. Weeds and bushes were growing over the dirt surfaces of graves and over some of the flat gravestones. On the bleak November day when his brother was buried the sky was grey and overcast, and the cemetery and the crowd of people dressed in black reminded him of Courbet's painting of the funeral at Ornans. On this later visit to his brother's grave the sky was immensely beautiful, bright and blue. He expected at any moment to hear the shrill cry of a chicharra. God! How that cry always brought back a flood of childhood memories.

Very likely, he thought mistakenly, the change in the condition of the Mexican cemetery was to be explained by the tremendous growth of Austin which had pushed the city limits far out in all directions, and Pflugerville, being very close, had become a kind of prestigious suburb, while remaining a small town. A great superhighway, Interstate 35, had made the old Dallas 81 highway obsolete and it made Pflugerville easily accessible to Austinites. Probably the townspeople decided to beautify their town, and that included the then barren Mexican cemetery. Very likely it occurred to the members of the town council, descendants of German immigrants, to hire a caretaker. But it was mainly the season, and, his mother would tell him two years later, that his own Uncle Frank Corral had taken it upon himself to become the Mexican cemetery caretaker.

He walked among the graves, stopping to read the dates on the markers, when the people buried there were born and had died. The dates always made him think of what was happening in history at the time, in the United States, or Texas even, or in Mexico or in Europe. But he always imagined the person buried there at the age that he or she died. If they were young he imagined them making love a few days before, or if they were old, he would think of how the old people stirred his imagination, because they too made love when they were young. Since junior high school he had developed this fascination with cemeteries. They were like ghost towns to him and in the silence of the late afternoon hours he could almost feel the presence of invisible people carrying on conversations as they did in life. When he was in the eighth grade he wrote an essay about a walk that he took through the cemetery at the French legation in Austin.

It struck him now, when he read the names of the Mexicans buried there, that in the very detailed histories of the town with which he was familiar, to which the descendants of German immigrants could point with pride, the Mexicans' names did not appear.

He paused at a number of graves bearing the same last name, Correa, obviously poor people, he gathered, from the modesty of the grave markers, and quite clearly a large family. Teodoro, Francisca, Epifanio, Alfredo, Cornelio, José, Federico, Catarino, Guadalupe, and others.

The Corral family was large, too. It was his family on his mother's side. He stood in front of the family graves. He remembered the Sunday visits when he was a child, his mother and father, and his grandmother and grandfather, and his aunts and uncles, all the grownups sitting around the table in the small kitchen talking for what seemed endless hours. The family graves brought back a great many recollections. He raised his eyes towards the immensity of the Texas sky. The memories were deeply engraved. Other people who lived and died in Pflugerville had names that included Robles, Gonzales, Rodríguez, Medina, Silva, López, Vallejo, Soto, Santos, Rojas, and many more. His mother and father had told him many stories about these people.

These historic names evoked in Miguel's mind the history of Texas and the U.S. Southwest when it was part of New Spain and later independent Mexican territory. In 1821 Moses Austin arrived with three hundred families, having obtained permission from the Mexican government to settle there, on condition that they respect the laws of Mexico. He died that year and his son, Stephen Foster Austin, took charge. Eventually, these Texans were supposed to become Mexican citizens. But a war between the United States and Mexico brought many changes, and history took a different course. By 1848 the United States had taken from Mexico approximately one half of its northern territories, and the Mexicans who chose to remain in these borderlands became American citizens when the Treaty of Guadalupe Hidalgo was signed. And strangers in their own land. To the day he died, his grandfather, don Miguel, never forgave the americanos for taking this territory. And to this day many Mexicans still maintain a psychological identification with the borderlands, and in their minds the border does not exist. To this town came Heinrich Pfluger with many German families in 1846. They settled here and prospered, and their descendants set aside this small piece of land for the Mexicans to be buried there, far from their own cemetery. In the history of this region the Mexicans have not been given their due place.

I too am a native of Pflugerville, and since my brother died my last name is here too, on a modest gravestone. Alejandro Velásquez, January 12, 1936–November 23, 1971. Death touched my immediate family for the first time and took my brother.

He could not allow his brother and the other people to pass into oblivion. The town of Pflugerville must go on the map of the world, and must include Mexicans who were born, who lived and died here.

On that day, he would realize it a few years later, the idea entered the mind of Miguel Velásquez, quietly and without his knowledge, to write about his family and the people they knew, about their hardships in that vast land called Texas, which is part of what Chicanos now call Aztlán, and about what it was like to live among these descendants of German immigrants. He did not know it that day, but this task would take on, ultimately, the dimensions of a mission.

His reflections on that day when he walked among the graves were to bear fruit eventually. These people buried here lived and suffered, fell in love, married, some had children and grandchildren. They were mothers and fathers who toiled the land, who cared for their children, watched them grow, could not send them to school. Some of them, like his uncles, fought courageously during World War II, and Alejandro had served in Korea when he was barely eighteen years old, at the end of the undeclared war. Yes, most of these people were a rural, farm-working people. Some Mexicans may not have known, as his grandfather did, that the lands on which they toiled for the descendants of German immigrants once belonged to Mexico. A task began to take shape in his mind. He must make and leave behind a record of these people, his people, among whom he was born. He must tell the stories of their sorrows and joys, which his mother and father had told him. He did not know until years later that on that day his spirit had come home. In the next few years the ties of blood and ancestry would slowly work on him. After travelling to many parts of the world, he had come home again. On another visit to the Mexican cemetery it became clear. Here I was born. Here my destiny began. At that time he did not know that years later one of the families buried there would provide him with a name for his fictional character.

The PSA 737 touched ground, bounced slightly once, twice. The engine of the plane roared when it dropped into a lower gear, became louder and slowed the plane abruptly. The seat belt tightened around his lap. He pushed against the arm rests to keep his body from going forward, keeping his back against the seat. The arrival at Oakland gave him a pleasurable sensation of being simultaneously in several places at once. He could close his eyes and be anywhere in the world.

Before the plane came to a complete stop some of the passengers began to stand up and to take their belongings from overhead compartments and from underneath the seats. His watch said 10:58 in the morning. Right on time. Two minutes or so later, when the plane had made a complete stop and the door was opened for the passengers to exit, Miguel Velásquez remained in his seat, watching some passengers at the front of the PSA 737, who, holding baggage in hand, were waiting impatiently for their turns to exit. One after another disappeared through the door. The airline stewardesses and the steward were standing by the door, smiling, thanking the passengers as they arrived at the door to exit, and wishing them a pleasant stay in the Bay area. Some of the passengers were probably already in the waiting room of the airport. The waiting room scenes were familiar to him, the hugs, kisses and endearments of welcomes and farewells. There would be no one to greet this solitary traveller, he thought, and that is as it should be. The voice-haunted passenger was going to be alone and free for a few days. He was going to be anonymous, a stranger among strangers. Such was his destiny.

He leaned over and took his briefcase from under the seat in front of his. It contained articles that he had started and abandoned years ago. The contents of the briefcase turned his thoughts to that amazing discovery . . . one day in the university parking lot . . . on the way to his car, it dawned on him unexpectedly . . . that the joint appointment had changed the whole direction of his life.

When he stood and moved out into the aisle, holding his briefcase, he stayed there for a moment to enjoy that strange and exhilarating sensation which is well known to those who are accustomed to long voyages and arrivals, a sensation of freedom which all solitaries know. As he walked slowly towards the front of the airplane he saw the last of the passengers disappear through the front door. Soon he would be at the Bayview Hotel in Berkeley. It seemed to him that some ideas for the novel had fallen together on this journey, but he still did not know how to begin. Halfway to the front of the airplane he heard snoring. The sight of the aging alcoholic, who had passed out, made him shudder. Poor man. He continued on and at the front of the plane the stewardesses and the steward greeted him with smiles.

"Good-bye, sir," said the attractive stewardess who had served him. "We hope you enjoy your stay in the Bay area, and thank you for flying PSA."

"Thank you," he said. Smiling, he caressed with his eyes her hair, her face, her neck, her shoulders, lovingly and tenderly. Finally, he looked deeply into her eyes and held his gaze there as if to say, My, but you are a very attractive woman. It was just for a moment, but long enough. Then he said good-bye. As before, she received the candid tenderness of his eyes graciously. He turned and stepped through the door.

For a traveller emerging from an airplane into the brisk, fresh air and the bright sunshine the scene of the Bay area with its crisply clear blue sky is breathtaking. A breeze, barely perceptible, passed through his hair and inside the open collar of his shirt, around his neck. Below, on the ground, two men were approaching with a wheelchair. Probably for that poor fellow. He stepped slowly down the ladder. Ahead was the airport, not too far away. It was under construction. Another level was being added and improvements were being made. He took a very deep breath and wondered how in the world he might be able to begin his novel.

*Suddenly* . . . no, that would never do, and yet . . . *Suddenly, Alejandro* . . . better perhaps, *Suddenly Teodoro Correa sat up in his coffin* and, yes, *he tossed his head back and laughed joyfully just like he used to when he was a child* . . . Can I pull that one off? He was not sure if it was appropriate for a writer to begin a novel with a dead man sitting up in his coffin and laughing. But in a moment of inspiration, without expecting it, he had hit upon a fictional name for his brother.

Stepping off the ladder, precisely at the moment when his left foot touched the ground, he was lifted up as if by some great spiritual and creative power. He trembled with a sudden and mysterious joy. All I need now is a first name for my own autobiographical character.

Riverside, California
July 1, 1987